POLITICS, TAXATION, AND THE RULE OF LAW

POLITICS, TAXATION, AND THE RULE OF LAW:
The Power to Tax in Constitutional Perspective

edited by

Donald P. Racheter
Central College and
Public Interest Institute, Iowa

and

Richard E. Wagner
George Mason University, Virginia
and Public Interest Institute, Iowa

SPRINGER-SCIENCE+BUSINESS MEDIA, B.V.

Library of Congress Cataloging-in-Publication Data

Politics, taxation, and the rule of law : the power to tax in constitutional perspective / edited by Donald P. Racheter, Richard E. Wagner.

p.cm.

Includes bibliographical references and index.

ISBN 978-1-4020-7154-6 ISBN 978-1-4615-1069-7 (eBook)

DOI 10.1007/978-1-4615-1069-7

1. Taxation--Law and legislation--United States. 2. Taxing power--United States. 3. Rule of law--United States. I.Racheter, Donald P II. Wagner, Richard E.

KF6289 .P65 2002

343.7304--dc21 2002075497

Printed on acid-free paper.

TO: *All students of freedom, who having read this volume, try to implement the principles of limited government.*

CONTENTS

List of Figures and Tables

Figures

Tables

CONTRIBUTORS

Donald P. Racheter is President of Public Interest Institute, Mount Pleasant, Iowa and Professor of Political Science at Central College, Pella, Iowa.

Richard E. Wagner is Chairman of Public Interest Institute's Academic Advisory Board and Professor of Economics, Center for the Study of Public Choice at George Mason University, Fairfax, Virginia.

Eric Mack is a Professor of Philosophy at Tulane University, New Orleans, Louisiana.

Gary Wolfram is a Professor of Economics at Hillsdale College, Hillsdale, Michigan.

Gary Anderson is Professor of Economics at California State University, Northridge, California.

Stanley L. Winer is a Professor of Economics at The School of Public Administration, Carleton University, Ottawa, Ontario, Canada.

Walter Hettich is a Professor of Economics at California State University, Fullerton, California.

Randall G. Holcombe is a Professor of Economics at Florida State University, Tallahassee, Florida.

Robert A. Levy is Senior Fellow in Constitutional Studies at Cato Institute, Washington, District of Columbia.

James L. Payne is President of Lytton Research at Sandpoint, Idaho.

Fred Foldvary is Professor of Economics at Santa Clara University, Santa Clara, California.

Samuel Staley directs the Urban Futures Program at the Reason Public Policy Institute, Los Angeles, California.

Bruce Yandle is a member of Public Interest Institute's Academic Advisory Board and Alumni Distinguished Professor of Economics and Legal Studies at Clemson University, Clemson, South Carolina.

PREFACE

Public Interest Institute began operations in 1992 as Iowa's only state-level, independent, research organization. As a public-policy research organization, our four principal goals are to become an information and analysis resource for all Iowans; provide local, state, and national policy-makers with a rigorous, objective, and understandable analysis of specific policy initiatives; identify practical alternatives for action on critical issues; and provide a forum for policy-makers and individuals to share ideas and concerns.

The Institute promotes the importance of a free-enterprise economic system and its relationship to a free and democratic society. It seeks to support the proper role of a limited government in a society based upon individual freedom and liberty. Concerned citizens are challenged to become better informed about public issues, for ideas have consequences, and involved individuals can make a difference.

Following the general treatment of how to achieve these ideals contained in *LIMITING LEVIATHAN*, we have continued our series of books designed to examine the topics raised there in greater depth. In *FEDERALIST GOVERNMENT IN PRINCIPLE AND PRACTICE* we developed the ways in which dividing governmental power between levels such as national and state can help citizens preserve their freedoms. In this volume we develop the ways in which property rights do the same.

If you have comments about this book, are interested in our other publications, or want to learn more about the work of Public Interest Institute, please visit our web site at www.limitedgovernment.org; contact us by mail at 600 North Jackson Street, Mt. Pleasant, Iowa 52641-1328 USA; by e-mail at public.interest.institute@limitedgovernment.org, by phone at 319-385-3462, or by fax at 319-385-3799.

The editors would like to thank each of the authors for their fine work and cooperative spirit in bringing this collaboration to fruition. We also thank Institute staff members Madeline Swailes and Amy Frantz for their assistance with typing, proofreading, and other administrative details in melding twelve independent efforts into a unified whole. Finally, we express our thanks to the staff of Kluwer Publishing, particularly Carolyn O'Neil, for their assistance.

Donald P. Racheter and Richard E. Wagner

1 THE CONSTITUTIONAL FRAMEWORK FOR DEMOCRATIC TAXATION

Donald P. Racheter and Richard E. Wagner

The essays in this book treat the relationships among politics, taxation, and the rule of law. A central tenet of democratic ideology is that taxation is something that we choose to do to ourselves, rather than being something that is imposed on us by some ruler. The basic ideology of the American constitutional founding is that government is not the source of our rights of person and property. To the contrary, government is something we establish with our prior rights of person and property to preserve and protect those rights.

The tasks of preservation and protection will require the generation of revenues to finance the operations of those who specialize in providing the preservation and protection of our rights. While taxation may thus be employed to provide these services, it may also be used in some contrary fashion. Consider a small town with only three residents, Primo, Secundo, and Terzo. Primo and Secundo like to play tennis; Terzo does not. Within the market framework of private property and freedom of contract that the town government is established to preserve and protect, Primo and Secundo could readily finance from their own funds the building of a court on which to play tennis.

It would be a legitimate use of the town's police power for the sheriff to prevent Terzo from pitching a tent or holding a picnic on Primo and Secundo's tennis court. It would also be a legitimate use of the town's police power for the sheriff to prevent Primo and Secundo from robbing Terzo to help them cover the cost of their tennis court.

Or would it? Primo and Secundo also comprise a voting majority, and they could play tennis more cheaply if they were to declare the provision of tennis courts to be a town activity. If we work with the simple assumption that town residents contribute equally to town taxes, Terzo would pay one-third of the cost of the tennis courts while getting no value from them. By contrast, Primo and Secundo would secure a price reduction. With town provision, they could play tennis for only two-thirds the cost they would pay with private provision. A government that fulfills its function of preserving and protecting would not allow Primo and Secundo to rob Terzo to subsidize their tennis matches. Yet majority voting accomplishes the same thing in this instance.

There is a potentially deep cleavage between democratic ideology and democratic practice. The ideology treats government as an institution of common benefit that people create to promote their common interests. The practice, however, seems often to clash with the ideology, as the simple example of Primo, Secundo, and their tennis court illustrates. To be sure, democratic practice is not simply a matter of majority voting. That practice is institutionally far more complex. Many layers of institutions impinge upon democratic practice. Many of those institutions make it more difficult for democratic politics to turn predatory, but other institutions doubtlessly work in the other direction as well, something that Bertrand De Jouvenal (1961) explains in a particularly pithy fashion.

While it is possible to articulate some intellectual notions about good government and appropriate taxation, it does not follow from the mere fact of this articulation that actual taxation works as articulated. Taxation may be a necessary means of preserving and protecting rights of person and property, but it might also operate in various ways to undermine, abridge, and erode those rights. The central tenet of democratic ideology, a tenet that is reflected thoroughly in the American constitutional founding, is that it is people's prior right to their property that limits the reach of government (Buchanan and Tullock 1962). This ideology rejects without a second thought any notion that government defines the limits of people's right to property. Yet democratic practice may well contradict and subvert democratic ideology, though the relationship between practice and ideology is not so simple as one being dominant over the other (Wagner 2002).

POLITICS AND THE THEORY OF PUBLIC FINANCE

The theory of public finance is primarily about the taxing and spending activities of governments. The appropriate perspective to bring to bear in addressing those two activities reveals a major fault line that runs throughout the theory of public finance, and has done so ever since two intellectual giants advanced their seminal articulations as the nineteenth century was ending.

One of those giants was Francis Edgeworth (1897), who construed taxation as something that a ruler does to improve the lot of his people. Public finance involved relationships of ruler and subject, and with a chasm, often dynastic, separating the two. The particular formulation that Edgeworth advanced concerned the extent to which a ruler could improve some notion of welfare within a nation by redistributing income. The analytical setting in this case was one where the utility that people were presumed to derive from their income was assumed to increase at a decreasing rate as their income increased. In the presence of such a declining marginal utility of income, a policy of redistributing income from people with high income to people with low income would increase total utility within the society, following the Edgeworthian presumptions.

The early interest in this sacrifice theory of taxation gave way to later articulations of optimal taxation. The analytical setting remained the same despite the change in the particular analytical formulations that were used. That setting was one where the state or ruler was treated as a smart and benevolent means for improving society. The theory of public finance was a choice-theoretic and not a catallactical enterprise, as examined in Richard Wagner (1997). This presumed analytical setting is surely an astonishing setting to pursue in democratic regimes, even though it might be suitable for a monarchical regime.

This sense of astonishment was expressed crisply by the other giant, Knut Wicksell (1896, translated 1958), who complained that the theory of public finance "seems to have retained the assumptions of its infancy, in the seventeenth and eighteenth centuries, when absolute power ruled almost all Europe" (p. 82). Wicksell articulated a catallactical approach to public finance, one whose ability to generate an alternative analytical agenda was illustrated nicely in James Buchanan (1967). The analytical orientation of this catallactical or Wicksellian approach is not upon how a ruler might somehow improve society, but rather is placed upon how people participate in and through government to achieve their various ends (Wagner, 1988). Public finance does not involve ruler-subject relationships in a democracy. There are no nobles, so there is no noblesse oblige to dispense. Democratic relationships might be ones of mutuality or they might be ones of domination-and-subordination, but in any case they involve relationships among people of the same rank.

Democratic fiscal practice might involve general gains for everyone, or it might involve cases where some people gain at the expense of other people. The catallactical approach to public finance places central importance on the institutional framework within which political and fiscal relationships are governed. To speak of a catallactical approach to public finance is not to assimilate public finance exclusively to a theory of voluntary exchange. It is rather to assimilate it to a theory of social interaction, as against being assimilated to a theory of individual choice. It is quite possible to recognize that fiscal processes involve duress and not just mutual consent, and yet take a catallactical rather than a choice-theoretic orientation toward the subject matter.

THE CONSTITUTIONAL FRAMEWORK FOR FISCAL INTERACTION

The extent to which fiscal interactions work for the general benefit of all, as against being a means by which some people gain advantage by imposing losses on others, will to an important extent be controlled by the constitutional framework that governs those interactions. Above the headquarters of the Internal Revenue Service in Washington, D.C., is chiseled the quotation: "Taxation is the price we pay for civilization." In one respect, Holmes's assertion seems eminently reasonable. Well-working governments that promote and maintain peace and tranquility are a blessing, and not a blessing that comes for free. These blessings are costly, and taxes are the customary means by which we pay the price to obtain peace and tranquility.

It would, however, be wrong to draft Holmes's assertion to the service of unlimited taxation and state power. Taxation is a form of Faustian bargain (Ostrom 1984, Racheter and Wagner 1999), in that it represents the use of an instrument of evil, violence of some people toward other people, to secure a common good: peace, tranquility, and the flourishing of civil society. If the alternative to taxation is the absence of government and civil order, some taxation is surely necessary to provide a framework for good civil order. In this respect, taxation is truly a price we pay for civilization.

It does not follow, however, that any and all forms and levels of taxation are warranted by the requirements of good civil order. The United States, after all, was founded on the proposition that taxes may exact prices that are too high and may thus impair the civilization that they are meant to serve. We can acknowledge with Holmes that proper taxation may well be a price we pay for civilization, while at the same time recognizing with our founders that taxation becomes destructive if it is too high or wrongly imposed.

THE ESSAYS TO FOLLOW

The essays in this book examine Holmes's assertion from several angles. In Chapter 2, Eric Mack explores the relationship between self-ownership and taxation in a democracy. The American republic was founded on the proposition that we have natural rights, and that government is constituted to preserve and protect those rights. Government may protect our rights, but it is not the source of those rights. Mack explores some of the implications of self-ownership for the power to tax in a democracy.

At its most fundamental level, taxation converts private property to a form of common property with the state as regulatory agent. Richard Wagner examines some aspects of this conversion in Chapter 3. What taxation does is apportion obligations among the citizenry to work to stock the common stores, as it were. The appropriations side of the budgetary process entails the granting of access to those stores to the citizenry, with individual citizens differing in the amount of access they are granted, just as they differ in the obligations to labor that are imposed on them through taxation.

Any principle of a rule of law requires some means for addressing claims that the principle has been violated in some fashion or another. In Chapter 4,

Gary Wolfram reports on various notions of taxpayer rights and how these might serve to limit the power to tax. In so doing, this chapter addresses taxation in what might be called a constitutional perspective.

A number of states make considerable use of referenda, even to the extent of subjecting tax measures to referenda. In one respect, referenda might seem to be means of subjecting taxation to some level of popular approval. Yet referenda would seem also to provide a means by which a majority of people can vote to tax people other than themselves. In Chapter 5, Gary Anderson examines referenda as a means by which tax measures are approved or rejected.

Taxes are legislated by political realists and not by tax philosophers. In Chapter 6, Walter Hettich and Stanley Winer examine some of the consequences of this simple recognition. The actual pattern of taxation in a democracy reflects such things as the relative ability of different interest groups to resist taxation through such things as securing privileges and exemptions. The pattern of democratic taxation reflects an underlying political and economic logic.

In a similar vein, Randall Holcombe focuses on excise taxation in Chapter 7. Excise taxes provide a rich opportunity to explore how interest groups influence the political processes through which tax legislation is enacted. The central point of departure here is the simple recognition that the best tax is always one that someone else pays, and this chapter pursues various lines of thought from this point of departure.

In days of old, rulers often retained tax farmers to collect taxes for them. The tax farmers were well rewarded for their efforts, and the rulers seemed generally to be quite happy with the revenues the tax farmers extracted. Perhaps lawyers are becoming the modern form of tax farmer. The tobacco litigation collected massive revenues for state governments and rewarded handsomely the lawyers who pursued that litigation in the process. In Chapter 8, Robert Levy examines how litigation is becoming an alternative form of taxation and considers some of the possible growth areas for this new form of taxation.

It is hard not to complain about the complexity of our tax system. The tax code becomes ever longer and more complex. More and more people have experts prepare their taxes for them. Periodically, proposals are advanced for simpler forms of taxation. But those proposals seem to go nowhere. In Chapter 9, James Payne shows why taxation is inconsistent with modern democratic values and sentiments and explains how complexity emerges out of this inconsistency.

In Chapter 10, Fred Foldvary presents a case for the taxation of site values as superior to other forms of taxation, both because it is more efficient and because it is more just. The single tax is most closely associated with Henry George in the nineteenth century, though it has been tried in numerous places. Indeed, it is in many respects misleading to refer to this as a tax, for in many respects it operates more like a means by which governments can charge prices for public services and improvements.

Cities have much scope for using regulation as an alternative to taxation. In Chapter 11, Samuel Staley examines some of these regulatory substitutes for taxation in urban areas. Zoning and the growing interest in what is called smart growth are examples whereby regulation accomplishes much the same thing that taxation could have accomplished. To be sure, the regulatory burdens are often placed on different people than those who would have paid the taxes, and this shift in burden surely has something to do with the apparent popularity of these measures.

Environmental justifications are given for numerous tax proposals. Carbon taxes are just one of many illustrations. In many cases, environmental problems arise because property rights are severely abridged. In Chapter 12, Bruce Yandle examines environmental taxes in relation to property rights, and considers how political and economic processes influence the apparent dominance of regulation and central control over taxation and decentralized choice.

REFERENCES

Buchanan, J. M. (1960). "The Italian Tradition in Fiscal Theory," In *Fiscal Theory and Political Economy*, Chapel Hill, NC.: University of North Carolina Press, pp. 24-74.

Buchanan, J. M. (1967). *Public Finance in Democratic Process.* Chapel Hill, NC.: University of North Carolina Press.

Buchanan, J.M. and Tullock, G. (1962), *The Calculus of Consent*, Ann Arbor, MI.: University of Michigan Press.

De Jouvenal B. (1961), "The Chairman's Problem," *American Political Science Review* 55, pp. 368-372.

Edgeworth, F. Y. (1897). "The Pure Theory of Taxation." In R. A. Musgrave and A. T. Peacock, (eds.), *Classics in the Theory of Public Finance*, London, UK.: Macmillan, 1958, pp. 119-136.

Epstein, R. A. (1985). *Takings: Private Property and the Power of Eminent Domain.* Cambridge, MA: Harvard University Press.

Gordon, S. (1999). *Controlling Government.* Cambridge, MA.: Harvard University Press.

Ostrom, V. (1984). "Why Governments Fail: An Inquiry into the Use of Instruments of Evil to do Good." In J. M. Buchanan and R. D. Tollison (eds.), *Theory of Public Choice II.*. Ann Arbor, MI.: University of Michigan Press, pp. 422-435.

Racheter, D.P. and Wagner, R.E. (1999), "Faustian Bargains and Constitutional Governance," In D.P. Racheter and R. E. Wagner (eds.), *Limiting Leviathan*, Northampton, UK.: Elgar, pp. 1-12.

Wagner, Richard E. "Choice, Exchange, and Public Finance," *American Economic Review*, Proceedings, 87, May 1997, pp. 160-163.

Wagner, Richard E. (1988). "The Calculus of Consent: A Wicksellian Retrospective."*Public Choice* 56, pp. 153-166.

Wagner, Richard. E. (2002), "Complexity, Governance, and Constitutional Craftsmanship," *American Journal of Economics and Sociology* 61, pp. 105-122.

Wicksell, K. (1896). "A New Principle of Just Taxation." In *Classics in the Theory of Public Finance,* R. A. Musgrave and A.T. Peacock (eds.), London, UK.: Macmillan, 1958, pp. 72-118.

2 SELF-OWNERSHIP, TAXATION, AND DEMOCRACY: A PHILOSOPHICAL-CONSTITUTIONAL PERSPECTIVE

Eric Mack

THE CONSTITUTIONAL PERSPECTIVE, NATURAL LAW, AND JOHN LOCKE

As F.A. Hayek says at the outset of volume one of *Law, Legislation, and Liberty,* "Constitutionalism means limited government." (p.1) To adopt a constitutional perspective is to focus on general principles that constrain the powers and conduct of government. If one holds to a constitutional perspective, the first question one will ask when a particular governmental action is under consideration will be, "Is this action constitutional?" That is, "Does this action fall within the constraints on governmental power and conduct that constitute the core of our constitution?" If the action under consideration contravenes constitutional restrictions, it must be foresworn even if it appears to have desirable results. The constitutional perspective presumes that the state itself is—and the individuals who act on behalf of the state are—subject to these constitutional constraints. Constitutionalism rejects the idea that nothing can stand as a limit to state authority; it rejects the idea that the state possesses unlimited sovereignty.

What, then, can be the source of the principles that limit the sovereignty of the state and its permissible modes of action? One possibility is that unlimited sovereignty does exist; but it resides, not in the state, but in the people. The rightful power of the state is limited simply because the people have not fully authorized the state to exercise all the sovereign powers of the people. However, this doctrine of the unlimited sovereignty of the people as the source of the limited powers of the state is neither plausible nor felicitous to the cause of constitutionalism. If some primordial collectivity called "the people" possesses an original unlimited sovereignty, why should it establish a state that is barred from fully carrying out its will? If the state is somehow the manifestation of the sovereignty and will of the people, it seems that constitutional restrictions on state action ought always to give way before the will of the people. On the other hand, if there are constitutional principles that ought not to give way before the will of the people, then the will and sovereignty of the people cannot be the source of those principles and barriers.

The great historical alternative to doctrines of unlimited state *or* popular sovereignty are doctrines of *natural law* according to which all human agents and all human institutions are subject to certain principles of justice or human rights. No human agent or institution—not even the state or the people—may lawfully do whatever he or it wills. For natural law, and not the will of any individual or collective agent, is the ultimate measure of whether the actions of agents are lawful and permissible. Natural law is natural in precisely the sense that it is not the result of any individual's or any collectivity's will or design. The idea that everyone, including the state and its minions, is subject to law—i.e., the idea that no individual's or collectivity's will stands above and determines the law—is a corollary of the idea that there is a natural moral law that governs human interactions.

There are, however, a variety of different types of natural law doctrine. The type of natural law doctrine that is central to the articulation and justification of the sort of constitutional order that was founded in the United States is the natural law doctrine that focuses on the natural *rights* of individuals. Indeed, the greatest single philosophical spokesman for this natural rights doctrine is the late seventeenth century philosopher, John Locke; and Locke was also the single most important intellectual influence upon Americans during the revolutionary and post-revolutionary period. It is a Lockean version of natural law that undergirds American constitutionalism. In this essay, I offer an essentially Lockean account of individual rights, including property rights, and explain how this philosophical understanding of rights implies a constitutional perspective that radically limits the lawful conduct of the state and its minions. I shall then briefly explore the implications of this philosophically derived constitutional perspective for taxation and democracy.

NATURAL RIGHTS AND THE RIGHT OF SELF-OWNERSHIP

The distinctive feature of the natural rights type of natural law theory is its underlying moral individualism. Natural rights theorists like Locke hold that each person's rational goal is the achievement of his own happiness and the crucial ingredient and condition of that happiness, which is his self-preservation. While everyone's happiness and self-preservation is ultimately valuable, each person has a special regard for his own happiness and self-preservation and, indeed, each has a duty to achieve and sustain *that* happiness and self-preservation. Each person, with propriety, devotes himself to sustaining his own life and well being; none is bound to sacrifice his life or well being for the sake of the alleged higher purposes of any other individual or of society as a whole. Thus, Locke—especially in his *Second Treatise of Government*—and other defenders of the natural rights tradition reject the idea that any individual is naturally subordinate to any other individual, to any political authority, or even to society as a whole. Each individual is free of natural subordination to others; each individual possesses a natural moral freedom.

The question that natural rights theorists such as Locke face is whether or not this liberation of the individual from natural servitude to some privileged personage or to the social whole means that the individual is free of *all* natural moral constraints in his interaction with other people. Or is there some natural principle that restricts how the individual may treat other people in the course of pursuing his happiness and self-preservation? The answer of the great mid-seventeenth century philosopher, Thomas Hobbes—especially in his *Leviathan*—was that there is no natural constraining principle. Each individual has, by nature, *unlimited* freedom to do as he sees fit in the pursuit of his own self-preservation. Each has a natural right to do anything whatsoever that appears to him to be necessary to his self-preservation.

> The Right of Nature... is the Liberty each man hath, to use his own power, as he will himself, for the preservation of his own Nature; that is to say, of his own Life; and consequently, of doing anything, which in his own Judgment, and Reason, thee shall conceive to be the aptest means thereunto. (Hobbes, p.189)

If it seems to person A that sneaking up on person B while she sleeps and slitting her throat would promote A's self-preservation, then A is perfectly morally at liberty to sneak up on B and slit her throat. Of course, knowing that A might conclude that he is perfectly at liberty to slit her throat might well indicate to B that she had better preemptively bash in A's skull and that she is perfectly morally at liberty to do this. And knowing that B may be thinking that she is at liberty to bash in his skull may precisely be A's reason for thinking that slitting B's throat is necessary to his self-preservation. We see here in microcosm Hobbes's reason for thinking that mankind's natural condition of unlimited blameless liberty entails the war of all upon all. This war does not arise out of any defect in human nature or human rationality. Rather, Hobbes's most central point is that, in a world in which there are no natural moral constraints on how individuals may promote their own desires and self-preservation, individuals will have no basis for expecting constraint on the part of other people. As a consequence, each will have ever more reason to be unconstrained in his or her own conduct. The result, as Hobbes emphasizes, is a world in which all individuals are markedly worse off than they would be if they were subject to natural constraints upon how they may seek their happiness and self-preservation and could expect one another generally to abide by these constraints. The state of nature descends into a state of war of all upon all precisely because the state of nature lacks a *moral constitution*; i.e., it lacks a set of restrictions upon how agents may pursue their ends.

Hobbes's own solution to the war of all upon all that, as he sees it, results from the absence of any natural moral constraints is the institution of absolute political authority. Such an absolute political sovereign will create *artificial* constraints on people's behavior by commanding that people foreswear certain ways of interacting with one another—e.g., slitting each others' throats or bashing in each others' heads—and by enforcing these commands with the threat of swift and fearful punishment. According to Hobbes, by issuing such commands and threats, the sovereign *creates* constraints upon A's conduct toward B. The sovereign thereby *creates* obligations upon A to desist from certain conduct toward B and, correlatively, *creates* for B "rights properly so-called" against A. For example, by commanding that A not engage in the unprovoked killing of B, the sovereign creates an obligation upon A not to kill B without clear provocation. Hobbes says that only when the sovereign sets his will against this killing and credibly threatens to punish it does it become *wrong* for A to engage in the unprovoked killing of B. Only in virtue of the sovereign's setting his will against this killing does B come to possess a right properly so-called against being killed. Only through the sovereign's promulgation and enforcement of such rights do these rights come into existence. By taking away people's natural unlimited liberty to do anything whatsoever and by imposing constraints upon them, the Hobbesian sovereign makes peaceful co-existence (and mutually beneficial interaction) among people possible. As Hobbes sees it, the sovereign thereby makes all the individuals who are subject to his power better off than they would be in their natural state of unconstrained liberty.

However, this Hobbesian version of the natural rights view is incompatible with the constitutional perspective. For that perspective, it will be recalled, centrally involves the idea that there exist principles that stand outside of and independent of the will of the sovereign and that limit how the sovereign and its agents may act. In contrast, the Hobbesian view is that no laws or no principles exist outside of the will of the sovereign. According to the Hobbesian view, the will of the sovereign is the *source* of all law, all rights properly so-called, and indeed all justice. Since the will of the sovereign is the source of all law, rights, and justice, *whatever* the sovereign wills or does or orders is lawful, right, and just. Hence, on this view, in principle there can be no constraints on the rightful power of the state. Hobbes attempts to solve the problem of everyone *naturally* possessing unlimited liberty by introducing a political sovereign who *artificially* constrains everyone else. But this leaves us with the problem of having a sovereign, in whom power is concentrated, who is unlimited in his liberty to do whatever *he* wills. To think that men would accept this solution is, Locke says, "to think, that men are so foolish, that they take care to avoid what mischiefs may be done them by *polecats, or foxes*; but are content, nay, think it safety, to be devoured by *lions*." (Locke, para.93)

Lockean natural rights theory joins Hobbesian natural right theory in emphasizing the rationality of each individual's pursuit of his happiness and self-preservation and the existence of each person's natural freedom from subordination to other agents. But Lockean natural rights theory denies that our natural freedom is an unlimited freedom to do anything whatsoever. Indeed, what makes any given individual's natural freedom especially valuable to that individual is that *other* individuals are *not* morally free to trespass upon that freedom. Each person possesses a sphere of rightful freedom within which he may do as he sees fit; but the existence of such spheres requires that no one may rightfully invade anyone else's sphere of rightful freedom. Each person has, not merely a blameless natural liberty to act as he sees fit within his own sphere, but also a natural *right* (i.e., a right "properly so-called") not to be interfered with by others when he does as he sees fit within his own sphere. The corollary of each person possessing such a natural right is that each *other* individual is naturally obligated not to invade or do damage to or take possession of the first agent's sphere. As Locke puts it, the state that all men are naturally in is "a *state of perfect freedom* to order their actions, and dispose of their possessions and persons, as they think fit, within the bounds of the law of nature, without asking leave, or depending upon the will of any other man." (Locke, para.4) If we ask how Locke can say that individuals possess a "perfect" natural freedom and yet are subject to certain natural constraints on how they may act, Locke's answer is that only if we are each bound by the law of nature not to trespass upon others' spheres can each of us have a genuine right (and, hence, a *perfect* freedom) to do as we see fit within our own spheres.

According to Lockean natural rights theory, each individual is naturally free to pursue his own chosen path to happiness and self-preservation; but each must foreswear paths that involve the violation of any other party's comparable rights. These rights are the *moral constitution* of the state of nature; to recognize such rights is to adopt the constitutional perspective. But this does not yet get us to the constitutional perspective applied to governmental power. For that we have to focus further on the Lockean natural rights view and its eventual implications for the role of government in a just society. We have to see how this moral constitution defines the purpose and sets the limits on the power of political society.

To begin with, we need to explore further the basis for belief in natural rights and in the rights of property. In the remainder of this section I want to describe briefly three of the arguments that Lockeans put forward for the reasonableness of belief in Lockean natural rights. In the next section, we will turn to property rights.

(1) The first Lockean argument centers on the idea that person A's interferences with person B *falsely* presume that B exists for A's purposes. Suppose that, without B's voluntary permission, A enslaves B or otherwise extracts labor or services from her or A kills or maims B in order to advance his own purposes. Any such action by A would treat B as though she were A's natural subordinate. Any such action presumes that she exists for A's own purposes. However, the fact that all (normal) human beings share one basic nature— that there is among us one "community of nature" (Locke, para.6)—is prima facie reason for believing that no one is anyone else's natural owner or master; no one is anyone else's natural slave or servant. We have prima facie

reason to believe, and no countervailing reason to disbelieve, that no individual is made for any other individual's purposes. Thus, the presumption involved in all acts of enslaving, extracting labor and service, killing, and maiming (to which the subject has not given consent) is false and all such actions are, therefore, unjustified. So we can say that each person possesses a natural right—a right that derives from his common human nature—not to be subjected to such interferences with and invasions of his person.

(2) The second Lockean argument centers on the idea that each individual rationally claims for himself a right to freedom and, hence, must recognize a like right in all morally similar agents. Each person rationally aims to promote his happiness and self-preservation. So each person has to be concerned with securing that general condition vis-à-vis all other individuals that will permit him to promote his happiness and self-preservation—either by way of his own separate actions or by way of his chosen interactions with others. The crucial general condition that permits such conduct is freedom from others' enslaving one, extracting labor from one, killing one, and so on. So every rational person claims for himself freedom from such interfering and invasive conduct. Every rational person claims a right against all others to dispose of his own person, faculties, talents, and energies as he sees fit. But, as beings with a common nature, none naturally superior or naturally inferior to another, we are moral equals. Whatever natural rights any one of us has, all must be recognized to have. Thus, if each of us rationally claims for ourselves a right to dispose of ourselves as we respectively see fit, each of us must also recognize a right in every other individual to do likewise.

(3) The third Lockean argument centers on the idea that a moral code that directs each individual to achieve his happiness and self-preservation must also direct individuals to abide by constraints on how they pursue those ends—precisely because such a moral constitution is essential to individuals achieving their respective happiness and self-preservation. The starting point for all natural rights theories is a moral individualism according to which each person's happiness and life is of ultimate separate value. A reasonable moral code liberates individuals from servitude to other individuals and to any encompassing collectivity; such a code of conduct endorses each individual being primarily concerned to discover and pursue the actions (and virtues) that will enhance his happiness and life. But we have also seen in our discussion of Hobbes that a code of conduct that tells people to be *unconstrained* maximizers of their interests will turn out to be self-defeating. That is to say, if people are guided by one and only one rule—"do whatever under the existing circumstances will maximize the pay-off to oneself"—*and* people anticipate each other being guided solely by this rule, then people will end up with pay-offs that are much lower than the pay-offs they will attain if they are not unconstrained maximizers. We also saw in our discussion of Hobbes that, if there are constraints upon how people may seek to advance their ends *and* people anticipate that others will tend to abide by those constraints, everyone will benefit. The war of all upon all will be avoided; peaceful co-existence and even mutually beneficial cooperation will

become possible. (We also saw that the Hobbesian introduction of constraints on the behavior of individuals by way of subjecting us to an *unconstrained* sovereign frees us from polecats and foxes only by way of subjecting us to lions.)

According to the Lockean formulation, the lesson to be derived from seeing the consequences of unconstrained interaction is *not* that we need an all-powerful Hobbesian ruler who creates constraint through the exercise of his unconstrained sovereign will. Rather, the lesson to be derived is about the structure of a rational code of conduct. We learn that a code of conduct that endorses each individual's pursuit of his own happiness and self-preservation must also include constraints upon how individuals may pursue their happiness and self-preservation *if that code of conduct is not to be self-defeating.*[1] If it is reasonable for a code of conduct to include a given rule, but that first rule must be complemented and constrained by a second rule if the code is not to be self-defeating, then it is reasonable for that code also to include that second rule. Thus, if it is reasonable to endorse the rule "each should devote himself to the fullest realization of his happiness and life," if, but only if, one *also* endorses the accompanying rule "no one may devote *other persons* (without their consent) to the realization of his happiness and life," then it is reasonable also to endorse that constraining second rule. Such a code says, in effect, that you may devote *yourself* to the fullest realizable of your happiness and life. But you are precluded from devoting *others* to your ends because, as equal right-holders, they may devote *themselves* to their own cherished ends. Although each person may properly pursue the ultimate good which is his own happiness and life, each person is constrained from sacrificing other people on the altar of this pursuit; each person is morally precluded from treating other persons as though they exist for his purposes. In a way that seems at first to be paradoxical, your being subject to such constraints in your conduct toward others is more advantageous to you than your not being subject to such constraints. It is more advantageous to you because others also are constrained in their conduct *and* because peaceful co-existence and mutually beneficial interaction is so much more apt to arise among agents who view themselves *and* each other as subject to constraining moral principles than among agents who view themselves and each other as morally free to do anything that will advance their interests. To understand this is to understand the rationale for moral constitutionalism.

The Lockean natural rights theorist holds that reflection upon what norms people have reason to endorse in light of the ultimate value of each person's happiness and self-preservation and the natural moral equality among persons reveals the rationality of the that each person has a right to dispose of himself as he sees fit consistent with his recognizing a like right in every other person. This right is a natural right in the sense that it is to be ascribed to individuals on the basis of philosophical reflection upon the nature of persons and the nature of their good and not on the basis of any special contracts that individuals have entered into or any acts or proclamations of government. To have such a right to control and dispose of one's person is to have moral ownership over one's self, i.e., a moral ownership of one's body, mind, faculties, talents, labor, and energies. Hence, the Lockean natural rights tradition often speaks of our most fundamental right being the right of self-ownership. In contrast to all versions of the view that some one agent (the king, the state, the people, or whatever) is *the* sovereign, the Lockean natural rights theorist maintains that each person is sovereign over his own life. Each person may do as he wills—within his own life. But these rights are not themselves the creature of any privileged agent's will.[2] Rather, these rights stand as rational limitations on every agent's permissible behavior.

PROPERTY RIGHTS

A considerable part of the appeal of the thesis of self-ownership is that it supports our belief that people ought to be able to so as they chose with their own lives "without asking leave, or depending upon the will of any other man." (Locke, para.4) However, almost all action involves not just personal resources but, also, extra-personal resources. Although *I* am writing this paper, I am doing so with my laptop computer (in a coffeehouse that provides me with a table and electricity in exchange for my patronage). There would be very little I could chose to do without extra-personal resources of my own or extra-personal resources of other people that they were willing to let me use—usually in exchange for my being willing to convey to them some resource of my own. The desire for a social scheme in which people will be able to live as they individually chose extends, therefore, to a desire for social principles that allow individuals to acquire (and transfer) rights over extra-personal resources that are comparable to the rights they possess over themselves. So it is no surprise that Lockean natural rights theorists offer a variety of arguments on behalf of the moral power of individuals to acquire rights to extra-personal resources. In this section, I will articulate two such arguments—arguments that, I believe, complement one another.

(1) The first argument for property rights centers on the idea that agents acquire property rights by extending their self-owned selves into the extra-personal world.[3] Locke himself famously and plausibly argues that individual rights in extra-personal objects arise through individuals exercising their rights of self-ownership. This exercise takes the form of individuals mixing their labor with natural materials. Since, as self-owners, individuals each have rights to their own labor and they do not abandon these rights when they invest that labor in the objects that they transform through that labor, they acquire rights to those transformed objects. (Locke, chapter V) It would be a clear violation of another's self-ownership rights were I to force her to bring her talents and energies to bear to clear an unowned field for me so that I could use that cleared field (or force someone else to use it!) to grow a crop. Such a seizure of the other's talents and energies would treat that person as a moral inferior who was made for my purposes. But I inflict the same wrong on that person if I slyly stand

aside while she clears that field and readies it for cultivation and *then* step in to seize the improved field. Seizing the labor as it is being produced and seizing it after it has been produced are morally on a par; if the first seizure violates the other's self-ownership—and it does—then so does the second seizure. But, if my seizure of what another has produced through her labor violates her rights, then she has a right—a property right—to the fruits of her labor. "Whatsoever then he removes out of the state that nature hath provided, and left it in, he hath mixed his *labour* with, and joined to it something that is his own, and thereby makes it his *property*. (Locke, para.27)

If one has, through one's labor, made some object part of one's rightful estate, then one may dispose of that object as one sees fit—subject, as always, to the constraint that one may not use the object to violate the self-ownership or property rights of another. One crucial use of one's property is the transference of it to another party in exchange for some property of the other or in exchange for the other providing one with some service that one may not seize from her. And, of course, one retains or even fortifies one's right to what one has gotten in trade from another if one further transforms that object through one's labor upon it. Another significant use of objects within one's rightful estate is the donation of those objects to a recipient of one's choice. Thus, although Locke's own discussion focuses almost entirely on the initial property rights that arise from individuals laboring upon natural materials, Lockean doctrine holds that individuals also have the moral power to convey the resulting property rights to others by means of exchange and donation. And it is, of course, only because we can convey to others rights to what we have produced and they can convey to us rights to what they have produced that we all have incentives to engage in and, hence, can gain from economic specialization.

(2) The second argument for property rights centers on the idea that only a "historical entitlement" regime of extra-personal holdings is compatible with respect for the rights of self-ownership. In his *Anarchy, State, and Utopia*, Robert Nozick employs the language of "distributive justice" to advance this historical entitlement view of persons' right to extra-personal holdings. Nozick distinguishes between "end-state," "pattern," and "historical entitlement" theories of distributive justice. In large part, he argues for the third of these alternatives by revealing difficulties that afflict the first two theories. Each end-state theory of distributive justice maintains that society should bring about the distribution of (lifetime) income that most accords with that theory's favored profile. End-state theories differ from one another by favoring different profiles. For instance, a strict egalitarian end-state theory holds that of all the distributions of income that society (through its political institutions) can bring about, it ought to bring about the distribution that is most equal. The end-state principle that John Rawls advocates in his *A Theory of Justice*— which he dubs the "difference principle"—calls for society to bring about the available distribution of income that maximizes the (lifetime) income of those in the lowest income group. One of Nozick's primary criticisms of all end-state

theories is that, according to each and every one of them, whether an individual has been economically productive or destructive is irrelevant to what the just distribution of income is; and yet, surely, says Nozick, whether a person has been economically productive or destructive *must* play a major role in determining what distribution of income is just. Table 1 helps illustrate these points.

Table 2.1

	person A's lifetime income	person B's lifetime income
distributive arrangement I	50	10
distributive arrangement II	25	15
distributive arrangement III	11	11

Simply on the basis of the numbers that appear in this table of possible distributions of income in the society composed of individuals A and B, the strict egalitarian will declare that distribution III is the just one, while the advocate of the difference principle will declare that distribution II is the just one. Now suppose certain facts obtain that are not (and *cannot* be) captured in this sort of a table. Suppose that, no matter which distributive arrangements exist in this mini-society, all the income is produced by A. Distribution I arises when A produces 60 units of income and, out of the goodness of his heart, gives 10 to B. Distribution II arises when the difference principle is imposed and the rate of transfer of income from A to B is set as high as will maximize B's resulting income. (Under arrangement II, A's production drops and/or the direct costs of redistribution mount) Distribution III arises when half of whatever A produces is redistributed to B even if this rate of transfer leads B to have less than he otherwise might. (Under arrangement III, A's production drops further and/or the direct costs of redistribution rise further.) Nozick points out that any reasonable theory of economic justice would take this information about whose productivity makes it possible that B have *anything* to be relevant to deciding which of these three arrangements is the just one. For example, before any reasonable theory condemns arrangement I as unjust and demands that A end up with less than 50 so that B can receive more than 10, it should consider the fact that the 10 that B has under arrangement I is already entirely due to A's productivity (and goodwill). But, for any end-state theorist, this information is irrelevant. All that matters are the numbers reported in the table. If one thinks that the information not reported in this sort of table is relevant to whether or not arrangement I should be condemned as unjust or whether or not arrangement III should be declared more just than arrangement II, one must reject the entire end-state approach to thinking about distributive justice.

In contrast to end-state theories, pattern theories of distributive justice do hold that one must know something about the relevant individuals or what they have done *before* one can say which of the available distributions of income is the just one. Each particular pattern theorist specifies some characteristic that individuals have or have displayed in their actions—such as moral virtue or productive effort—and declares that the state should arrange the distribution of income within society so that people receive income in proportion to their possession or display of the specified characteristic. (Of course, pattern theorists disagree with one another about what characteristic should guide the allocation of income or holdings just as end-state theorists disagree with one another about what profile of income must guide the state's allocation of income.) Each pattern theorist believes that he has specified the one characteristic (or the one weighted set of characteristics) that explains the extent of each individual's claim to a share of the total income or total extra-personal resources within his society. And each pattern theorist is committed to the proposition that, at least for the most part, agents of the state will be able to know when this characteristic (or weighted set of characteristics) is possessed by individuals or displayed in their actions *and* know the extent to which it is possessed or displayed. Needless to say, these beliefs are highly problematic. Even if we were to seem to agree in the abstract that moral virtue (or productive effort or some weighting of the two) ought to be the measure of each person's just share of society's income, when it came to judge actual cases, we would quickly discover that our agreement was mostly illusory. We would discover that our verbal agreement masked deep and difficult to articulate disagreements about what moral virtue (or productive effort) really is—disagreements that only emerge when we attempt to assess particular cases of reputed moral virtue (or productive effort). And even if we found ourselves in agreement about whether the favored characteristic was present in a particular case, we would quickly discover significant differences of opinion among reasonable people about the extent to which that characteristic was present in those cases.[4] Hence, no pattern theory can do what it purports to do, viz., give determinate guidance to state officials about who should received what share of societal income.

Notice also that pattern theories share a deep presumption with end-state theories. This is the presumption that the actual particular actions whereby individuals produce objects, reconfigure and transform them, add value to them, discover more valuable uses for them, discover how to put them to more valuable use, or trade for them in light of such discoveries do not themselves generate entitlements to the particular objects that are produced, transformed, or acquired through trade. Rather, the deep presumption of both end-state and pattern theories is that all such actions contribute to "society's" income and then society"—through its political institutions—has to exercise its authority over this "social income" by arranging its proper distribution among individuals. Advocates of both types of theory presume that a social income pie gets created and that it is within the authority of "society" to decide what the fair or just division of this social pie is. But the fact of the matter, Nozick insists, is that the particular parts of the income pie are generated by specific individuals exercising their natural and developed talents, their alertness and judgment, their entrepreneurial verve, and their effortful perseverance. For the state to treat the resulting values as part of a social income pie over which it has legitimate authority and which it ought now to distribute in accordance with some end-state or pattern theory of justice is for the state to assert authority over at least a portion of the talents, judgments, and efforts of those specific individuals. For the state to have a standing policy of exercising control over what it will describe as "society's income" out of allegiance to some end-state or pattern theory is for the state to institute partial ownership over *the people* whose talents, judgments, and efforts have produced that "social income." But, any such non-consensual institution of partial ownership over people is unjust. It is unjust precisely because it contravenes the basic right that at root condemns all forms of partial or complete slavery—the right of self-ownership.[5] End-state and pattern principles are unjust because they "involve a shift from the classical liberals' notion of self-ownership to a notion of (partial) property rights in *other* people." (Nozick, p.172)

According to Nozick, the plausible alternative to both end-state and pattern theories of distributive justice will direct our attention to the specific acts of production and transfer that particular individuals have engaged in and that entitle them to the particular items that have thereby been produced or transferred. This is how in everyday life we determine whenever an individual has a genuine property right in some extra-personal item. We inquire about whether that agent has produced this item with labor that was rightfully his out of material to which he had rightful access or whether he received this item via voluntary transfer from someone who produced it with labor that was rightfully hers or herself got it through voluntary transfer from some third party who was genuinely entitled to it. According to the historical entitlement view, to show that an individual has a genuine property right in X is to show that the history of his coming to possess X has consisted of acts of just initial acquisition and/or actions of just transfer. A historical entitlement theory of justice in holdings spells out the various ways in which, in light of the conventions and mutual understandings within a given society, individuals in that society are reasonably judged to obtain property rights through acts of initial acquisition and acts of voluntary transfer.[6]

According to historical entitlement theory, then, the justice of A's possession, control, and use of X is entirely a matter of the propriety of the *processes* through which A has come to have X. The justice of A's possession of that item is not at all a matter of A's possession complying with any pre-ordained profile or pattern of holdings (or income) across members of A's society. The overall just distribution of holdings (or income) is simply *whatever* set of holdings (or *whatever* accumulation of incomes) individuals have become entitled to through procedures of just acquisition. If A has obtained vast holdings through entitlement conferring or conveying processes, then the just overall distribution will include A's possession and control of those holdings. But if A had acted differently— if he had he devoted himself to beachcombing rather than building a profitable enterprise—then he would not have legitimately obtained vast holdings and the just overall distribution of holdings would not include his possession and control of those (or any) vast holdings. There is no pre-ordained profile or pattern that the overall set of holdings (or incomes) must comply with in order to be just. Conversely, if B has acquired holdings by improper processes—e.g., by the non-consensual acquisition of other people or their labor or by forcible or fraudulent acquisition of their holdings—then B is not entitled to those holdings no matter how much they accord with some prized overall profile or pattern of holdings. (A third component of the historical entitlement doctrine requires that, insofar as is feasible, the beneficiaries of such unjust acquisitions make restitution to the victims of those acquisitions.)

In essence, the entitlement theory says that a just distribution of holdings within a society is the unintended effect of a free market economic order. If you want economic justice, work for a market order that allows people to acquire in entitlement-conferring and entitlement-conveying ways and for legal institutions that seek to prohibit unjust acquisitive processes and to nullify the unjust acquisitions that do occur. One should endorse this conception of economic justice because the alternative views, end-state and pattern doctrines, are deeply flawed. And one deep flaw that they have in common is that instituting any one of them would, in contravention of the rights of self-ownership, institute partial ownership of some people by other people.[7]

THE ROLE OF GOVERNMENT AND THE STATUS OF TAXATION

Rights are especially stringent moral demands. For, if one has a right over X, one is justified in requiring that others leave one to one's peaceful possession, control, and enjoyment of X. If one has a right over X, one may not merely reasonably request that others not seize or destroy or interfere with one's control of X; one may use force or authorize others to use force to suppress attempts by others to seize or destroy or interfere with one's control of X. Moreover, from the Lockean perspective, the *only* justifiable use of force is, indeed, to suppress the violation of individual rights. It may be morally desirable that A be chaste rather than promiscuous. It may morally desirable that A be charitable rather than miserly. It may morally desirable that A show contempt for all politicians rather than respect for them. But A's being promiscuous, miserly, and *even* his being respectful of politicians violates no one else's rights (assuming that he has not contracted to be chaste, to be charitable, or contemptuous of politicians). A's acting in any one of these morally undesirable ways would, in fact, be an exercise of his rights over himself or his duly acquired property. In each case, A would be acting entirely within his protected sphere of freedom. In each case, the forcible suppression of A's morally undesirable conduct would itself be a violation of his rights.

The state is, above all else, a wielder of force. Indeed, the state is the institution within a given territory that claims to have the final say about when force will be used and is fairly successful at enforcing this claim to have the final say. From the Lockean perspective, states or, more precisely, the particular individuals who hold office within states, have no special, privileged moral standing. States and the individuals who hold office within them are subject to the same basic moral constraints that apply to all private individuals. If the state or its officials engage in actions that would be judged criminal when performed by one private individual upon another, then the actions of the state or its officials must also be judged to be criminal. "The injury and the crime is equal, whether committed by the wearer of a crown, or some petty villain. The title of the offender and the number of his followers, make no difference in the offence, unless it be to aggravate it." (Locke, para.176) From the Lockean perspective, the only legitimate use of force by the state or its officials is use that suppresses the violation of rights. Legitimate states are formed by people for "the mutual *preservation* of their lives, liberties, and estates, which I call by the general name, *property*." (Locke, para.124) "The great end of men's entering into society [is] the enjoyment of their properties in peace and safety..." (Locke, para.134)

Legitimate states may use force only in order to protect individual rights of life, liberty, and property against domestic and foreign threats to those rights. Such states may establish only those institutions—e.g., registries of property, courts, and police forces—that are necessary and proper for the protection of these rights. The use of state coercion for any other purpose—e.g., for the purpose of making people chaste or charitable or even duly contemptuous of politicians—contravenes the rights of those who are subjected to that coercion. The constitutional perspective that emerges from the philosophical considerations presented here sees legitimate state power as radically constrained by people's individual rights. An actual political constitution is worthy of veneration to the extent that it or its amendments either explicitly or implicitly *acknowledge* these constraining rights. A venerable constitution does not pretend to *grant* these rights as though it is within the sovereign power of the state or those who composed its constitution to withhold recognition of them. Of course, an actual political constitution will also set out the institutional structure of government. An actual constitution that is worthy of our allegiance will set out a structure that itself makes it difficult in practice for the state or for factions within the state to trample upon the rights that a constitution explicitly or implicitly recognizes.

The permissible and constitutional defense of people's rights and the rectification of violations of those rights requires resources; and this need for resources raises the difficult question of how the state can acquire the resources to carry out its proper function without violating the very rights it purports to protect. More specifically, how can the state acquire the funds to carry out its constitutional mandate without violating the property rights that it is supposed to be protecting? The traditional answer of classical liberals such as Locke is that we have all joined in a social contract in which we have agreed to be subject to taxation to fund the state's legitimate activities. This traditional answer will not withstand critical scrutiny. On the one hand, if we operate with anything like the ordinary idea of contract, it is obvious that very few if any individuals in, e.g., the United States, have voluntarily entered into a contract to pay taxes—even taxes solely for the purpose of financing the protection of their rights. On the other hand, suppose we water down the idea of contract enough so that everyone (or nearly everyone) in the United States can be said to have contracted to pay taxes. We might say, e.g., that not leaving the country counts as (tacitly) entering into a loving agreement to be taxed. We will then have so watered down the idea of contract that everyone (or nearly everyone) who does not flee from a country will count as having consented to whatever the state governing that country does to him. But, then, the idea of (tacit) consent will not do the job originally assigned to it. For it will vindicate the authority of *every* existing government (over all those who have not fled from their control); hence, it will not allow us to distinguish between legitimate and illegitimate governments.

It seems, however, that the very doctrine of rights that has been sketched in this essay points to an alternative to the flawed idea of a general *social* contract. That doctrine of rights ascribes to A rights against B (and against C) not to be disturbed in his peaceful enjoyment and use of his person and property. If B assaults or kidnaps A, B violates these rights as would C if C were to join in this assault or kidnapping. But suppose instead that C, while capable of forcibly suppressing B's assaulting or kidnapping A, *refrains* from this forcible suppression. Such omissions on C's part would *not* violate any right of A's. For A does not have a right to C's saving him from B's assault or kidnapping. A has no more right to this valuable service than A has a right, in the absence of an ordinary contract with D, to D's service of mowing A's lawn. These propositions hold true even if C is not a single bystander but rather a set of individuals who comprise an organization (called "the state") that has a specialized capacity for suppressing assaults and kidnappings. This in turn suggests that the protection of an individual's rights ought to be thought of as a service relevantly like other services that an individual may hope to enjoy—but must expect to acquire in the marketplace.

The government (we have been presuming) will be the monopoly supplier of this service.[8] But, since the protection of rights is a service to which individuals do *not* have natural rights, it is permissible for the government to provide that service on a voluntary fee-for-service basis. Since we can assume that there is, among almost all individuals, considerable demand for the various measures that will protect their rights, it seems as though we can explain how the provision of those services will be funded without any need to appeal to the idea of a general social contract. It will be funded by people purchasing those protective services from the government. If we were confident about this fee-for-service solution to the problem of funding legitimate governmental activities, we could add a further highly restrictive plank to our constitutional perspective: Government must fund its legitimate protective activities entirely by *selling* its services to willing customers; it must not engage in taxation in any normal sense of the term.

Unfortunately, we cannot be confident about the voluntary fee-for-service solution. For we cannot be confident that the protection of the rights of individuals is *enough* relevantly like the desired services that are readily supplied in the marketplace. The well-known problem here is that various aspects of the protection of people's rights have the characteristics of public goods. Most saliently, if the protection is produced, it will impossible or at least very costly to prevent individuals who have not paid for protection of their rights from also benefiting from the protection. For example, if an effective system of national defense against foreign threats is produced, it will be impossible or at least very costly to exclude individuals who have not paid to be defended from enjoying the benefits of that defensive system. The serious problem here is *not* that some individuals may manage to free ride on other people's funding of defensive services. Rather, the serious problem is that so many people may attempt to free ride that the defense system will not get funded (or will be markedly under funded); hence, *no one* will get the desirable ride. The result of a resolve to fund the protection of rights solely on a voluntary fee-for-service basis *may* be the very undesirable situation in which many people who would strongly prefer to get the defensive services over holding on to a certain amount of money end up holding on to that money but not getting those services. Many highly beneficial exchanges that would have the particularly salutary effect of securing people's rights against violation *may* not take place. For the sake of seeing its constitutional implications for taxation and democracy, let us make the pessimistic *assumption* that the special problems of securing people's voluntary contribution to the funding of institutions and activities that are protective of rights will not be solved. Let us *assume*, that is, that structures for the protection of rights will only be adequately funded if individuals are coercively required to contribute to their funding.[9]

Now, in general, if one takes rights seriously, one will continue to respect people's rights even if doing so leads to a situation that one correctly judges to be undesirable. Rights give people discretionary control over their lives and holdings—including the freedom to act sub-optionally. So the person who takes rights seriously cannot and should not move *quickly* from (1) the assumption that respecting people's rights over themselves and their possession leads to some undesirable outcome to the conclusion that (2) those rights should not be respected and, instead, may permissibly be violated. But the undesirable outcome that consists in the non-production of protective services seems to be a special case. First, the undesirable outcome consists in people being subject to the particular evil of rights violations. Second, being subject to these rights violations may well be disastrous to people in terms of loss of happiness and life. Third, the likely outcomes may well be disastrous to people in terms of their own actual values—not merely in terms of some other party's view about what these people should value. So, in this special case, if individuals are required to contribute to the funding of protective services, they will all be net gainers both in the sense that they will suffer less in the way of infringement of their rights than they otherwise would and in the sense that, by their own lights, their life situation will be more desirable than it otherwise would be. Moreover, there is a fourth interesting feature of this sort of case. Recall that our pessimistic assumption is that, if people are morally at liberty to free ride upon others' non-coerced financing of rights-protective services, then so many (too clever for their own good) people will attempt to free ride on others' voluntary financing of those services that the outcome will be that all those people will end up without protection for their rights. If the pessimistic assumption is correct, people having the moral liberty not to contribute to the funding of protective services will be *self-defeating* in very much the same way that people having the *unconstrained* moral liberty to pursue their own ends would be *self-defeating.*[10]

Previously (especially in section 2-3) I argued that, if a moral code includes the rule, "seek your individual happiness and self-preservation," then it is reasonable for that code also to include a second and constraining rule that prevents general compliance with the first rule from being self-defeating. We saw that general compliance with this first rule will be self-defeating, i.e., individuals will end up with markedly less happiness and self-preservation, unless the conduct of persons is constrained by a second rule that says, "respect each person's discretionary possession and enjoyment of their own persons and just holdings." And we concluded that, therefore, a reasonable moral code would also include this constraining second rule. What we have before us now is the prospect that unqualified compliance *with this constraining second rule* itself will be self-defeating because it will result (if the pessimistic assumption is correct) in people being bereft of protection for their rights. Since the rationale for the adoption of this constraining second rule is to prevent compliance with the first rule (the "seek your own happiness and self-preservation" rule) from being self-defeating, it seems reasonable to restrict this constraining second rule if this is necessary to prevent compliance with this second rule from being self-defeating. This restriction upon the second rule would be a third rule to the effect that people do not have the right to withhold payment for the protection of rights if (but only if) their possessing this right to withhold payment would result in the non-protection of rights. If this third rule is part of a reasonable code of conduct, then a monopoly provider of protective services may permissibly *require* individuals to contribute to the financing of those protective services *if (but only if)* the pessimistic assumption is correct. If (but only if) that assumption is correct, the government's requiring people to make these payments will be unlike all other coercion of peaceful individuals; it will leave all those individuals better off by their own lights.

But let us be clear what has and what has not been justified on the basis of the pessimistic assumption. Only coercive taxation for the funding of the state's *rights protecting* activities has been vindicated. Moreover, for each individual, the loss imposed upon him by taxation must be less than the benefit to him of the protective services he receives. Only if *every* individual who is subject to the taxation is a net beneficiary will the provision of protective services by way of mandatory funding be a genuine public good.[11] So the vindication of *non-voluntary* fee-for-service funding of protective services points to two severe constitutional constraints upon the taxing power of the state. First, taxes may only be imposed to fund the protection of people's rights. Second, the loss imposed through taxation on any given individual must be less than the gain to that individual of the protective services.

Of course, there are extraordinary problems in determining how much a service is worth to individuals who are not free to decline to purchase that service. Because of these problems and the natural tendency of any state to take whatever it can get away with, each individual should have the opportunity to challenge in court the fee-for-service that is imposed upon him on the grounds that this fee equals or exceeds the benefits of the service to him. This opportunity would be built into a reasonable constitutional structure. In fact, such an opportunity *is* built into our constitutional structure if one follows the robust reading of the fifth amendment's takings clause that is proposed in Richard Epstein's *Takings*. There, in effect, Epstein holds that the only constitutionally *justified* taxes are takings of funds for public purposes such that the benefit of the resulting public good that is enjoyed by each person who is deprived of property is great enough to provide just compensation (in kind) for that deprivation. On Epstein's reading all other taxation is constitutionally defective—just as, on the philosophical-constitutional perspective developed here, all taxation that is not part of a scheme of mandatory funding that is *necessary* for the provision of protective services is morally impermissible.[12]

RIGHTS, CONSTITUTIONAL CONSTRAINTS, AND DEMOCRACY

Constitutionalism restricts state power whether that power is lodged in a single individual, or a single class, or the majority of the people as a whole. Nevertheless, even if governmental power is duly restricted, choices will have to be made between the production of innumerable distinct packages of protective services. Some decision mechanism will have to exist to choose which affordable mix of courts, investigative agencies, defensive weaponry, and penal institutions will be created with which technologies, employment practices, and oversight structures. Who should have what sort of a say—either directly or through their representatives—in the basic decisions about how the resources legitimately available to the government should be allocated for protective purposes? It seems pretty clear that *everyone* who contributes to the fund of available resources should have a say.[13] And I shall assume this calls for a system of one man one vote—although a system that weights each person's vote in proportion to his contribution certainly deserves consideration.

If one has a system of one man one vote, one must require *at least* a majority vote for determining whether or not a given option will be adopted or not. For, if less than a majority were to suffice, then there could be enough votes to adopt the option and, at the same time, enough votes to reject it. But there seems to be no general reason why a simple majority of votes in favor of a proposal should be enough for that proposal to be adopted. And there seems to be a good general reason against decision by simple majority. That reason is that simple majorities can too readily be assembled to endorse measures that actually do not on net make everyone better off. Under the guise of protecting everyone's rights, simple majorities may readily adopt measures that especially protect everyone's enjoyment of certain rights, but disproportionately burden some people with the costs of that protection. Worse yet, under the guise of choosing among constitutionally permissible institutions and policies, simple majorities may readily provide members of the majority coalition with goods and services to which they have no rights in ways that necessarily violate the moral and constitutional rights of the minority. Under a venerable constitutional structure such measures would be struck down by a duly vigilant and right-thinking judiciary. But it is too much to hope that, even in the context of a venerable constitutional structure, the judiciary will in fact always be vigilant and right-thinking—especially if it is continually confronted with the need to stand athwart a torrent of unconstitutional (yet popular) governmental action.

One partial solution is constitutionally to require super-majorities for the adoption of any proposed plan of governmental action. Super-majorities, of course, have the virtue of being inherently more difficult to assemble. Moreover, the larger the required super-majority is, the more concentrated and visible must be the burden placed upon the super-minority by any exploitative proposal favored by that super-majority. If, e.g., a proposal requires an 80 percent vote to be adopted, then if it is exploitative, all of the gains to the 80 percent will have to be extracted from the 20 percent. The exploitative (and unconstitutional) character of this measure will be much more visible than the exploitative (and unconstitutional) character of a measure that extracts as much from 49 percent of the people for the benefit of 51 percent. And the more concentrated prospective victims of the measure would be, the more likely the victims would be able to organize effectively against it. In fact, a system that requires simple majority votes in both chambers of Congress and a Presidential endorsement (or a two-thirds vote in both chambers) for legislation to be adopted does, in effect, require a super-majority.[14] And this type of requirement does seem to give potentially exploited minorities a greater chance to resist unjust extractions than they would have in a single-chamber parliamentary system. Unfortunately, this understanding of the constraining tendency of these current constitutional requirements for valid legislation is naively optimistic. For it naively assumes that elected officials do actually represent their constituents at large rather than the special interests that own—or at least rent—them. So it seems worthwhile to look for some other and more direct ways to implement super-majority voting as a constitutional device for limiting the extent to which government actually benefits some individuals at the expense of others and their rights.

The device that I would suggest as worthy of consideration is that the basic tax structure of government be subject to approval by direct popular vote and that the necessary vote for approval be a large super-majority, e.g., 80 percent. This proposal has the virtue of requiring a very simple tax structure, e.g., a national sales tax or a flat rate income tax or an income tax with a small number of brackets. Under such a constitutional rule, a proposed tax structure will be adopted only if it is pretty obvious to at least 80 percent of the voters that the individual costs to them under that structure will be less than the benefits to them individually of the rights protection that the structure will fund. And, for it to be pretty obvious to 80 percent of the voters that they will be net beneficiaries in this way, it will probably have to be true that *almost all* voters will in fact be net beneficiaries under that structure. What about a proposed structure that is likely to be adopted because it benefits almost everyone, but to a significant degree provides some of those benefits through the exploitation of a small minority? The exploitative character of such a structure will at least be highly visible. This may dissuade people from voting for it; and it *should* engender judicial nullification of that structure for its being in violation of the takings clause. Such a super-majority referendum system for taxation would not *guarantee* that only taxes that satisfy the philosophical-constitutional strictures developed in this essay would be adopted and allowed to stand. But it might come as close to a guarantee as one can reasonably expect when one attempts to apply to the real world the insights about moral rights, property rights, and the limits of legitimate government that are found in philosophical reflection.

ENDNOTES

1. Unconstrained maximization may not be *as immediately* self-defeating as consideration of such a one-time encounter between A and B suggests. For, even if A and B are *unconstrained* maximizers, if they are facing an open-ended future of many possible mutually advantageous interactions, they each will be motivated to conduct themselves during present encounters so as to preserve opportunities to benefit from future cooperation. Also, they each may eschew present aggression in order to sustain their reputation for being cooperative among third parties with whom they hope to have gainful interactions. In short, unconstrained maximizers will have reasons to behave as though they are constrained maximizers. The question then becomes whether individuals who all take themselves at root to be unconstrained maximizers will behave enough like constrained maximizers to do as well as constrained maximizers. If the answer is negative—as I believe it is—then the code that calls for unconstrained maximization still is self-defeating.
2. Except that, on some readings of Locke, the rights of human beings are the product of *God's* will.
3. A somewhat different account of private property rights is offered in Mack, "Self-Ownership and the Right of Property."
4. These sorts of points about our inability to reach agreement about what moral virtue or productive effort (or so on) really is and to know how much of it is present in particular individuals take center stage in F. A. Hayek's critique of "social justice." On can agree with these Hayekian points without accepting Hayek's bolder claim that the concept of "social justice" is a meaningless. See especially, volume two of Hayek's *Law, Legislation, and Liberty*.
6. Rawls, e.g., acknowledges that the presumption that people's talents and willingness to produce are "collective assets" is built into the structure of his theory of justice.
7. I have provided a highly condensed and stylized statement of Nozick's contentions. See pages 149-178 of *Anarchy, State, and Utopia* for his own contrast between the historical entitlement theory and end-state and pattern theories and pp. 183-231 for his overwhelming critique of Rawls and the difference principle. See Mack, "Self-Ownership, Marxism, and Equality; Part I, for a reformulation of an important argument by Nozick against end-state and pattern theories that is not presented here.
8. Perhaps no state can be legitimate because no organization can maintain itself as the *monopoly* protector of rights without violating the rights of those who aspire to compete with it (as a protector of rights). If the protection of rights really is a service akin to other desirable services, isn't it impermissible for the state to suppress competing providers of this service? I skip past this crucial issue here. But see part I of Nozick and Sanders and Narveson.
9. Talk about adequate funding embodies the dubious contention that, in the absence of market choices, we have some way of determining what the adequate (or even "optimal") spending on some public goods would be. Insofar as we can talk in this way, we can say that any system of coercive funding is *over-funding* the production of the public good. Coercive funding of protection will always tend to become a "protection racket." For a sampling of skepticism about the assumption that coercion is needed see Cowen, Foldvary, Mack (1986), Sanders and Narveson, and Schmidtz.
10. One way of seeing the similarity of the situation of individuals who confront one another as unconstrained Hobbesian agents and the situation of individuals who confront one another as agents who are morally free not to contribute to the funding of protective services is to see that each situation can readily be presented as a prisoner's dilemma. In both cases, the absence of the relevant constraint leads both agents into non-cooperative conduct and, hence, to payoffs that are less desirable for each than would obtain if both had engaged in cooperative conduct.
11. Each person being a net beneficiary is actually too weak a condition. An appropriately stronger condition would require that no individual be made to contribute out of proportion to the benefits to him of the protective services.
12. But Epstein does not restrict justifiable coercive funding of *protective* services.
13. And, it seems, that those who do not contribute, i.e., those who receive a free ride vis-à-vis protective services because they cannot contribute to their funding, ought not to have

a say about which particular rights-protecting institutions and policies are funded.

14. Throughout this discussion, I am thinking of the federal government in the United States. But my points apply to any government.

15. Unlike the voluntary fee-for-service system, under this sort of regime, if enough voters approve of a measure, those voters bind both themselves and those who have not signed on.

REFERENCES

Barnett, Randy. (ed.) (1989) *The Rights Retained by the People*, volume one. Fairfax,VA: George Mason University Press.

Cowen, Tyler. (ed.) (1988) *The Theory of Market Failure.* Fairfax, VA: George Mason University Press.

Epstein. Richard. (1985) *Takings*. Cambridge, MA: Harvard University Press.

Foldvary, Fred. (1994) *Public Goods and Private Communities.* Brookfield, VT: Edward Elgar Publishing, Limited.

Hayek, F.A. (1973) "Rules and Order." *Law, Legislation, and Liberty*, Volume One, Chicago, IL.: University of Chicago Press.

Hayek, F.A. (1976) "The Mirage of Social Justice." *Law, Legislation, and Liberty*, volume two, Chicago, IL.: University of Chicago Press.

Hobbes, Thomas. (1968) *Leviathan*, C.B. MacPherson (ed.). London, UK.: Pelican Books.

Locke, John. (1969) *Two Treatises on Government,* Peter Laslett (ed.). Cambridge, UK.: Cambridge University Press.

Mack, Eric. (1986) "The Ethics of Taxation: Rights versus Public Goods?" In Dwight Lee (ed.) *Taxation and the Deficit Economy*, San Francisco, CA.: Pacific Research Institute,. pp. 487-514.

Mack, Eric. (1990) "Self-Ownership and the Right of Property" *The Monist*, Vol.73, No.4 (October 1990)

Mack, Eric. (2002) "Self-Ownership, Marxism, and Equality: Part I. Challenges to Historical Entitlement." *Politics, Philosophy, and Economics,* London, UK.: Sage Publication, Volume 1, Issue 1.

Mack, Eric. (2002) "Self-Ownership, Marxism, and Equality: Part II. Challenges to the Self-Ownership Thesis." *Politics, Philosophy, and Economics,* London, UK.: Sage Publication, Volume 1, Issue 2.

Nozick, Robert. (1974) *Anarchy, State, and Utopia.* New York, NY.: Basic Books.

Rawls, John. (1971) *A Theory of Justice.* Cambridge, MA: Harvard University Press.

Sanders, John T. and Narveson, Jan (eds). (1996) *For and Against the State.* Lanham, MD: Rowman and Littlefield.

Schmidtz, David. (1991) *The Limits of Government.* Boulder, CO.: Westview Press.

3 PROPERTY, TAXATION, AND THE BUDGETARY COMMONS

Richard E. Wagner

The central concern of economic analysis has been to explain how a market economy generates an orderly pattern of economic activity even though there is no person or office that creates this order. The order that we observe emerges as if it were imposed by an invisible hand. Only there is no hand. Rather, many hands participate in the generation of orderly economic life. What promotes the coordinated patterns of our economic life is the framework of institutional rules within which people conduct their activities. This institutional framework is characterized mainly by the principles of private property and freedom of contract. Economics is centrally concerned with explaining how it happens that when economic relationships among people are governed by the principles of private property and freedom of contract, productive patterns of economic activity emerge and societies flourish.

One question that arises is how government relates to this institutional framework. Nearly all schools of thought assign to government an important role in maintaining and preserving this institutional framework. This leads to justifications for such things as military, police, and courts as instruments for preserving and maintaining this institutional framework. But modern governments do far more than this. Through their budgetary operations, governments provide a wide array of services, including parks, schools, retirement annuities, medical insurance, and weather forecasts, to mention but a few examples.

In this vein, James Buchanan (1975) makes the conceptual distinction between the protective and the productive states. By protective state, Buchanan refers to the state's maintenance of a framework of property and contract within which people relate to one another. It is helpful to think of economic life as a kind of game that people play, in which personal conduct is governed by rules regarding such things as property and contract. In a market economy, personal conduct is governed by the rules of private property and freedom of contract. In this setting, the protective state is a type of referee or umpire that seeks to ensure that people play by these rules. By contrast, the productive state is a player in the organization of economic activity. The productive state arises when people use their rights of property and contract collectively to form state enterprises. The formation of such state enterprises as schools and subway systems, according to the logic of the productive state, follows the same principles as the formation of such private enterprises as restaurants and hardware stores. People thus buy some services from privately organized vendors and other services from publicly organized vendors.

For the most part, the theory of public finance treats public budgeting as simply a different type of market transaction. Taxing and spending are treated as if they were merely different uses of property and alternative forms of contract. Public budgeting reflects simply different particular uses to which people put their property. People might buy shoes from a retail store, and at the same time they might buy parks from a city. Where they would pay market prices for their shoes, they might pay taxes for their parks. Taxation changes the identity of the vendor from whom purchases are made and to whom orders for production are placed, and nothing more. It is simply one particular use that people make of their private property. Different rates of tax correspond to different collective choices regarding the uses to which people put what is still their private property.

This paper challenges directly this common institutional presumption about property and governance. It does so by treating budgetary operations as vehicles for transforming private property into common property, thereby changing the governance relationships that operate within a society. At its most fundamental level, taxation converts private property to common property, with the state serving as the arena where rules for governing the commons are made. The tax side of the budget is where obligations to stock the common stores are apportioned among the citizenry. The appropriations side is where citizens compete for access to those common stores. As a result of this competition, individual citizens differ in the amount of access they secure, just as they differ in the obligations to stock the commons that they are forced to bear. Where standard fiscal analysis treats taxation as one component of a private property order, here taxation is treated as a means of transforming property, as well as the associated patterns of governance, from private to common.

TAXATION AS A USE OF PRIVATE PROPERTY

It should be said at the outset that not all budgetary operations or processes necessarily convert private property into common. The history of fiscal scholarship contains a good number of formulations whereby state budgeting is thought to act consistently with a framework of private property and freedom of contract. Surely the best known of these formulations is Knut Wicksell's (1896) contribution to justice in taxation. This formulation plays a central role in constitutional political economy, as articulated initially in James Buchanan and Gordon Tullock (1962) and as elaborated in Richard Wagner (1988).

Wicksell thought that it would be possible through proportional representation to select a parliament whose members would be broadly representative of the society from which they were selected. If the parliament were a small-scale replica of the society at large, and if members of parliament were subject to the same laws, obligations, and privileges as everyone else in society, a rule of approximate unanimity within parliament would correspond to approximate unanimity within the society at large. In this case, the conflict between private and collective property would be eliminated through the incorporation of the state into the order of private property. Political enterprises would compete on equal terms with private enterprises.

While Wicksell's formulation is best known in the history of fiscal thought, the Cameralist originators of the theory of public finance, who thrived throughout the Germanic lands from roughly 1650 to 1850, had a similar orientatrion (see Jürgen Backhaus and Richard Wagner [1987]). For the Cameralists, taxation was a last resort method of public finance. States possessed property, and the Cameralists argued that princes should be able to manage their property so as to generate sufficient revenue to provide public services throughout their lands. A prince who resorted to taxation was a failed prince who at the same time was impeding the well being of those who lived within his lands. In the Cameralist orientation, as in the Wicksellian framework, state budgeting was conceived ideally as something that took place within the framework of property and contract, as against transcending or transforming that framework.

Site-value taxation, as explored by Fred Foldvary's chapter in this book, in principle can operate as a variation on the Cameralist theme. To the extent that public services make location within the boundaries of that government more desirable, land values will increase. A government that finances its services from those increases in land values is actually charging people something like market prices for the services its provides. In this case, site-value taxation becomes a form of market price. To the extent this happens, government is acting as but one participant among many within an economic process that is governed uniformly by the principles of property and contract.

DEMOCRACY AND THE BUDGETARY COMMONS

Whether government acts within the rules of property and contract or whether it acts to transform those rules is a knotty institutional question that lies at the confluence of fiscal philosophy and fiscal practice. Just as we can distinguish between types of property, so can we distinguish between forms of democracy. Democracy is commonly taken to mean any system of governance where political offices are filled by periodic election. There is nothing particularly wrong with this minimalist approach to definition. Yet it is no more informative than describing a group of people as "playing ball."

When faced with such a statement, we may be sure that those people are not playing with cards. But we learn no more than this from this description.

Similarly, to hear that a system of governance is democratic tells us only that people are invited periodically to vote, which thereby tells us that they are not governed by generals or by royal families. While we learn something when we hear that people are playing ball or are being governed democratically, we do not learn much. If we wanted to learn more about their play, we would need to learn more about the particular types of ball they were playing. This desire would lead us into an inquiry about how different rules governing play correspond to different particular ball games. It is the same for systems of democratic governance. Different rules would generate different patterns of democratic governance and different political outcomes, partly because of differences in incentives that are created and partly because of differences in knowledge that are generated within different systems of governance, as explained in Dan Usher (1992).

With respect to democratic governance, what is of central importance is the relationship between property and democracy, as noted in the various essays in Charles Rowley (ed.) (1993). The fundamental disjunction lies in whether property is prior to and a limitation on democracy, or whether is a creation of democracy. The vision that dominated the American constitutional founding was clearly the former. People and their rights of person and property are prior to government. Governments are created to preserve and protect those rights. The powers of government are derived from the consent of the governed. This is a vision of a limited government, with the limitation residing in the superior claim of people to their own property. In the limit, a government is treated as just another form of voluntary association. People may agree to join a swimming club, but the jurisdiction of the club is only what those people have agreed to. The club is in no sense a source of rights, but rather is merely a reflection of those peoples' uses of their prior and superior rights.

This principle of governance constitutes liberal democracy. Human relationships are governed within a framework provided by the legal principles of private property and freedom of contract, and government itself is constituted consistently with those principles. This framework for governance generates the pattern of commercial activities that constitute an open or competitive market economy. In such a system of freedom of competition, commercial activities are organized consensually. People are free to do as they choose within the framework of property and contract. Someone who wants to start a newspaper can do so, and there is no particular person or office of authority that can prevent that project from going forward. The publisher will have to convince all kinds of people, including writers, advertisers, and customers, to support his project if it is to be successful. But all of these choices are made voluntarily, and there is no particular person whose permission is necessary and without which the project cannot go forward. This freely competitive economy is the economic instantiation of a system of liberal democracy, where government itself acts within, and is limited by the principles of private property and freedom of contract.

If private property is instantiated politically as liberal democracy, social democracy is the political instantiation of common property. In this setting, property is held commonly and the state serves as the arena within which access to the commons is governed. What are treated as rights of property evolve out of the activities that take place within the arena that comprises the state. What is regarded as property in this case results either from a direct grant by the state or from a disinterest of the state in asserting its prerogatives. Property in broadcasting, to mention but one of numerous possible illustrations, comes through grants from the state. No one can broadcast without permission of the Federal Communications Commission. Property in this instance is more on the order of a usufruct. What can be done, or what must be done with that property is defined and controlled by the state, and may be amended pretty much at the state's choosing.

There are also many areas where the state shows no interest, at least to date, in exerting control. Grass cutting and babysitting, for instance, are still organized through open competition within a framework of private property and freedom of contract. Even here, however, there is no principled reason under social democracy why the state could not exert control over these matters. The state simply cannot be involved in everything, so there will exist spheres of individual autonomy. What limits the reach of state action, however, is simply a calculus of state interest, and not some principled limit on the reach of the state.

A system of social democracy generates a system of regulated or closed competition, under which the principles of property and contract are relegated to the background, as the foreground comes to be occupied by the relevant regulatory edicts. Some of these edicts will be general in their coverage, as in such things as the myriad rules governing discrimination. Other of these edicts will be specific to subsets of activities, as illustrated by marketing orders in agriculture or the creation of particular minimum wage requirements in construction, the proliferation of which are examined in Richard Epstein (1995).

There is an economic logic to the entire range of undertakings and outcomes of any political regime. The pattern of political activities conforms as fully to an economic logic as does the pattern of economic activities. This insight from the scholarship on public choice has now become common knowledge among students of political economy, as explained in William Mitchell and Randy Simmons (1994). Within the rules that characterize a particular political regime, there will exist a pattern of outcomes and policies that emerge from the interactions among the participants within those regimes. The set of rules that characterize a system of social democracy will generate a set of policy outcomes that has survival power within that regime.

Social democracy and liberal democracy are polar models of democratic governance, just as private and common property are polar models of property rights. The United States was founded as a system of liberal democracy, and has undergone a widespread transformation into a system of social democracy. This is not to say that this transformation has gone smoothly and without resistance. Nor is it to say that it is complete—or irreversible. There is resistance to that transformation, and in scattered places there are even signs of some possible reversal. Still, recognition that there are two ideal forms of democracy corresponding to two ideal forms of property rights will be important in thinking through the relation between state budgets and market processes.

THE FISCAL COMMONS

For the most part, particularly at the national level of government, state budgeting transforms private property into common, as explained in Richard Wagner (1992). To be sure, not all collective budgeting takes place on a fiscal commons. A good deal of such budgeting takes place within a framework of private property. Among other things, there are a large number of clubs, civic associations, and even local governments that engage in budgetary operations without exhibiting phenomena associated with the tragedy of the commons. For the most part, common property budgeting arises at the level of the nation state.

With the fiscal commons, the produce from the commons is provided not by Mother Nature but through taxation. The fiscal commons is stocked through taxation, with the tax code stipulating the liabilities of different people within a society to contribute to that stocking. For instance, a flat-rate tax of 20 percent on income would require each person to devote 20 percent of his productive effort to stocking the fiscal commons. The spending side of the budget reflects the efforts of people and their interest groups to compete for shares of this budgetary commons. Those people who are more effective at political organization will fare better and gain larger shares of this budgetary commons.

To be extent public budgeting takes the form of a fiscal commons, we should expect to observe various phenomena associated with the tragedy of the commons. When property is owned privately, the owners of property individually bear responsibility for the value consequences of their actions. When property is owned in common, those value consequences are diffused throughout the relevant society. It is this diffusion of consequences that was described as the "tragedy of the commons" by Garrett Hardin (1968). While Hardin's essay attracted strong attention, the economic consequences of common property were explored well before Hardin, for instance by Frank Knight (1924) and H. Scott Gordon (1954). With private property, individual owners can exclude others from using that property without receiving the owner's permission. With common property, there is no such right to exclude. In some cases, access to a commons will be open to everyone. This situation is the pure or classic form of common property. More generally, common property refers to some form of collective ownership where property is held jointly by some collective body, and where ownership shares are not distributed severally among the members of that body. Governance of the commons thus takes place through some process of collective decision making (Ostrom [1990] and Yoon [2000]).

In the development of the economic analysis of common property settings, natural resource situations have supplied many examples. Oyster beds, as discussed by Angello and Donnelley (1975), provide an interesting illustration of the familiar "tragedy of the commons" model. Oyster beds within the United States are subject to private ownership in some states and common ownership in other states. When oyster beds are owned privately, owners have a strong incentive to seek to maximize the value of the oyster bed. Among other things, this requires that owners avoid harvesting oysters that are immature. It also requires that they replenish the clutch, the deposits of rock or shell that are vital for the growth of oysters and which are scooped up along with the oysters.

Under common ownership, farmers have little incentive to return immature oysters or to replenish clutch. The bulk of any increased value that would result from doing these things would benefit everyone else who harvests the common oysters. States where common property is maintained have recognized these incentive problems, and have imposed restrictions on the minimum size of the oysters that can be harvested and have imposed requirements for the replacement of clutch. Regulations, however, can never replace fully the effectiveness of the incentives that private ownership generates naturally. Indeed, Agnello and Donnelley estimate that a conversion of commonly owned oyster beds to private ownership would increase the value of the output from the farming of oysters by about 50 percent.

In the presence of common property budgeting, as in the presence of common property generally, the self-interests of fiscal participants cannot be relied upon to promote good fiscal order. Individual oyster fishermen will not harvest oysters prematurely when they own the beds. When the beds are held in common, this is no longer true. The promotion of good economic order in this case requires auxiliary controls imposed by some regulatory authority. Such regulation, however, will never work perfectly and costlessly. Regulation will impose its own costs, and it will follow a political calculus that may differ sharply from the economic calculus that private property entails.

The phenomena of common-property budgeting occur on both the taxing and spending sides of the budget. The taxing side is a political arena where obligations to stock the fiscal commons are imposed. From an individual's perspective, the best tax is invariably one that other people pay. With wide differences in political effectiveness across people and the interest groups with which they are associated, widespread discrimination in the distribution of tax liabilities characterizes democratic processes, as Walter Hettich and Stanley Winer explain in their chapter in this book.

Through taxation, a structure of politically generated prices would replace the market prices that would arise under private property budgeting, a point that was set forward in Maffeo Pantaleoni (1911) and elaborated in Richard Wagner (1997)(1998). These political prices involve price discrimination, with those who are politically favored receiving lower prices. In turn, those lower prices are made possible by imposing higher prices on everyone else. To be sure, the state does not have unlimited ability to practice fiscal discrimination because people can to varying degrees withdraw their contributions to the tax base. Still, the state does have considerable ability to discriminate among taxpayers in ways that would have allowed opportunities for arbitrage in private markets.

Political price discrimination expands the scope for venality in politics. Political offices become more valuable objects to possess. The possession of an unlimited power to tax by the state increases the value of holding political offices for two reasons, reasons that are political cousins to bribery and extortion. The political cousin to bribery is called "rent seeking" by economists. If tax discrimination is a permissible outcome of tax legislation, interest groups will seek to secure favorable tax treatment. This will take the form of exemptions, deductions, or exclusions from the tax base, the consequence of which is to generate a higher rate of tax applied to a narrower base. There will be, as it were, a market for tax legislation, whereby interest groups lobby for particularly desired tax provisions.

The political cousin to extortion is "rent extraction," which is explored in Fred McChesney (1997). Rent extraction is represented by threats to tax that are rescinded if the tax target responds as desired by the threatening politician. A possible change in a tax provision can be announced and a hearing scheduled, only later to be canceled if sufficient opposition materializes, with opposition being signified by such things as campaign contributions. In this case, money is being paid for nothing but a continuation of the present tax status. In contrast, with rent seeking money is being paid to secure some change in tax status.

At first glance it might seem as though legislative positions with responsibility for drafting tax legislation would be undesirable. It might seem to be far better to be able to hand out appropriations on the spending side of the budget than to collect revenues on the taxing side. Yet the facts are sharply the reverse. Members of the revenue-raising committees capture about twice the campaign contributions as other Legislators. Members of the revenue committees also receive significantly larger honoraria and in-kind perquisites than other Legislators. The opportunities for fiscal discrimination that accompany the fiscal commons makes the opportunity to influence tax legislation particularly valuable. Citizens will pay for influence that might translate into favored tax treatment. They will also pay for influence that will prevent them from being on the losing end of tax discrimination. They will pay the political cousin of bribery to secure tax favors, and they will pay the political cousin of extortion to avoid tax harms.

On the expenditure side of the budget, life on the fiscal commons will also entail higher production costs than would be found with private property. Government is inherently a high-cost provider of whatever it provides, as compared with what would result under private-property governance. This theme is elaborated cogently in William Peirce (1999). The high-cost character of government enterprise is due to the separation of choice from liability that common property creates. Ordinary self-interest cannot be relied upon to secure efficiency on the fiscal commons. For instance, a government agency has few incentives to refrain from spending what has been appropriated because the savings cannot be carried forward to the next year. Moreover, a failure to spend the full appropriation may even be taken to indicate that the past appropriation was unnecessarily high. Additional layers of auditing, inspections, and other forms of bureaucratic control will be made necessary by common-property governance, and which will entail costs that are not present with the private ordering of economic transactions.

PROPERTY, FISCAL SOCIOLOGY, AND TECTONIC POLITICS

Carolyn Webber and Aaron Wildavsky (1986) argue that budgetary choices involve much more than a choice about how much people will spend at public-goods stores relative to private-goods stores. They are fundamentally conflict-laden choices among people over how we are to lead our lives. Private property and common property represent the basis for two alternative regimes for ordering human relationships, and these two regimes clash in important respects. Public spending takes place through various programs that constitute identifiable political enterprises, each with their particular clients and supporters. An interest group, moreover, has weak incentives to reduce its budgetary requests, because such reductions will simply leave more money available for other interest groups to harvest.

One implication of the relative inefficiency of the political enterprises that are established within the fiscal commons is that their very existence will create potential profit opportunities for competitive private enterprises. To the extent those private enterprises are able successfully to exploit those profit opportunities, the basis of support for the political enterprise will erode. To prevent this erosion, the political enterprises will have to erect auxiliary controls over the competitive efforts of private enterprises. For instance, in many cases political enterprises practice price discrimination. Through such discrimination, price reductions to favored clients are financed by the higher prices charged to other customers. Those higher prices, in turn, often create incentives for private enterprises to serve those customers at lower prices.

Understandably, political enterprises and their supporters seek to preclude such "cream skimming," for this would otherwise undermine the price discrimination that is essential for the support of the political enterprise. In any case, there will be a continual churning in the structure of regulatory restrictions within the fiscal commons, in response to the continuing cat-and-mouse game that the fiscal commons creates.

This clash between governing regimes can be illustrated by considering alternative approaches to the organization of transportation in urban areas. Such transportation could be organized wholly through private ordering. The mix among such things as cars, busses, and trains would depend on the choices of entrepreneurs, customers, and other market participants. It is surely conceivable that someone might invest in a fleet of busses. The success of this bus enterprise would depend on its ability to offer an attractive product to people who face such other options as driving their own cars, forming car pools, and moving closer to their places of work.

Suppose urban transportation had been organized wholly through private ordering, and now a publicly organized bus service is established. To the extent this bus service could not be competitive with private enterprises because of its higher cost character, the public enterprise could not survive competition with the private enterprises. For the public enterprise to become competitive, it will have to use political power to gain some competitive advantage. There are several ways this can be done. One is for the state to subsidize the public enterprise. This subsidy would allow the public enterprise to charge lower prices than it would otherwise have to charge, thereby strengthening its competitive position. Another way is for the state to impose particular disabilities upon competitive private enterprises. Taxes can be imposed on private busses to increase their costs of operation. Regulations can be imposed that require drivers to be full-time employees, again increasing costs of operation and strengthening the relative competitive position of the political enterprise. Obstacles can also be imposed on services and activities that are competitive with the political enterprise. For instance, taxes can be imposed on private parking garages and restrictions can be imposed on the sizes of such garages. These taxes and restrictions increase the cost of using private cars, which again strengthen the relative competitive position of the political enterprise. An almost endless array of taxes, subsidies, and regulatory restrictions can emerge to strengthen the inherently weak competitive position of the political enterprise. This is an element of the dynamics of the mixed economy, as noted by Sanford Ikeda (1997).

MITIGATING THE TRAGEDY OF THE FISCAL COMMONS

Above the entrance to the headquarters of the American Internal Revenue Service is chiseled a quotation from Oliver Wendell Holmes: "Taxation is the price we pay for civilization." A surface reading might suggest that we should acquiesce in whatever taxes are imposed on us, because the alternative would be even more painful that the taxes we pay. A deeper reflection on Holmes' statement, however, reveals ambiguity about taxation. That some taxation may strengthen civil society does not mean that any and all taxation will do so. If taxation is too heavy or is otherwise inappropriate, it will erode rather than support the flourishing of civil society.

Taxation most surely represents a form of Faustian bargain, for reasons presented by Vincent Ostrom (1987). Taxation is an instrument of evil, in that it injects the use of force into what should be peaceful, voluntary human relationships. We countenance the evil because we think the alternative will be an even worse evil. If the alternative to taxation is the absence of government and civil order, some taxation is necessary to provide a framework for good civil order. In this respect taxation is truly a price we pay for civilization. That some taxation works to our common benefit does not, however, mean that any and all taxation does so. We can acknowledge with Holmes that proper taxation may well be a price we pay for civilization, while at the same time recognizing with our forebearers that taxation becomes destructive if it is too high or wrongly imposed.

Some taxation is surely necessary simply to secure an economic order grounded in private property. If taxes were replaced by voluntary contributions, it would be impossible for anyone to claim that the state was involved in expropriating private property. At the same time, however, people would have strong incentives to take free rides on the contributions of others. As a result, such common valued services as civil order and national security, which require expenditures on military, police, and courts, are likely to be under funded. Taxation thus represents a type of "forced exchange," as Richard Epstein (1985) notes. This term might appear a bit oxymoronic at first glance, but it conveys an important truth. Government is not limited to purely voluntary exchanges, in part because of disabilities such as those posed by free riding. Yet, while government thus possesses a power to tax, the use of that power is limited normatively by the requirement that it conform reasonably well to the exchanges that ideally would have been made, but which were precluded by such things as free riding. Taxes should mirror the voluntary payments that would have been made were it not for the problems of free riding. The difficulty, of course, is that there is no way truly to know what the pattern of those voluntary contributions would have been.

The principle of forced exchange treats taxation as a means of pricing state-supplied services to the citizenry. This treatment of taxation comprises a long and respected tradition among tax philosophers, and has come to be known as the benefit principle of public finance. This treatment is useful because it recognizes that there is a purpose to taxation, which is to allow people to provide valued services for themselves that they would be unlikely to secure nearly so fully or efficiently if the state did not possess the power to tax. When Justice Holmes was speaking of taxation as the price of civilization, he was touching upon some of the central features of the benefit principle of public finance.

To speak of taxes as prices also has its problematical side, however, because this simile is easily corruptible (as noted in Racheter and Wagner [1999]). In some cases the forced exchanges that taxation makes possible will be beneficial to all. But in other cases, taxation will be used as an instrument for the deprivation and abridgement of property. The dark side of the Faustian bargain is that the power to tax can also be used to expropriate property, which would never happen with truly voluntary contributions. Among three adjoining neighbors, two might steal asparagus from a patch owned by the third. Should the three neighbors comprise a government and the majority support a tax on asparagus, what otherwise would have been theft will have been converted into tax policy. The best tax, after all, is always one that someone else pays, and governments offer plenty of scope to do just this.

The central feature that enables government to abridge rights of property through taxation is its ability to practice tax discrimination. This can be seen by comparing a state that possesses an unlimited power to tax with one whose power to tax is limited by a constitutional requirement of generality or nondiscrimination in taxation (see Hutt 1975). It is a quite different matter to tax asparagus if only one neighbor grows it than if all three do so. In the former case, the majority is agreeing to tax the minority. In the latter case, it is far more plausible to claim that the three neighbors are agreeing to tax themselves.

A principle of generality in taxation leads naturally to support for broad-based taxation. Although broad-based taxation would not eliminate all possible claims of tax discrimination, it would severely restrict the practice, as examined, for instance, in James Buchanan and Roger Congleton (1998). A broad-based tax on income, where the entire base is taxed at the same rate, would conform to reasonable notions of generality in taxation. There would be no scope for political position to influence a person's tax liability. The same rate of tax would apply to everyone, and each person's tax liability would depend simply on his own income or consumption in conjunction with the tax rate that was enacted through the political process.

Broad-based, nondiscriminatory taxation impedes efforts to use taxation to reward or punish certain forms of activity. The very principle of nondiscrimination is one that asks the state to be neutral toward all kinds of activities. Yet a great deal of tax legislation rewards or punishes specific forms of activity. The principle of nondiscrimination clashes with the use of taxation to punish and reward. Once a government acquires the habit of rewarding or punishing particular types of activity, the principle of broad-based, nondiscriminatory taxation quickly evaporates under the heat of politics. What results is an unlimited power to tax, where the only limit on the reach of the tax collector is the pragmatic one of political pressure and votes.

Economists use the prisoners' dilemma to illustrate situations where a sequence of choices may yield outcomes that are harmful to nearly everyone, even though each of the individual choices might have seemed wise to the person making the choice. A similar dilemma exists when approaching the issue of discrimination in taxation. A requirement of nondiscrimination would be a fairly strict limit on the power to tax, and would prevent progressive taxation, along with a plethora of exemptions, deductions, and the like.

There is no doubt that sincere people can come up with compelling reasons why exceptions to the principle of nondiscrimination should be made. Proponents of such purportedly good discrimination can find some support among the tax philosophers. Tax policy, however, is made by political realists and not by tax philosophers. The elimination of nondiscrimination as a constitutional principle invites the political realists as well as the tax philosophers to think of ingenious ways to use taxes as a form of political and social control. Rent seeking and rent extraction will flourish once a principle of anything goes replaces nondiscrimination as a guiding norm. There is almost no cause that cannot be claimed to be a good one if it is supported by taxes placed on other people.

REFERENCES

Agnello, Richard J. and Donnelley, Lawrence P. (1975) "Property Rights and Efficiency in the Oyster Industry." *Journal of Law and Economics* 18, pp. 521-533.

Backhaus, Jürgen and Wagner, Richard E. (1987) "The Cameralists: A Public Choice Perspective." *Public Choice* 53, pp. 3-20.

Buchanan, James M. (1975) *The Limits of Liberty*. Chicago, IL.: University of Chicago Press.

Buchanan, James M. and Congleton, Roger D. (1998) *Politics by Principle, Not Interest: Toward Nondiscriminatory Democracy,* Cambridge, MA: Cambridge University Press.

Buchanan, James M. and Tullock, Gordon. (1962) *The Calculus of Consent*. Ann Arbor, MI.: University of Michigan Press.

Epstein, Richard. (1985) *Takings: Private Property and the Power of Eminent Domain.* Cambridge, MA.: Harvard University Press.

Epstein, Richard. (1995) *Simple Rules for a Complex World.* Cambridge, MA.: Harvard University Press.

Gordon, H. Scott (1954) "The Economic Theory of a Common-Property Resource: The Fishery." *Journal of Political Economy* 62, pp. 124-142.

Hardin, Garrett. (1968). "The Tragedy of the Commons." *Science* 162, pp. 1243-1248.

Hutt, William H. (1975) "Unanimity versus Non-discrimination (as Criteria for Constitutional Validity)." In *Individual Freedom: Selected Essays of William H. Hutt*, Svetozar Pejovich and David Klingaman (eds.) Westport, CT.: Greenwood Press, pp. 14-33.

Ikeda, Sanford. (1997) *Dynamics of the Mixed Economy*. London, UK.: Routledge.

Knight, Frank H. (1924). "Some Fallacies in the Interpretation of Social Cost." *Quarterly Journal of Economics* 38, pp. 582-606.

McChensey, Fred. (1997) *Money for Nothing: Polictians, Rent Extraction, and Political Extortion.* Cambridge, MA.: Harvard University Press.

Mitchell, William C. and Simmons, Randy T. (1994) *Beyond Politics: Markets, Welfare, and the Failure of Bureaucracy*. Boulder, CO.: Westview Press.

Ostrom, Elinor (1990). *Governing the Commons*. Cambridge, MA.: Cambridge University Press.

Ostrom, Vincent. (1987) *The Political Theory of a Compound Republic*, 2nd ed. Lincoln, NE.: University of Nebraska Press.

Pantaleoni, Maffeo. (1911) "Considerazioni sulle proprieta di un sistema di prezzi politici." *Giornale degli Economisti* 42, pp. 9-29, 114-133

Peirce, William S. (1999) "Government: An Expensive Provider." In *Limiting Leviathan*, Donald P. Racheter and Richard E. Wagner (eds.) Northhampton, MA: Edward Elgar, pp. 56-73.

Racheter, Donald P. and Wagner, Richard E. (1999). "Faustian Bargains and Constitutional Governance." In *Limiting Leviathan*, Donald P. Racheter and Richard E. Wagner (eds). Northhampton, MA.: Edward Elgar, pp. 1-9.

Rowley, Charles K., ed. (1993), *Property Rights and the Limits of Democracy*. Hants, U.K: Edward Elgar.

Usher, Dan. (1992). *The Welfare Economics of Markets, Voting, and Predation*. Ann Arbor, MI.: University of Michigan Press.

Wagner, Richard E. (1988). "The Calculus of Consent: A Wicksellian Retrospective." *Public Choice* 56, pp. 153-166 .

Wagner, Richard E. (1992) "Grazing the Budgetary Commons: The Rational Politics of Budgetary Irresponsibility." *Journal of Law and Politics* 9, pp. 105-19.

Wagner, Richard E. (1997) "Parasitical Pricing, Economic Calculation, and the Size of Government: Variations on a Theme by Maffeo Pantaleoni." *Journal of Public Finance and Public Choice* 15, pp. 135-146.

Wagner, Richard E. (1998) "Social Democracy, Societal Tectonics, and Parasitical Pricing." *Constitutional Political Economy* 9, pp. 105-111.

Webber, Carolyn and Wildavsky, Aaron. (1986) *A History of Taxation and Public Expenditure in the Western World.* New York, NY.: Simon and Schuster.

Wicksell, Knut. (1896; 1958) "A New Principle of Just Taxation." In *Classics in the Theory of Public Finance*, Richard A. Musgrave and Allan T. Peacock (eds.) London, UK.: Macmillan, pp. 72-118.

Yoon, Jong J. (2000). "Politics as Tragedy: The Logic of Common Access to Social Value." *Journal of Public Finance and Public Choice* 18, pp. 23-34.

4 TAXPAYERS RIGHTS AND THE FISCAL CONSTITUTION

Gary Wolfram

"Taxes are what we pay for a civilized society"
Oliver Wendell Holmes, inscribed over the entrance to the Internal Revenue Service Building in Washington D.C.

"The power to tax involves the power to destroy."
Chief Justice John Marshall, *McCulloch v. Maryland*

As Shakespeare might say, "there's the rub." If we believe that Thomas Hobbes was correct in his observation that life without government was solitary, poor, nasty, brutish, and short, then in order to save ourselves from the dark world of anarchy we form a government. One of the primary ways of funding government is taxation, and thus Oliver Wendell Holmes' statement. However, as Hobbes and many others have pointed out, there is a tendency for governments to grow in coercive power. Taxation is one of the coercive powers of government that holds the possibility of being used to destroy business entities, organizations, or individual liberty. A fundamental question then is how do we form a government that protects the taxpayers from the coercive power of those in control.

This is no idle question. Charles Adams, in *For Good and Evil: The Impact of Taxes on the Course of Civilization* hypothesizes that taxes are a primary explanation of the history of society. He begins with the ancient Egyptians and traces tax revolts throughout history to argue that

> taxes are a powerful mover of people, more than governments care to admit or to realize...Indeed it will seem axiomatic that behind most of the great events of history—the prosperity of nations, revolts and revolutions, liberty and slavery, and most of all war—taxes have played an important role that is easily lost sight of in the drama of great events. (xvii)

Adams' view of history is a series of events where government increases its tax burden beyond what the taxpayers are willing to stand. This is then followed by taxpayer revolt, violence, and drastic changes in the structure of society. To the extent that Adams is correct in his view, had an effective fiscal constitution existed, world history might very well be completely different.

Any discussion of taxpayers' rights and the fiscal constitution must begin with a recognition of the fundamental problem of political economy: it is likely that government is needed to minimize or limit coercion of the individual, but how can we limit our government once it is granted coercive power? Some, such as Friedrich Hayek argue that it is possible to limit the coercive power of government through institutional structures, such as a written constitution, while others might argue that there is no effective way to limit government from assuming despotic powers. As Harold Groves once pointed out: "Public Finance has a root in political science as well as one in economics, and some conception of the state and how it makes its decisions is linked to taxation." (1974, 4) In the course of this paper we will examine the proper role of government, outline the characteristics of laws that protect taxpayer rights and different views of the fiscal constitution, include an example of a state fiscal constitution, and discuss whether one can construct a fiscal constitution that effectively limits the federal government.

THE ROLE OF GOVERNMENT: NATURAL RIGHTS

Herbert Spencer, writing in the middle of the 19th century, spoke to the importance of establishing what he called the proper sphere of government:

> It need no arguments to prove that there is a boundary beyond which no legislative control should pass—that there are individual and social requirements whose fulfillment will be better secured by moral stimulus and voluntary exertion, than by artificial regulations—that between the two extremes of its possible power, the *everything* and the *nothing* with which a government might be entrusted, there must be some point which both principle and policy indicate as its proper limitation. This point, this boundary, it behooves every man to fix for himself...Before he ventures to entertain another opinion upon what a government should *do*, he must first settle for himself the question—What is a government *for*? (1982, 269)

A discussion of the literature on the role of government would take volumes. For a good overview, see *Limiting Leviathan* and *Federalist Government in Principle and Practice*, edited by Racheter and Wagner. (1999, 2001) Our discussion will be much more limited. In this paper we will look at it from

Spencer's perspective, that government's role in public policy, and thus its need for tax revenues to fund that role, must be founded in some general principle of what government is for. However, to discuss what a government is for, we must first establish what the rights of the individual are, and then whether government is useful for protecting those rights.

One of the fundamental principles of the relationship of the individual to government is natural rights theory as developed by John Locke in, among other writings, *Second Treatise on Civil Government.* Locke's position was trying to "show how men might come to have a property in several parts of that which God gave to mankind in common, and that without any express compact of all the commoners."(21) Locke's basic premise was that we have a right to ourselves, our bodies. He then extends this to the idea that we have a right to property that has come about through our own work effort. "Whatsoever, then, he removes out of the state that nature has provided and left it in, he hath mixed his labour with, and joined it to something that is his own, and thereby becomes his property."(22) Locke was discussing the idea of property in a world where the average person made things or grew them, rather than produced computer software. However, in the broadest sense, I think that Locke would agree that if you go to work for General Motors and they pay you $40,000 per year, then you have a natural right to that $40,000. Thus natural rights theory would say that we have a natural right to property, our bodies, and whatever we make through our effort.

In terms of taxpayers' rights, we would begin with Locke's idea and say taxpayers have a right to whatever they produce, and thus government has no right to take their property through coercion. The problem with this position is that there would be no government in such a world. We could have voluntary associations whereby we paid dues, but not government as we normally think of it. So why would we form a government?

Locke suggested that we form government to escape from the problems of an anarchist world of complete individualism. In particular he writes, "The great and chief end, therefore, of men's uniting into commonwealths, and putting themselves under government, is the preservation of their property; to which in the state of nature there are many things wanting."(102) So men form governments chiefly for the protection of property. Locke's point is that the primary concern of government should be the protection of the taxpayer's property. However, he obviously does not take the position that there should be no government, and since government must be funded, it must be acceptable for government to tax its citizens in a sufficient amount to pay for the protective services of government.

As Roger Pilon (1993, 1999) has aptly pointed out, the founders of the United States were squarely in the Lockean tradition of natural rights to property. The founding documents make this clear. The Declaration of Independence speaks of "the separate and equal Station to which the laws of Nature and of Nature's God entitle them." It declares that "We hold these truths to be self-evident, that all men are created equal, that they are endowed by their Creator with certain unalienable rights, that among these are Life, Liberty, and the Pursuit of Happiness—That to secure these Rights, Governments are instituted among Men, deriving their just powers from the consent of the governed..." The Founders thus established the natural rights of men and then made it clear that the role of government is to protect these rights.

In *Federalist #1* Hamilton promises to show in the remainder of the *Federalist Papers* why adoption of the Constitution preserves Republican government as well as liberty and property. As one reads through the *Federalist Papers* it is evident that the primary reason given for replacing the Articles of Confederation with the new Constitution is the failure of the latter to provide sufficient protection of property and liberty. While it is possible today to look upon Locke as a political philosopher whose quaint writings are of only scholarly interest, the people writing the Declaration of Independence and the Constitution were using his work as a blueprint for what the new Republic should look like. They were attempting to establish a government that would protect the natural rights of man. In *Federalist #84*, Hamilton demonstrates that many of the provisions of the Constitution are to protect the rights of individuals. Indeed, the preamble to the Constitution states that it is established "to secure the Blessings of Liberty to ourselves and our Posterity," a Lockean notion of government to protect our rights rather than provide for us.

The Lockean natural rights theory is very consistent with the writings of Frederic Bastiat, a strong advocate of limited government, although the angle is a little different. Locke is basically making the point that natural law gives us the right to property, and that men form governments to protect this natural right. He then examines government and its limitations from the view that man has natural rights which he may voluntarily give up to the commonwealth, but the power of the commonwealth is limited to what the individual could give up. Since the individual has no arbitrary power under natural law over another individual,

> but only so much as the law of nature gave him for the preservation of himself, and the rest of mankind; this is all he doth or can give up to the commonwealth, and by it to the legislative power, so the legislative can have no more than this. Their power in the utmost bounds of it, is limited to the public good of the society. It is a power that hath no other end but preservation, and therefore can never have a right to destroy, enslave, or designedly to impoverish the subjects. (111)

For Locke government is limited by natural law to the protection of the life, liberty, and property of the individual members of society.

Bastiat, comes to the same conclusion, but was concerned with what a just government would be like. In his 1850 book, *The Law*, Bastiat begins with the hypothesis that each person has a natural right to defend his person, liberty, and property. He then argues "If every person has the right to defend—even by force—his person, his liberty, and his property, then it follows that a group of men have the right to organize and support a common force to protect these rights constantly." (2) So men have the natural right to form a government. He then argues that a just government cannot exceed the limits of protection of life, liberty, and property:

> The law is the organization of the natural right of lawful defense. It is the substitution of a common force for individual forces. And this common force is to do only what the individual forces have a natural and lawful right to do: to protect persons, liberties, and properties; to maintain the right of each, and to cause justice to reign over us all. (3)

Bastiat believed that government could not be used to take from one person and give to another. This he calls legalized plunder. If a law does such a thing, Bastiat's recommendation is:

> Then abolish this law without delay, for it is not only an evil itself, but it also is a fertile source for further evils because it invites reprisals. If such a law—which may be an isolated case—is not abolished immediately, it will spread, multiply, and develop into a system. (17)

Taxpayers of a government that is just, from Bastiat's perspective, would only fund the police function of the state.

Bastiat's answer to the question of what the scope and power of government ought to be is straightforward. "I do not hesitate to answer: *Law is the common force organized to act as an obstacle to injustice.* In short, *law is justice.*" (68) Law should be limited to the protection of life, liberty, and property. A taxpayer cannot be plundered in order to provide goods and services for another.

Bastiat held out the United States, whose constitution in 1850 still served to protect the rights of the taxpayer, as the best example of a nation that had a government that met this standard of justice. His caveat was that in two instances, tariffs and slavery, the United States government had overstepped the bounds of justice and that this defect would lead to a political crisis. Of course, the events of eleven years later proved him correct.

Bastiat understood the point made by Groves as quoted above, that there is a relationship between economics and politics. Bastiat writes:

> A science of economics must be developed before a science of politics can be logically formulated. Essentially, economics is the science of determining whether the interests of human beings are harmonious or antagonistic. This must be known before a science of

politics can be formulated to determine the proper functions of government. (68)

If a society of individuals acting together is harmonious, then there might be little need for government. If, on the other hand, individuals unrestrained by government act in a fashion that leads to a world that is impoverished and coercive, then we might need a strong government.

THE ROLE OF GOVERNMENT: SOCIAL HARMONY AND THE WEALTH OF THE NATION

Adam Smith, famously addressed this issue about the harmonious actions of individuals in the absence of government by arguing that through the market process each individual acting according to his own plan and interest will lead to a society of wealth and harmony. In his *An Inquiry into the Nature and Causes of the Wealth of Nations*, Smith argues for government more limited in scope than that of his time, using his discussion of how markets work to explain the benefits of reducing restrictions on trade, limiting the public debt, etc. An economic system that produces great wealth through voluntary social cooperation requires less government than would be the case if human action were naturally antagonistic.

David Hume, also writing around the time of the Founding, understood that there was a relationship between the political system and economic prosperity: "The greatness of a state, and the happiness of its subjects, how independent so ever they may be supposed in some respects, are commonly allowed to be inseparable with regard to commerce." (1970,5)

The emphasis of the Founders that the purpose of the constitution was protection of individual rights of life, liberty, and property was not only based upon a natural rights argument, but also on the realization that limited government would result in greater prosperity and peaceful interaction of individuals. In Federalist #11, Hamilton discusses in detail the positive effects the new constitution would have on the "commercial prosperity" of the Union. It is clear that the Founders foresaw that the Constitution would lay the foundation for a prosperous economy that would lead to economic, political, and military strength sufficient to protect the new nation from attack. This would allow for the peaceful carrying on of trade and commerce both within the boundaries of the Union and with foreign nations.

The Austrian school of economics explains why the Founders were correct in their belief that a limited government would lead to a free and prosperous people. Ludwig von Mises laid out the foundations of Austrian thought in several works, but his most comprehensive one is *Human Action*. One of the fundamental principles of the Austrian school is that the market is a system of voluntary exchange and social cooperation. No one is coerced and thus the market results in a positive sum game, where all parties are made better off. As Adam Smith demonstrated, this system of voluntary exchange allows for specialization of labor and increased productivity.

Mises, and later Friedrich Hayek, emphasized the fundamental problem of decentralized information and the market as a solution. Since each of us has the best knowledge of what our wants and talents are, a central planner cannot possibly accumulate enough information on a timely basis to know how much of what goods to produce, and how they are to be produced, if he is charged with creating the highest possible standard of living. This information problem is insurmountable for the central planner. The planner is forced to impose his own wishes for what goods and services are to be provided and how they are to be produced and distributed. This results in totalitarianism, and in a low standard of living.

Perhaps the cleverest presentation of this thought is Leonard Read's "I, Pencil", published in 1958. Professor Read discusses the incredibly complex series of transactions that must occur just in order to produce a pencil. Wood must be gathered from Oregon, graphite mined from Sri Lanka, rubber from Malaysia, etc. It is only through a system of voluntary exchange and market prices that such coordination is made possible.

The point of this train of thought that is relevant to our discussion is that government plays a limited role in the market system. Mises, in explaining the foundations of classical liberalism in 1927 wrote: "as the liberal sees it, the task of the state consists solely and exclusively in guaranteeing the protection of life, health, liberty, and private property against violent attacks. Everything that goes beyond this is an evil."(1985, 62) This is not an anarchistic philosophy. It does not advocate a system of no government.[1] As the quote above demonstrates, it is more in the line of Locke and Bastiat, that individuals gather together to form governments to protect themselves. Governments that go beyond this create a threat to personal property and to justice. However, governments are necessary to preserve the system of social cooperation that is the market system.

The important thing for Mises is less a concept of what is moral than what is practical. Yet it is relatively easy to make the case that the market system is a particularly moral order. No one is forced to act against his or her will. You are not forced to work where you don't want to, nor buy goods for which you have no desire. The only way to attain wealth in a market system is by providing for others in society. If you don't produce what others want, or provide a service they desire, you cannot force these upon them. Since the market system is the system that creates the most prosperity, then the governmental structure consistent with the market system is the most desirable. Again, taxpayers need only be burdened with the police functions of government.

Hayek in *The Constitution of Liberty*, follows much the same train of thought. Since information is decentralized, central planners cannot efficiently allocate resources. The social system of the market developed as a mechanism for solving this decentralization problem. The voluntary actions of individuals acting in concert with one another results in the most efficient use of knowledge and resources in society. This market mechanism requires that individuals be free to act according to their own plan. You must decide what you can best provide to society in terms of resources or products, what you are willing to purchase of goods at various relative prices, etc. Uncoerced action is fundamental to a system of voluntary exchange.

As a consequence, the system of government that best serves the market system is one that minimizes the total amount of coercion. Hayek agrees with Mises that anarchy will result in coercion of the weak by the strong. Hayek defines coercion as "when one man's actions are made to serve another man's will, not for his own, but for the other's purpose." (133) The purpose of government is to create "an assured free sphere" of action. Hayek argues that "the rights of the individual are the result of the recognition of such a private sphere." (139) But the question is who decides what is in each person's private sphere of action?

> If people are to make the best use of their knowledge and capacities and foresight, it is desirable that they themselves have some voice in the determination of what will be included in their personal protected sphere. The solution that men have found for this problem rests on the recognition of general rules governing the conditions under which objects or circumstances become part of the protected sphere of a person or persons. (139)

Hayek believes that the political institution by which men govern themselves must have certain characteristics. The laws that are acceptable must be general, that is they should not be in the form of a command. The Legislature should not know beforehand to whom the law will apply. Laws should be known, that is citizens should be able to know what the laws are. They should be predictable. If you are to make decisions about what to produce or how to produce, you should be able to have some confidence about what the rules of the game are going to be. This is especially important in an economy with methods of production which are long-lived, such as the production of autos. Laws should be made such that individuals can comply with them. Finally, the laws should apply equally to all persons.

The point is that if laws have such characteristics, then it will be difficult for those who make up the government to coerce the citizenry. Notice how similar Hayek's admonitions about the characteristics of law are to what Madison had to say in Federalist #62.

> It will be of little avail to the people if the laws are made by people of their own choice, if the laws be so voluminous that they cannot be read, or so incoherent that they cannot be understood; if they be repealed or revised before they are promulgated, or undergo such incessant changes

> that no man who knows what the law is today can guess what it will be tomorrow. (1982, 317)

According to Hayek, the mechanism by which we ensure that the laws have such characteristics is a written constitution. The constitution sets forth what the general beliefs of society are about the sphere of action in which individuals are able to act without coercion of their government. The purpose of a constitution is to limit the temporary majority to actions that are consistent with these general beliefs of society. The constitution can be altered, but only when the general beliefs of society have changed. In the context of this discussion, a fiscal constitution is what ensures the rights of the taxpayer.

CHARACTERISTICS OF LAW AS APPLIED TO TAXPAYER RIGHTS

Taxpayers have the right to their property, whether because of natural law, as put forth by Locke and to a certain extent Bastiat, or because this results in the highest standard of living for society, as the Austrian school argues. Hayek, in the spirit of Madison has laid out what laws in general, and therefore tax laws in particular ought to be like if the rights of taxpayers are to be protected.[2] This is the basis for a fiscal constitution.

First, tax laws should be general, in the sense that taxpayers should not get special benefits or burdens because they are favored or disliked by the majority of the Legislature. The Congress should not pass tax legislation where it knows who is going to benefit from the legislation prior to passage. For example, suppose ACME Computer Company is the only company that produces a particular type of software. The Congress should not be able to pass legislation that taxes ACME in particular greater than other computer companies, nor tax them less than other companies. If it passes a law that taxes all companies that produce this particular brand of software, of which ACME happens to be the only firm, the law should not be enacted in order to benefit or burden ACME. There must be some reason that is not particular to ACME that the producers of such software should be treated differently.

The tax law should be known by all taxpayers, or at least capable of being known by all taxpayers. If the tax law is not known, then individuals or businesses can make plans and decisions that run afoul of the law after the fact. The idea of law is, as Hayek says, to create a landscape which is known to the individual, who then can make decisions given the constraints of the landscape. If the landscape is unknown then it will be difficult for the taxpayer to make decisions that result in efficient use of resources, and it will make it easy for the state to coerce the unsuspecting taxpayer. Given that the Internal Revenue Service has authority to seize property and place the taxpayer in prison, tax laws that cannot by fully known by taxpayers can easily lead to a government that exceeds the level of coercion that is necessary to minimize total coercion in society.

The tax laws should be predictable. If, for example, you are deciding to invest in real estate development that will take two years to come to fruition, you need to be fairly certain that the tax treatment of this investment will not change wildly during the interim. Unpredictable tax laws will lead to less willingness to engage in capital investment, since this roundabout production takes time and is subject to extra uncertainty from a Congress that moves the tax code about in unpredictable ways.

The tax laws should be such that the taxpayer is capable of complying with them. Tax laws that require record keeping that is prohibitively complicated or expensive subject the taxpayer to coercion from a government agent who might dislike the taxpayer for some reason. If the tax code is such that taxpayers cannot reasonably comply with the requirements of the code, the Congress might use the tax code to punish those whose plans are not the same as the planners wish them to be.

Finally, the tax laws should apply equally to all persons. If ACME Computers and Bayview Resorts are in similar circumstances with regard to the tax base, then they should bear equal tax burdens. If the tax law need not apply equally to all taxpayers, then the state can use the tax code to impede the plans of certain individuals, and induce other individuals to alter their plans. In a sense, the government is saying: we will take away your property if you act according to your plan. We will give you someone else's property if you act according to our plan. This type of government behavior leads to a loss of individual freedom and an inefficient use of resources.

CHARACTERISTICS OF LAW: THE CURRENT SITUATION

Let us briefly examine whether the current tax laws meet any of the characteristics that Madison or Hayek believe are necessary to limit Leviathan government from exceeding the amount of coercion that is necessary to sustain the market process or to protect life, liberty, and property. Anyone who has ever had reason to do research in tax policy has probably had to look at the Internal Revenue Code at some point. The most obvious aspect of the Internal Revenue code is that it is voluminous. The current Internal Revenue Code and its regulations are more that 17,000 pages long. This comes to more than five and one-half million words of text. In addition there are thousands of pages of Tax Court decisions and IRS letter rulings that are necessary to truly know what the Code is. It is clear that the code is so voluminous that it cannot be read. What about coherent?

I have chosen at random a page of the internal revenue code to quote:

> If the amount of the net unrealized built-in gain or net unrealized built-loss (determined without regard to this subparagraph) of any old loss corporation is not greater than 25 percent of the amount determined for purposes of paragraph (A)(i)(1), the net unrealized built-in gain or net unrealized built-in loss shall be zero....For purposes of subsection (b)(3)-(A) in applying subparagraph (A) thereof, taxable income shall be computed without regard to recognized built-in gains and losses, and described in paragraph (1)(C) for the year, and (B) in applying subparagraph (B) thereof, the section 382 limitation shall be computed without regard to recognized built-in gains, and gain described in paragraph (1)(C), for the year.(IRC 26, Sec. 382)

Reading this, it is pretty clear that the Code is so incoherent that it cannot be understood, at least by this reader. If the average person were to try to read through the Code, it would be impossible to figure out what the tax law was. Indeed, professionals do not know what the code means. *Money* magazine conducted a survey of tax experts in 1988. Fifty estimated a hypothetical taxpayer's liability. Each of the fifty gave a different answer. When *Money* repeated the experiment the next year, the results were the same. In 1990 *Money* received 48 wrong answers out of 50 when conducting its survey for the 3rd time, 49 wrong out of 50 in its 1991 survey, 50 wrong out of 50 in its 1992 test, and 41 wrong out of 41 in the 1993 test.

The Internal Revenue Code is so incoherent that the Internal Revenue Service itself does not know what the tax code is. A study by the General Accounting Office found that callers who did get through to the Internal Revenue Service received a wrong answer about their tax situation 47% of the time.(Mitchell, 2001) When the GAO sent representatives to IRS offices, it found that they received a wrong answer regarding their tax predicament 49% of the time.

The Internal Revenue Code can hardly be called predictable. If one looks at the hard copy of the Internal Revenue Code, there is what is called the pocket packet at the end of each volume. This is because the law changes so frequently that by the time a book is published the law has been changed. So each book has a pocket in the back of the volume for an insertion that contains the amendments to the code. But these packets can only be so up-to-date. So even if you look at the pocket packet you cannot be sure what the law is.

In today's world, if you have access to the Internet, you can get what the law currently is. But, of course, this does not give you an idea of what the law might be tomorrow. As the House Ways and Means Committee is not bound by any requirement for predictability, there is little certainty that if you know what the law is today that you know what it will be six months from now. Indeed, the 1986 change in the tax law with regard to passive losses altered the value of real estate investments, which in turn affected the portfolios of savings and loan institutions, and affected the wealth of individual taxpayers. This change might have been predicted if the taxpayer were keeping a careful eye on the happenings in Congress, but most likely could not have been predicted very far in advance of the tax change.

But even the most dedicated tax watcher would have a hard time figuring out what the tax law may be in the near future even if he or she knew what the law is today. The 1997 Budget Act added 820 pages to the code alone. In 1997 the IRS added 271 new regulations to the code. The Research Institute of America needed 3,132 pages to explain the changes in the tax law in 1997. Major sections of the tax code were amended 878 times between 1955 and 1994. The number of cumulative changes in tax law between the 1986 Tax Reform Act and April 15, 1998 was more than 5,400. (Mitchell, 1998)

It is relatively clear that the laws do not apply equally to all persons, unless persons are defined rather narrowly. Although the U.S. Constitution has an equal protection clause, it is not hard to find instances where two taxpayers would be treated differently. If you produce or purchase certain products, for example cigarettes, you will be taxed more than someone who purchases or produces another product, for example tobacco. If you produce oil you may have a different method of depreciating your assets than if you produce natural gas. It is true that if the law is construed to mean that you must be treated the same as someone who is an identical circumstance, there is equal protection. But the purpose of this characteristic of the law is to limit the coercive power of government. The concept is that if I tax you in order to redistribute your wealth, then I must tax everyone. This makes it more difficult to form coalitions where the majority may steal from the minority. If the Congress may pass a tax law that taxes only boat dealers and redistributes their property to the rest of society, it is easier to form a majority coalition to do so then if the tax has to apply to all retailers.

Notice that if the role of government is primarily or exclusively to defend life, liberty, and property—the police or defense function—then the amount of revenue that must be raised to support this function of government will be limited. This allows for some leeway in creating a tax code that satisfies Hayek's conditions for proper law. A tax structure that raises $100 million from the U.S. taxpayers can stray fairly far away from the ideal system without severely infringing upon the right of taxpayers to their property. On the other hand, a tax structure that must raise $2 trillion is more likely to infringe on taxpayers rights and must adhere more closely to Hayek's characteristics.

This is much the same argument that Bastiat made with regard to the voting franchise. His position was that if government were limited to justice, that is the protection of life, liberty, and property, then it would matter little who was able to vote. It is only when government may take from one person and give to another that the degree of enfranchisement is of great importance.[3]

VIEWS ON THE FISCAL CONSTITUTION

The Founders addressed the problem of how to form a government that saves us from the Hobbesian world of anarchy yet does not force us into a situation where in order to gain security we give up our freedoms to a Leviathan government. Richard Epstein (1985) discusses how they accomplished this. "The basic constitutional plan seeks to limit government by indirection...At every turn the constitutional concern is with preventing the concentration of power in a few hands." (16) The constitution is a set of procedural safeguards that indirectly protect the rights of the taxpayer. But a review of the Internal Revenue Code and today's level of taxation are sufficient evidence that this approach has not been entirely successful in protecting the rights of taxpayers.

If one were to adopt Hayek's hypothesis, that a written constitution could limit the coercive power of the temporary majority, what form should this constitution take? Following upon the idea that the purpose of government is to minimize the total amount of coercion, or to maximize the sphere of free action where an individual may act according to his or her own plan, then it makes sense for the constitution to require that laws have the characteristics outlined above. The purpose of the constitution is to serve as a higher order of law that limits ordinary law. (1972)

Some state constitutions have provisions that attempt to ensure that laws will satisfy the conditions Madison and Hayek suggest. For example, the Constitution of the State of Michigan requires that notice of all committee hearings and a clear statement of all subjects to be considered at each hearing be published in the journal of each House in advance of the hearing. (IV, 16) It also has a provision that all bills must remain for at least five days in each House of the Legislature. (IV, 26) The purpose of this provision is to give time for individuals to know what laws are being passed. There is also a provision that unless given immediate effect by a 2/3 vote of both Houses, laws do not take effect until 90 days after the end of session.(IV, 27) This also is an attempt to give people due notice about what the law is going to be. Certain other provisions attempt to limit the ability to pass statutes that specifically benefit certain individuals or communities. Section 29 of Article IV specifies that: "The Legislature shall pass no local or special act in any case where a general act can be made applicable, and whether a general act can be made applicable shall be a judicial question." In addition, no local or special act can take effect without a 2/3 vote of both Houses of the Legislature and a majority vote of the citizens in the affected district. (IV, 27) There are a number of other provisions in the Michigan Constitution to ensure notice and understanding of legislation. There are also provisions that attempt to limit and to prevent the state from borrowing money to assist individuals or firms.[4]

One approach to a federal fiscal constitution would be to set out the proper role of government and then establish a general principle of legislation that limits government to that role. Such an approach would concentrate on ensuring that laws are general, known, predictable, apply equally to all, and can be complied with. This would entail a constitutional amendment that would add provisions similar to those of the Michigan Constitution discussed above. It certainly appears that little harm could be done by requiring the Congress to open its legislative process, making each act clear and known to the general public, and limiting the ability of Congress to enact statutes that take effect immediately.

Of course, as is well known from the public choice literature, it is likely that the average taxpayer will remain rationally ignorant of legislation, even if given due notice. However, it is not necessary that every taxpayer be well-informed. Associations of individuals would find it easier to determine the law and what might happen during the legislative process and then alert their members on issues important to their special interest. For example, an association of retailers could find it easier to track legislation on a potential federal sales tax. This association could then notify its members who could in turn notify their Congressman. Clearly this is what is going on at the current time, but the transaction costs of following legislation are higher than need be, thus limiting associations that are effective to those who can hire specialized personnel to follow legislation. Due notice requirements in the federal Constitution would reduce these transaction costs. Thus, local and regional associations and newspapers would find it easier to protect the public against coercive activity by the federal government.

This approach would be consistent with Buchanan's emphasis on a contractarian basis for a fiscal constitution. Buchanan recognized that looking at the tax side only of a fiscal system was inherently flawed. Doing so implicitly assumes that the benefits from the expenditure side of government are equally distributed among the members of the polity. (1999) Thus looking at "taxpayers' rights and the fiscal constitution" is limiting the discussion. In the absence of the assumption of equal benefits from government expenditures, we should be looking at economic rights and the fiscal constitution.

This concept is consistent with our argument so far. The Locke-Bastiat view expressed above implicitly looks at both the expenditure side and the taxation side. The role of government is to protect life, liberty, and property. Just law does not take from one person and give to another. Thus, the expenditure side of the fiscal constitution is what is emphasized when determining the proper role of government. But, the taxation side is implied as well. If one cannot take from one person and give to another, and the role of government is to protect property, then it would seem to imply that taxation should be based upon the degree of protection of one's property that is afforded by the state. This is what Adam Smith suggested in his *Wealth of Nations*.

> The subjects of every state ought to contribute towards the support of the government as nearly as possible, in proportion to their

irrespective abilities; that is, in proportion to the revenue which they respectively enjoy under the protection of the state. (825)

The concept is that those who are wealthier obtain this wealth through a system of protection by the government. Thus, proportional taxation would be consistent with Smith's thought, and the implications of Locke and Bastiat, and the fiscal constitution would encompass both the taxation and expenditure side of the fiscal system. We will discuss proportional and progressive taxation in Section VII below.

This approach of examining the entire system of government is also consistent with the discussion of Mises and Hayek above. The characteristic of a good law that Hayek postulates applies both to laws that provide for taxation and also for laws that deal with government appropriations and regulation. The role of government is limited to minimizing total coercion in order to allow for the maximum use of individual knowledge and action, and this bears on both expenditure and revenue bills.

Another approach to a fiscal constitution is taken in the Taxpayers' Bill of Rights recently enacted by the U.S. Congress. While hailed as a "Taxpayers' Bill of Rights" the legislation does not make any radical changes in the tax collection system. Its primary effect is to give the taxpayer some legal leverage in dealing with the IRS. For example, prior to the legislation, when the taxpayer went to Tax Court it was presumed that the IRS' determination of the taxpayer's tax ability was correct. The burden of proof was on the taxpayer to prove the IRS wrong. Now, under certain circumstances, the IRS must show that the taxpayer was wrong. A few of the other provisions include: (1) if the taxpayer prevails in court, the IRS must pay a minimum amount of the taxpayer's legal costs; (2) permitting taxpayers to sue the government for damages caused by the IRS overstepping its legal bounds; (3) extending the privilege of confidential communication between client and attorney to tax practitioners advising a taxpayer on tax matters; (4) codifying IRS administrative procedure for seizure of taxpayer's property; and (5) requiring the IRS to provide taxpayers paying under installment agreements with annual statements of their accounts. As one can see from these examples, most of the law's provisions deal with notification and clarification. Even the burden of proof provision is limited. Under the new law the IRS will bear the burden of proof only when disputed cases reach the Tax Court, and then it does not apply if the taxpayer has more than $7 million in assets. Only 29,000 cases per year out of approximately 2 million audits ever reach Tax Court, and about 75% of these are settled without going before a judge. (Dodge, 1998)

There is one aspect of the Taxpayers' Bill of Rights that has had some effect on the system, and that is Section 1203. This section clarifies and encodes behavior by IRS staff that could result in dismissal. There are 10 provisions that include, for example, falsifying or destroying documents to avoid uncovering mistakes made by an IRS employee with respect to a taxpayer matter, and threatening to audit a taxpayer for the purpose of extracting personal gain or benefit. There have been reports that enforcement officers have declined to collect revenues owed to the IRS because of the effects of the new Act. (Morrison, 2000) However, with the exception of a provision against violating the civil rights of a taxpayer or other IRS employee, and violations of the Internal Revenue Code, Treasury Regulations, or policies of the IRS for the purposes of retaliating or harassing a taxpayer or other IRS employee, all of the forbidden acts are clearly defined. Even with respect to these two provisions, it is clear that IRS personnel must take willful actions. Any violation must be deliberate. If Section 1203 has had the effect of conspicuously limiting the collection action of the IRS, it is another example of how in need of amendment the Internal Revenue Code is.

There are several reasons why this Taxpayers' Bill of Rights is limited in its ability to serve as a fiscal constitution. It really is not a bill of rights in the sense that any provision of the legislation can be repealed or altered by a simple majority of the Congress. The purpose of a constitution is to limit the temporary majority. As Hayek notes, the constitution puts forth the general principles of how society is to be governed. While it may be useful for the Legislature to be required to state these general principles when justifying its actions,

> it will clearly be more effective if only another body has the power to modify these basic principles, especially if the procedure of this body is lengthy and thus allows time for the importance of the particular objective that has given rise to the demand for modification to be seen in the proper proportion. (1972, 180)

In other words, a legislative taxpayers' bill of rights would not be a true bill of rights because it can hardly be a principle that binds the temporary majority if the temporary majority may alter the general principle whenever it has the votes. It is true that some degree of comfort may be taken by taxpayers from the existence of certain provisions in the bill, since it is always more difficult to pass legislation than to block legislation. If the Congress wished to reinstate powers of the IRS then it would require action to get a majority of both Houses and the signature of the President. However, an actual taxpayers' bill of rights would be a set of principles that would require long deliberation and a change in the general principles of society to be amended.

The Taxpayers' Bill of Rights is not comprehensive, in that it doesn't establish the role of government, nor does it limit the ability of the federal government to use taxation to coerce us. It merely sets some procedures that the IRS must follow when auditing taxpayers and collecting taxes. While these procedures may be important in limiting the coercive actions of individual IRS agents, and perhaps the IRS as an agency, it only marginally protects the rights of the individual taxpayer.

Another approach is to adopt the concept that limiting the revenue requirements or the ability of the government to raise revenue is the strongest protection of taxpayer's right to property. As discussed above, if the revenue that has to be raised to fund the actions of government is small, then there is room for error in meeting the characteristics of law that would protect the free sphere of action of individuals. A good deal of effort was expended in the 1970s on this approach. A particular example of this is the Headlee amendment to the Michigan Constitution discussed in Section VI below.

Using another approach, Buchanan and Wagner came to similar conclusions about the necessity of a fiscal constitution. They argue in *Democracy in Deficit* that prior to the Keynesian revolution there was an unwritten fiscal constitution at work in the United States. This unwritten constitution was that public debt was to be limited. As David Hume put it in 1752, "For why should the case be so different between the public and an individual, as to make us establish different maxims of conduct for each?" (1970, 91) Or as Adam Smith put it more famously, "What is prudence in the conduct of every private family, can scarce be folly in that of a great kingdom." With the advent of Keynesian macroeconomics, this general principle held by society that the government should balance its budget, saving up in prosperous times against the necessity of spending more than it takes in during time of emergency such as war, was overturned. The nullification of the belief in the necessity of government to balance its budget led, in the context of representative democracy, to a situation where the public is misled about the true cost of government. Politicians running for office offer voters spending without taxation.

The problem with this scenario is that the federal government will spend more than it would if the true cost of government services were not masked by borrowing instead of taxing. The federal government then piles up debt, which puts pressure on interest rates. The Federal Reserve, in response to the interest rate pressures, monetizes the debt. This causes inflation and the attendant problems associated with a decline in the value of the medium of exchange. Thus a cycle of expanding government, increasingly large debt, and price inflation is a result of the collapse of the unwritten constitution.

For Buchanan and Wagner this leads to a breakdown in what one might think of as a contractarian constitution. Taxes are raised without having to be voted on by the Legislature. This occurs because taxpayers are driven into higher tax brackets as their nominal income rises. Savings are taxed away as the value of the medium of exchange declines. Buchanan and Wagner's suggestion is an amendment to the Constitution that would require a balanced budget. It would do so by requiring the President and Congress to work with a balanced budget in determining outlays and in the event that budget deficits actually occur due to projection errors, outlays will be automatically adjusted downward to restore the projected balance within three months. If a surplus exists, it would be used to reduce the national debt. The budget provision could be waived if 2/3 of both Houses of the Congress declare a state of national emergency and this is approved by the President.

Notice that Buchanan and Wagner are not necessarily concerned with a fiscal constitution that limits the size of government, but rather wish to limit deficits because they obscure the price of government and lead to an expansion that would not have been agreed upon with better information of the taxpayer. It is not their position in *Democracy in Deficit* that a fiscal constitution is needed to limit a Leviathan government, but rather that a growing government is the result of Keynesian economics altering the unwritten fiscal constitution of a balanced budget. The Buchanan and Wagner amendment is merely to ensure taxpayers understand the true cost of government. (1977)

Buchanan and Wagner were writing in 1977, when the U.S. government had 8 years of uninterrupted deficits and had only one balanced budget from 1960 to 1977. Deficits continued and actually got much larger for the next twenty years after Buchanan and Wagner's writing. However, in 1992 things changed in the unwritten fiscal constitution. Ross Perot, an independent candidate for President, ran an effective campaign arguing that one of the greatest threats to the American economy was federal deficits. Eventually, both major parties adopted this position as well after Mr. Perot spent several million dollars in campaign commercials on the topic. In effect, Mr. Perot reestablished the unwritten fiscal constitution regarding budget deficits. The result has been that in 1998 the federal government ran its first budget surplus since 1969, and is projected to run surpluses on a regular basis over the next several years barring a national emergency.

Milton Friedman, in *Capitalism and Freedom* argued in a somewhat similar fashion that the adoption of Keynesian economic theory of "priming the pump" in order to forestall a repeat of the Great Depression led to a systematic expansion of federal spending and the inability to reduce the tax burden. (76) Friedman suggests that politicians use the expenditure side of the fiscal equation to maintain aggregate demand, rather than reducing taxes, because it is in the politicians' best personal interest to expand government. This has been made possible

> because of the existence of other forces making for increased governmental expenditures; in particular, the widespread acceptance by intellectuals of the belief that government should play a larger role in economic and private affairs; the triumph, that is, of the philosophy of the welfare state. (77)

The implication is that the general belief about the role of government had by 1962 been established as gong far beyond what Bastiat thought in 1850.

Friedman did not offer a solution to the problem of what he called "the balance wheel" theory of fiscal policy in *Capitalism and Freedom*. But by 1979 he and Rose Friedman offered in *Free to Choose*, a constitutional amendment to limit federal spending. This amendment was prepared by the Federal Amendment Drafting Committee of the National Tax Limitation Committee. In *Free to Choose*, Friedman expanded his discussion of the political system, arguing that the democratic political system itself generates expanded government. The primary reason this occurs is that government benefits are targeted and the costs of government programs are widely dispersed. Therefore, special interests that stand to gain large amounts for each of their members will dominate in a political process where the cost of each particular program is so widely spread among taxpayers that no one taxpayer has an incentive to oppose a politician based upon the cost of any particular program. (292) Friedman suggests we do as Hayek suggested, use the constitution to lay down broad rules of the game that may deny us our small special interest, but save us more in the long run since the process will deny everyone else their special interest as well. "We should not consider each case on its merits, but lay down broad rules limiting what government may do." (299)

The Friedmans call for an economic Bill of Rights in order to reverse the trend toward ever-bigger government. The proposed amendment would among other things, limit increases in federal spending to the increase in GDP. It would also require that if revenues exceeded outlays, the excess would have to be used to reduce the national debt. The concept is to limit a government that has an inherent bias towards growth because of the political process of modern democracy. Government could not increase relative to the size of the economy. The amendment does not address the role of government; it addresses a flaw in the process of determining how much government will spend and tax over time.

Martin Anderson makes the case that the time preferences of politicians create a bias towards growth in government. While Anderson focuses on federal deficits, he suggests the same constitutional amendment proposal as did the Friedmans. Anderson argues that politicians find that constituents desire social programs and defense as well as lower taxes. The reason the federal government runs large deficits is that the political costs of reducing spending are immediate while the costs of deficits are in the future. And as Anderson puts it: "the time preference of political decision makers is such that they will almost always heavily discount anything that happens in the future. When the future is defined as sometime beyond their next election, the discount is nearly total." (1984)

Anderson's point regarding the present costs and future benefits from limiting government is relevant. While limiting the growth of government will pay off with a greater standard of living in the future, the increase may not be discernable in 24 months, the length of time between elections for a Congressman. On the other hand, reduction in programs will be clearly discernible in that time period. So a politician must be fairly assured of a safe seat to be willing to make major changes in the government tax and expenditure policy.

Walter Williams used The Frank M. Engle Lecture at The American College to argue that "while the U.S. Constitution is a brilliant document, it has one glaring defect. There is little in our Constitution that protects our economic rights." Along with the Friedmans and Anderson, Williams calls for enactment of the constitutional amendment of the National Tax Limitation Committee. (1993)

When the Friedmans, Anderson, and Williams were writing in support of the Constitutional limitation, there was a good deal of momentum for such a proposal. At one point 32 states had passed a resolution calling for a Constitutional Convention seeking some form of amendment to limit government spending and taxation policy. After the election of Ronald Reagan in 1981 much of the steam was let out of the constitutional amendment engine. This is probably due to the conservatives getting an income tax reduction and a rise in defense spending in return for maintenance of domestic programs. The Reagan administration ran high deficits (as did the George Bush administration) and the conservative forces were reluctant to force the issue of limitations on deficits and spending for fear it would hamper the advances they were making in defense and taxes. Although there have been congressional resolutions offered, in particular ones by Kyle of Arizona and Nick Smith of Michigan, none have seen committee hearings and there is little chance that a Constitutional Convention will be convened on the issue. However, the state of Michigan did pass a limitation in 1978 similar to that called for by the National Tax Limitation Committee.

THE MICHIGAN TAX LIMITATION AMENDMENT

In November of 1978 the people of the State of Michigan adopted a constitutional amendment, the Headlee Amendment, that limited the growth of state government.[5] While the amendment covers several sections of the Constitution, we outline its basic provisions. The most important provision for the purposes of drawing an analogy to the federal government, is in Section 26 of Article IX. This section "established a limit on the total amount of taxes which may be imposed by the Legislature in any fiscal year on the taxpayers" of Michigan. The limit is a percentage of tax revenues to state personal income. This ratio was set as the total state revenues in the fiscal year 1978-79 divided by state personal income of Michigan in 1977. At the time of the election, this number was not known, but was chosen to basically fix state revenues at the same share of personal income as existed at the time of the election. Section 28 limits expenses of state government in any fiscal year to the revenue limit plus federal aid and any surplus from a previous year. Thus the Headlee Amendment limits both state spending and revenue.

The ratio of revenues to personal income is slightly less than 9 and one-half percent.

The Headlee Amendment also addressed the possibility that the state Legislature might circumvent the amendment by imposing spending requirements on localities, thus maintaining government programs and increasing the taxpayer's local tax burden in response to a requirement to limit the state tax burden. Section 30 of Article IX requires that the proportion of total state spending paid to local units of government shall not be reduced below that proportion in effect in fiscal year 1978-79. Section 29 prohibits the state from reducing the state-financed proportion of the necessary costs of any existing activity or service required of local governments and requires that any new activity required of local units be accompanied by a state appropriation sufficient to pay for any necessary increased costs to the local government. Any proposed limitation on the spending or revenue of the federal government would require a similar provision, ensuring that the federal government does not circumvent limitations on its taxing or spending authority by requiring state governments to undertake programs that would otherwise have been done at the federal level.

The Headlee Amendment has served to limit the growth of state government relative to personal income. One anomaly was that using the formula of state revenues in FY 1978-79 to personal income in 1977 resulted in an unusually high ratio, since state personal income was low in 1977 and state revenue had climbed in the following year as Michigan pulled out of the recession it was in during the early to mid 1970s. However, the limitation has been binding or close to binding in some years and the Legislature is aware of the limit when setting budgets.

In the first twenty years of the revenue limit that began with the fiscal year 1979-80, the limit was exceeded twice, in 1994-95 and in 1998-99. (See Table 1.) The formula resulted in a revenue limit that was 9.49 percent of personal income. In the first year, FY 1979-80, revenues subject to the limit were 6.86 billion and the revenue limit was substantially above that, at $7.4 billion. By the 1982-93 fiscal year, the amount of revenue subject to the limit was $8.1 billion, which was $1.3 billion under the cap. So although revenues grew by 18% over a 3 year period, the limit grew by 27%. The limit thus didn't serve as much of a deterrent. However, by 1984-85 the limit was almost exceeded. In fact litigation at the time resulted in a more careful examination of the limit, and the end result was a declaration that the $9.86 billion in revenue was $6.1 million under the limit.

Table 4.1: **Michigan State Constitution Revenue Limit**

Fiscal Year	Revenue Subject to Limit (millions of dollars)	Revenue Limit (millions of dollars)	Amount Under Limit (millions of dollars)
1979-80	6870.1	7396.9	526.7
1980-81	7043.0	8215.7	1172.7
1981-82	7348.9	8763.0	1414.1
1982-83	8103.5	9424.9	1321.4
1983-84	9243.5	9488.1	244.6
1984-85	9861.6	9867.7	6.1
1985-86	10483.8	10857.3	373.5
1986-87	10891.9	11736.6	844.7
1987-88	11472.3	12822.2	1349.9
1988-89	12087.9	13439.5	1351.6
1989-80	12363.1	14513.4	2150.3
1990-91	12311.9	15351.4	3039.5
1991-92	12540.2	16288.2	3687.9
1992-93	13453.5	16583.8	3148.5
1993-94	15473.2	17624.2	2151.0
1994-95	18585.4	18475.8	(109.6)
1995-96	19798.8	19982.0	183.2
1996-97	20694.3	21672.2	977.9
1997-98	22072.3	22712.4	640.1
1998-99	23208.5	23186.8	(21.7)

Source: Senate Fiscal Agency, State of Michigan, *2000 Statistical Report*, pg. 9.

From FY 1984 to FY 1991-92 the limit grew swiftly, with the result that by FY 1991-92 the revenue of $12.54 billion was under the limit by $3.6 billion. This allowed for a major shift in education funding from local property taxes (which are not subject to the limit) to state sales taxes (which are subject to the limit) in the 1994 constitutional amendment entitled Proposal A. However, the limit did become binding in the first year of the tax shift, in 1994-95, as revenues of $18.586 billion exceeded the limit by $109.6 million. The limit has remained fairly constraining; with revenues of $23.2 billion exceeding the limit in FY 1998-99 by $21.7 million.

After 20 years of the Headlee Amendment, state revenue increased by 237%, and the revenue limit increased by 213%. Part of the revenue increase occurred due to the large shift from local property taxes to state taxes to fund K-12 education in Michigan. The limit was actually made more binding as a result of Proposal A, resulting in a slower growth in state government than would probably have been the case in the absence of Proposal A. In the absence of the shift from local to state taxes, the revenue limit would never have become binding. Nonetheless, the existence of the limit may have altered budget recommendations and had some downward pressure on state spending. In any event, it is clear that if a revenue limit is set, the limit should be chosen in a fashion that has some actual effect other then being simply symbolic.

If such an amendment were to be placed in the U.S. Constitution, it would make more sense to choose a ratio of revenues relative to gross domestic product or national income, or whatever might be the relevant choice to measure the size of the economy, that was consistent with recent history and fix it as a hard number rather than leaving the ratio up to the outcome of a particular economic situation.

PROGRESSIVITY, EFFICIENCY, AND PROCESS

Rather than take a broader view of the fiscal constitution, some authors have focused on particular aspects of a tax structure. An important aspect is whether to allow progressive taxation. Hayek discusses progressive taxation in some detail in his *Constitution of Liberty*. His main point is that progression of the tax system as a whole cannot be reconciled with a free society. Particular taxes may be progressive, such as the income tax, if they are to offset the regressive nature of other taxes, such as a poll tax. But when taken in its entirety, the tax structure cannot be progressive if the society is to be free.

Progressive taxation is for the purpose of redistribution of income. Karl Marx and Frederick Engels propose that in order for the proletariat to centralize all instruments of production in the hands of the state, a heavy progressive income tax will be necessary. (1987, 33) Hayek argues that an argument for any degree of progression can be used to justify any greater degree of progression, which eventually leads to the goal of Marx and Engels of state takeover of the means of production and elimination of the sphere of free action that makes up individual liberty. He writes, "Unlike proportionality, progression provides no principle which tells us what the relative burden of different persons ought to be." (1972, 313)

Hayek argues for proportional taxation for the following reason:

> It is the great merit of proportional taxation that it provides a rule which is likely to be agreed upon by those who will pay absolutely more and those who will pay absolutely less and which, once accepted, it raises no problem of a separate rule applying only to a minority. (314)

Proportional taxation is a general principle by which society may be governed. It, by definition, applies equally to all persons—an important characteristic of tax law as discussed earlier in Section III.

Proportional taxation would fit with Adam Smith's ability to pay principle if one presumes that the value of protection afforded individuals by government is in proportion to their wealth. The wealthy would pay more than the poor, but in Hayekian fashion, the general principle would be established, known, and predictable. Michigan's State Constitution has a provision that precludes an income tax that is "graduated as to rate or base." (IX, 7) Although this technically allows for a certain amount of progression due to the existence of exemptions, it is a definite limit upon the degree of progression that the state can impose upon the taxpayer. It is possible for the entire tax structure to be progressive under this provision, nonetheless, this is unlikely since the income tax and consumption taxes together make up 2/3 of the state tax revenues, and the net effect of these two is likely to be proportional or slightly regressive.[6]

Brennan and Buchanan (1980) present a thorough discussion of the importance of the analytics of a fiscal constitution. They argue that the proper analysis of taxation must include a discussion of how governments actually do behave or can be predicted to behave. They show that much of the economics literature on taxation presumes a model of a benevolent government that would follow the economist's advice on the most efficient or equitable taxation system. Their analysis begins with the supposition of a Leviathan government and they then demonstrate how many of the recommendations of economists with regard to efficient taxes are turned on their head under this assumption.

They do not attempt to provide a model for the optimal constitutional constraint, but discuss what sort of constitutional structure might be agreed upon by citizens under a veil of ignorance—a contractarian approach to a fiscal constitution. They make two important points. One is that constraints on fiscal matters can be surmounted by a government bent on maximizing its power, most obviously through using its regulatory power. The second is that economists should discuss limiting government through the process of making decisions, such as super majority votes for new taxes, and special assemblies for taxation as suggested by Hayek, rather than focusing on direct limitations on government actions.

CAN A FISCAL CONSTITUTION PROTECT TAXPAYERS' RIGHTS?

We observed in Section VII that the taxpayers of Michigan were able to place a tax and expenditure limit in its Constitution, and that the Michigan experience has seen growth of government consistent with growth of the state's personal income. I am not aware of a study that looked at how much responsibility the Headlee Amendment had on the state's growth. As mentioned in Section VII, the limit has become binding and it is considered by the Legislature in adopting the state's budget.

Dean Stansel has examined the effectiveness of state government tax and expenditure limitations in restraining state government expansion. Stansel presents evidence that properly designed limitations can and do limit the growth of state taxes and spending. The growth rate of per capita state spending in states that had enacted tax and spending limitations fell from 0.8 percentage points above the U.S. average in the five years preceding enactment to 2.9 percentage points below the U.S. average in the five years after enactment. (1994)

Stansel's main argument is that to be effective tax and expenditure limitations must have certain characteristics:

1. Originate with and be approved by, the voters, where possible, rather than the Legislature.
2. Be constitutional rather than statutory.
3. Apply a cap to 100 percent of the budget rather than to only certain categories.
4. Cap spending rather than revenue or taxes.
5. Limit the growth of spending to the growth of population plus inflation rather than to the growth of personal income.
6. Require voter approval for its provisions to be circumvented.
7. Apply to both state and local governments, and allow for transfer of responsibility to local government with the appropriate adjustments in each jurisdiction's limits.
8. Not require additional action by the Legislature for implementation.
9. Give taxpayers standing to sue to enforce its provisions, and require injunctive relief to prohibit any illegal taxes or spending while suit is pending.

Looking down the list, one notices that these characteristics conform to Hayek's view that the limitation on government should reflect the general belief of the populace and therefore be constitutional. Stansel is making the point in others that, as noted above, Legislators have little incentive to enact a binding limitation on themselves. The other characteristics reduce the ability of the state to continue to increase the size of government by requiring local units of government to provide increased services.

Michigan's Constitutional Amendment has a number of these characteristics. It originated with the voters, is constitutional, caps both spending and revenue, applies to 100% of the budget not funded by federal dollars, does not allow the transfer of responsibility to local governments, and gives taxpayers the right to sue to enforce. The Headlee Amendment's weaknesses are in the two areas where it does not meet Stansel's criteria. It does require some additional action by the Legislature for implementation, although this has not in general been a problem. As noted above, it does limit growth of spending to growth of personal income rather than population. This, as noted in Section VII, did limit its effectiveness prior to the change in K-12 education funding.

Stansel found that among the several states, tax and expenditure limitations varied in their effectiveness, depending on how they are structured. But suppose one could construct an effective constitutional limitation. There are two questions to be asked. First, could such an amendment be passed. Second, could such an amendment long be effective.

As Hayek noted, the constitution is a statement of the general principles of governance that society has adopted. It should be difficult and slow to amend the constitution since an amendment should signify a change in the underlying principles of society. Thus, a constitutional limit on taxation and spending should not be easily obtained. While one can never say never in things political, it is quite unlikely that a constitutional amendment that limits the Congress could ever be adopted.

It is not in the interest of the Legislators, nor the President to limit their power. It may be beneficial to certain Representatives and Senators to offer such an amendment, if their constituents are of such a mind as to wish to limit the growth of their government. Leadership of the Congress can let even a majority of its members support such an amendment, but it certainly would be on the near side of ridiculous to suppose that two-thirds of the members of the House and the Senate would vote to put such an amendment before the states for approval.

If the unlikely were to happen and the Congress were to move such an amendment to the states for approval, the likelihood that three-fourths of the state Legislatures would approve is very small. It would be very easy to argue that such a limitation would reduce federal revenues coming to the state and would result in increased state taxes or reduced state services that the state Legislators would be blamed for. Some might fear that the federal government would find a way to require states to provide new services without compensation. And many state Legislators might see themselves as future Congressman and not desire constraints on their ability to bring home the bacon for their constituents.

Even if a fiscal constitution were to be constructed and adopted, is it possible that such a constitution would protect the rights of a taxpayers over any length of time? John C. Calhoun felt that the courts were part of the government, and thus any limitations on government that were left to the courts, would be interpreted as a mechanism for increasing the power of government. (1953) Murray Rothbard agrees completely with this point. Professor Rothbard, in *For A New Liberty*, wrote:

> All Americans are familiar with the process by which John C. Calhoun's prophetic analysis has been vindicated; the State's own monopoly judiciary has inexorably broadened the construction of State power over the last century and a half...If a judicial decree of 'unconstitutional' is a mighty check on governmental power, so too a verdict of 'constitutional' is an equally mighty weapon for fostering public acceptance of ever greater governmental power. (1978, 65)

Whether one believes that a constitutional limitation on government spending and taxation can be effective rests to a certain extent on one's belief that there truly exists a separation of power between the different branches of government. Clearly Calhoun and Rothbard do not agree with Alexander Hamilton, who suggested in Federalist 78 that

> Whoever attentively considers the different departments of power must perceive, that in a government in which they are separated from one another, the judiciary, from the nature of its functions, will always by the least dangerous to the political rights of the constitution; because it will be least in a capacity to annoy or injure them.... (1982, 393)

They see the separation of powers as ineffective in limiting government, and believe that the judicial branch combines with the other branches to justify expanded government. For Calhoun, the only effective limitation on a central government was secession, and for Rothbard it was the elimination of government altogether.

Niskanen provides an interesting discussion of the effect of constitutional constraints in his 1990 article, "Conditions Affecting the Survival of Constitutional Rules." In this paper Niskanen contends

> The structure of the government authorized by the Constitution has proven to be remarkably stable for 200 years. That structure, however, has not proven to be sufficient to avoid a massive change in the effective constitution, especially as it bears upon the economic powers of the government.

Niskanen suggests that further research into the maintenance of the constitutional contract is needed to discover why some particular constitutional provisions are effective over time and others are not. He proposes three general principles in this regard: (1) a specific constitutional rule will be maintained only if it serves the interests of a succession of dominant coalitions; (2) the effective constitution will change when the dependence of the dominant coalition on those outside of the coalition changes, and (3) the effective constitution will change in response to changes in the probability that members of the dominant coalition will be replaced.

A question for research in this area is whether or not an effective constitutional limit that protects taxpayers' rights can even be crafted and enacted. One may take a position alongside Calhoun, Rothbard, or Niskanen, or one may find their positions simply alarmist. However, it is undeniable that the federal government has increased its role in the economy substantially from the founding, especially in the last sixty years. There is a large body of literature documenting and attempting to explain this phenomena, but the Economic Report of the President in 2001 gives an order of magnitude to the problem. In 1940, federal revenues were $6.5 billion and by 2000 revenues were in excess of $2 trillion. As a percentage of GDP, federal revenues were less than 8 percent in 1940, and were in excess of 20.6 percent in 2000.(B-79, B-80) Those who would argue that a fiscal constitution is an effective mechanism for protecting taxpayer rights surely have the burden of proof on their side.

WHAT CAN WE DO?

There is really only one way to protect taxpayers' rights against a Leviathan government, and that is for the general belief of society about the proper role of government to change. An amendment to the federal constitution patterned after the Michigan Headlee Amendment would no doubt prove useful in limiting government intrusion on the rights of taxpayers. However, such an amendment is unlikely to pass without a fundamental change in the unwritten fiscal constitution. Ross Perot demonstrated that such a change can occur, but this change must precede any proposed amendment.

The real issue is how to alter the beliefs of people about the role of government. Hayek argued that those who believe in the fundamental rights of individuals must bring the discussion of these issues to the forefront. Mises wrote that classical liberals must become engaged in the battle of ideas and declared in *Liberalism* that it is ideas that will determine how we are governed. Those who understand the market process will have to convince the rest of society that a social order based upon voluntary exchange and social cooperation is superior to one based upon central planning and coercion. They will also have to explain why limitations on government are vital to the maintenance of the market process. When these tasks are accomplished then an effective fiscal constitution that protects taxpayers rights will come to fruition.

ENDNOTES

1. Mises makes this explicit when he writes "Liberalism is not anarchism, nor has it anything to do with anarchism." (Liberalism , 37)

2. This can be found in greater depth in Hayek's *Constitution of Liberty*, Chapter 9.

3. Bastiat, *The Law*. This same argument is made in the "optimal taxation" literature. In examining what kind of tax creates the lowest excess burden, it should be kept in mind that tax systems that are not required to raise much revenue can be constructed fairly suboptimally and still have low excess burden. Tax systems that raise large amounts of revenue can create substantial excess burden even if they are close to the "optimal" structure.

4. See Article IV Section 24, Article IV Section 30, and Article IX Section 18.

5. Approved November 7, 1978; Effective December 23, 1978.

6. Total state tax revenues were $22.017 billion in FY 1998-99. Consumption taxes were $7.925 billion, and income taxes were $7.394 billion. Source: Senate Fiscal Agency 2000 Statistical Report, p. 6.

REFERENCES

Adams, Charles. (1993) *For Good and Evil: The Impact of Taxes on the Course of Civilization*. Lanham, MD.: Madison Books.

Anderson, Martin. (1984) "An Economic Bill of Rights." Reprinted from *To Economic Prosperity: US Domestic Policy in the Mid-1980s*. Stanford, CA.: Hoover Institution.

Anrig, Greg. (1988) "Even Seasoned Pros Are Confused This Year," *Money*: March.

Anrig, Greg (1989) "The Pros Flunk Our New Tax-Return Test," *Money*: March.

Bastiat, Frederic. (1998, 1850) *The Law*, 2nd ed. Irvington-on-Hudson, NY.: Foundation for Economic Education.

Brennan, Geoffrey and Buchanan, James (1980) *The Power to Tax: Analytical Foundations of a Fiscal Constitution*. Cambridge, MA.: Cambridge University Press.

Buchanan, James and Wagner, Richard. (1977) *Democracy in Deficit*. London, UK.: Academic Press.

Buchanan, James. (1999) "The Pure Theory of Government Finance." *The Collected Works of James Buchanan*. Indianapolis, IN.: Liberty Fund.

Calhoun, John. (1953) *A Disquisition on Government*. New York, NY.: Liberal Arts Press.

Citizens of the State of Michigan. (1963) *The Constitution of the State of Michigan*. Lansing. MI.

Dodge, Robert. (1998) "A Taxing Proposition," *Dallas Morning News*: August 4th.

Epstein, Richard (1985) *Takings: Private Property and the Power of Eminent Domain*. Cambridge, MA.: Harvard University Press.

Friedman, Milton. (1962) *Capitalism and Freedom*. Chicago, IL.: University of Chicago Press.

Friedman, Milton and Rose. (1980) *Free to Choose*. New York, NY.: Harcourt Brace Jovanovich.

Groves, Harold. (1974) *Tax Philosophers*. Madison, WI.: University of Wisconsin Press.

Hamilton, Alexander. (1982, 1788) "Federalist Numbers 1, 11, 84 and 85." *The Federalist Papers*. New York, NY.: Bantam Books.

Hayek, Friedrich. (1972, 1960) *The Constitution of Liberty*. South Bend, IN.: Gateway Publishing.

Hume, David. (1970, 1752) *David Hume's Writings on Economics*. Rotwein, Eugene, ed. Madison, WI.: University of Wisconsin Press.

Locke, John. (1971, 1689) *Second Treatise of Civil Government*, 8th edition. Chicago, IL.: Henry Regnery Company.

Madison, James. (1982, 1788) "Federalist No. 62." *The Federalist Papers*. New York, NY.: Bantam Books.

Marx, Karl and Engels, Frederick. (1987, 1848) *The Communist Manifesto*. New York, NY.: Pathfinder Press.

Mises, Ludwig. (1963) *Human Action*, 3rd ed. Chicago, IL.: Contemporary Books.

Mises, Ludwig. (1985) *Liberalism*, 3rd ed. Fairfax, VA.: Institute for Humane Studies.

Mitchell, Daniel. (1998) "737,734,941,858 Reasons...And Still Counting: Why a Flat Tax is Needed to Reform the IRS," *Heritage Foundation Backgrounder* 1170.

Mitchell, Daniel. (2001) "Tax Day Nightmare Gets Worse," *The Heritage Foundation*: April, 11th.

Morrison, Sylvia. (2000) *IRS Restructuring and Tax Law Compliance, CRS Report for Congress RL 30536*. Library of Congress.

Niskanen, William. (1990) "Conditions Affecting the Survival of Constitutional Rules." *Constitutional Political Economy* Vol. 1, Number 2: 53-62.

Pilon, Roger. (1993) "Freedom, Responsibility, and the Constitution: On Recovering Our Founding Principles." In Boaz, David and Crane, Edward (eds). *Market Liberalism: A Paradigm for the 21st Century*. Washington, D.C.: Cato Institute, pp. 1-52.

Pilon, Roger, (1999), "The Purpose and Limits of Government," Racheter, D.P. and Wagner, R.E. (eds.), *Limiting Leviathan,* Cheltenham, UK.: Edward Elgar

Racheter, Donald P. and Wagner, Richard E. (eds.) (1999), *Limiting Leviathan*, Cheltenham, U.K., Edward Elgar.

Racheter, Donald P. and Wagner Richard E., (eds.) (2001), *Federalist Government in Principle and* Practice, Norwell, MA.: Kluwer Academic Publishers.

Read, Leonard. (1958) "I Pencil." *The Freeman*, December: 32-37.

Rothbard, Murray. (1978) *For a New Liberty: The Libertarian Manifesto.* San Francisco, CA.: Fox and Wilkes.

Smith, Adam. (1981, 1776) *An Inquiry into the Nature and Causes of the Wealth of Nations,* Indianapolis, IN.: Liberty Fund.

Spencer, Herbert. (1982, 1843) *The Man Versus the State.* Indianapolis, IN.: Liberty Classics.

Stansel, Dean. (1994) "Taming Leviathan: Are Tax and Spending Limits the Answer?" *Cato Policy Analysis* 213: July 25th.

Topolinicki, Denise. (1990) "The Pros Flub Our Third Annual Tax-Return Test," *Money*: March.

Tritch, Teresa, and Deborah Lohse. (1991) "The Pros Flub Our Tax Test (Again)," *Money*: March.

Tritch, Teresa, and Deborah Lohse. (1992) "Tax Payers, Start Worrying," *Money*: March.

Tritch, Teresa. (1993) "Keep an Eye on Your Tax Pro.." *Money*: March.

United States Federal Government. Internal Revenue Service. (2001) *Internal Revenue Code.* Washington D.C.

Williams, Walter. (1993) "The Legitimate Role of Government in a Free Economy." Bryn Mawr, PA.: The American College, (Video).

5 REFERENDUM, REDISTRIBUTION, AND TAX EXEMPTION: A RENT-SEEKING THEORY OF DIRECT DEMOCRACY

Gary M. Anderson

INTRODUCTION

The central focus of research into the fiscal behavior of the public sector has long been the distribution of the benefits and costs associated with government activities. The traditional explanation of this pattern of largesse was, of course, that government was an agency that consistently (although somewhat mysteriously) sought to maximize the welfare of society and organized its fiscal activities accordingly. Thus, public spending and the taxing of private production were conducted in such a way that the tendency of the free market to "fail" to optimally provide various and sundry "public goods and services" didn't reduce the welfare of Society. This "public interest" model of government implied that the State was in effect the "backstop" supporting the market economy, making available those goods and services with "publicness" characteristics (i.e., non-rival and non-excludable in consumption) which private, for-profit enterprise was supposedly unable or unwilling to provide to consumers. Government was therefore viewed as the *deus ex machina* of the economy, promoting efficiency and increasing the social welfare by way of slaying the dragon of free-ridership.

There was only one problem with this nifty story of efficiency-promoting government behavior it was entirely unmotivated, and hence, almost completely unconvincing. The "public interest model" has been virtually annihilated—at least, among economists—by the concentrated (and comprehensive) assault on it undertaken by the Public Choice movement (mostly) over the course of the last 30 years. Study after study, article after article, and paper after paper have relentlessly destroyed the notion that the government is the selfless maximizer of the well-being of society, and that it engages in the activities we observe solely because that's where the pursuit of free-ridership has taken it. No, government decision-makers are grubby economizers like the rest of the human race, and behave in the way they do because those activities promise to reward their self-interested wealth maximization. The elegant vision of the public sector grandly and selflessly intervening in order to overcome the free-rider problem has been revealed to be merely a fantasy, a statist fairy tale. The State is not the agency that nobly and conveniently steps in to correct the supposed deficiencies of the free market, but a giant rent-seeking machine that provides coercive wealth transfers to the highest bidder (albeit in a fairly efficient market).

By now, this Public Choice explanation of the pattern of government activity—the less romantic, but more realistic, model—is generally accepted by scholars of public finance; there are almost no living, breathing, analysts of the public sector who continued to hold to the traditional Pigouvian alternative. However, on the other side the *essence* of the "public interest model" remains alive and well. Although it is widely conceded that the growth of government spending is a function of the lobbying by organized pressure groups, the defenders of various different purported "restraints" on that spending still profess to believe that the mechanisms they support (e.g., the balanced-budget constitutional amendment, the Presidential or Gubernatorial line-item veto, and the supermajority restriction on new spending and/or taxation) are by contrast the *really* selfless and social welfare-maximizing efforts associated with public policy. One such allegedly selfless mechanism is the institution of the initiative (and the referendum), the tools of what is sometimes termed "direct democracy."

The initiative provides ordinary voters with the direct ability to enact rules, regulations, and laws. The referendum gives voters the ability to effectively veto rules, regulations, and laws previously enacted by elected Representatives in the Legislature. Politicians ("elected Representatives"), when left to their own devices, will typically fail to accurately represent the true preferences of their constituents and instead at the margin pursue their own personal agendas, or simply shirk. Direct democracy provides voters with the ability to compensate for this "failure to represent", and avoid the middleman (so to speak).

In other words, the institutions of direct democracy in the form of the initiative/referendum amount to a kind of constitutional constraint on the behavior of governmental decision-makers. The availability of these devices to voters serves to render rent seeking (at least, in certain forms) by politicians less lucrative, given that the most pork-laden piece of legislation will be rendered less secure, and hence less valuable to special interest groups; regardless of the apparent success an interest group has achieved in lobbying for (say) a statutory entry barrier, that success will prove evanescent if the electorate can merely turn around and veto the measure by means of a referendum.

Of course, this is predicated on the presumption that the correct expression of the "true" preferences of the electorate will result in a restrained and smaller government redistribution machine; if rent seeking by elected representatives is merely taking the form of greater shirking on their part, and the median voter urgently *wants* bigger and more expansive government, the exercise of direct democracy might well lead to an *increase* in the size and scope of that government's activity. [To anyone intent on reducing the size of government, shirking by politicians will be a desirable outcome.] However this may be, it seems clear that the majority of scholars who focus their attention on the initiative/referendum perceive these devices as constraints on government, institutions which tend to reduce the tendency of the "monopoly on coercion" to grow regardless of the preferences of the median voter that it do otherwise.

However, a serious problem remains, one that tends to get lost amidst the enthusiasm (of both proponents and opponents) about "direct democracy": a careful study of the effect of initiatives and referendums on the budgetary behavior of governments appears to find little impact. Initiatives and referendums are apparently not having dramatic effects, and on the surface it would seem that the impassioned controversy is essentially misguided and pointless.

These studies also establish that the exercise of the initiative and the referendum do not have a consistent effect on the size and scope of government. Sometimes the utilization of direct democracy seems to restrain the growth of the State; but at other time, these devices would seem to have exactly the opposite effect. Those who base their support for, or opposition to, these mechanisms on the assumption that they operate as effective constraints on government growth are sadly mistaken.

Regardless of the impact of these electoral devices on the measurable dimensions of governmental performance, there remains the question of whether there are implications of the employment of the initiative and the referendum relevant to the wealth positions of those parties who bear the burden of the taxes and receive the benefits of the spending resulting from the exercise of direct democracy.

Whenever government imposes coercive levies (taxes) on society, whether in pursuit of revenue, or else seeking to discourage certain forms of behavior (e.g., smoking), a tax burden results (which may include deadweight cost) that will be allocated between the producers and consumers. This allocation process is accessible to private interest groups who may invest resources for the purpose of affecting this burden distribution in their favor.

It turns out that upon close examination initiatives and referendums frequently function to redistribute the wealth burden imposed by either taxation or government spending. Direct democracy provides special interest groups with wealth transfers in the form of tax exemptions that have greater durability and security then what the Legislature might have provided to them.

The purpose of this chapter is to provide an overview of the "direct democracy" phenomenon, focusing on the U.S., and to argue that the initiative/referendum process (whatever it's other impacts or implications) functions as a means by which the tax burden is rearranged to the benefit of particular interest groups and to the detriment of others; in other words, a coercive wealth transfer.

The paper is divided into six sections. Section 2 outlines the basic terrain of initiatives and referendums at the state level in the U.S. Section 3 discusses the debate between the advocates and the detractors of these mechanisms, explores the economic rationale behind the idea that they function to constrain government to follow the true preferences of voters, and reviews the empirical evidence of the actual effects of "direct democracy" on the public fisc. Section 4 discusses the function of initiatives/referendums as alternative devices to coercively transfer wealth available to government. Section 5 summarizes the recent history of tax-related initiatives and referendums and considers how they impact the distribution of wealth. Section 6 concludes the paper.

DIRECT DEMOCRACY IN PRACTICE: THE AMERICAN EXPERIENCE

> Power to tax is vested in the political branches of state and local governments... [and is] subject to political check of the ballot box. Political accountability for taxation is particularly strong because decisions about taxes are extraordinarily visible and sensitive. Thus, the power to tax, perhaps more than any other governmental power, resides ultimately in the electorate. (La Pierre 1993, p. 30).

In a modern representative democracy, the preferences of the median voter are not solely expressed directly, but are usually "filtered" through politicians (i.e., elected officials). But this isn't the only way to run a railroad; in many countries, institutions exist which allow the electorate to make various public policy decisions directly. These institutions are the "initiative" and the "referendum."

An initiative allows voters to concoct a law by gathering enough signatures via petition to place a measure on the ballot (Schmidt 1989, p. 3) In a referendum; the vote takes place after the law has actually been enacted by the Legislature (ibid.) Twenty-four states provide initiatives on statutory, constitutional, or both types of measure (Council of State Governments [1992], p. 29).[1] In almost all states (the sole exception being Vermont), citizens have the opportunity to vote on any constitutional change, either by initiative or referendum (ibid., pp. 329-343). In many cities, counties, and other local jurisdictions across the U.S., the voters using one or both of these devices can subject laws to scrutiny (ibid). Moreover, direct democracy constitutes a quite substantial part of total lawmaking. In fact, these devices of "direct democracy" are extremely common and used quite frequently. For example, in the 1998 elections, over 200 initiatives and proposed constitutional amendments were place on the ballot in 16 states (Verhovek 1998).

The initiative and referendum allow voters to directly determine the political agenda by either subjecting statutes, and constitutional amendments to the ballot, or by vetoing laws produced by Legislatures. In the U.S., these tools are only available at the state and local levels; but in some other federal government systems (e.g., Switzerland) they are available at the level of the central government.

Using the initiative, private citizens may in effect write statutes which will subsequently be put before voters assuming that enough (valid) petition signatures are gathered. Initiative sponsors—in states that provide both of these devices—will often submit their measure as a (constitutional) initiative because of its "more secure" legal standing. Constitutional initiatives can generally be changed only by a subsequent vote of the general electorate, although statutory initiatives in most states can later be amended by the Legislature. Initiatives that meet the signature requirement go either directly to the voters or are placed on the state Legislature's agenda, where, if that body fails to enact the initiative within a specified time, the proponents have the option to gather additional signatures and place the measure on the ballot. Five states permit both types of initiative, and initiative sponsors typically prefer to take their issue directly to the voters.[2]

By contrast, the referendum allows the voters to rule on laws previously enacted by state or local legislative bodies. Again, a predetermined number of valid petition signatures are normally required. An example would be the case of the California "fair housing" law that was overturned by referendum in 1964 (see Wolfinger and Greenstein 1968). Referendums can also be called by the Legislature. For instance, all states (except Delaware) require that constitutional changes go before the voters in a referendum, and many state Legislatures place measures on the ballot in order to secure voter approval.[3]

These measures were mostly adopted during the first two decades of the last century (i.e., during the so-called "Progressive Era") in the western U.S.—America's first two statewide initiatives were put on the ballot in Oregon (Piper 2000, p. 1)—but a number came into existence in the rest of the country since 1975. The major issues bandied about in western politics were drawn from the Progressive agenda (e.g., the income tax, the direct election of U.S. Senators, women's suffrage, and so on), and the Progressives dominated the governments in those states (Price 1975). East of the Mississippi only a few states (8) have the initiative and/or referenda, while west of the Mississippi only a few states (6) *lack* these instruments, in any form (Magleby 1994). (Some states east of the Mississippi have only part of the total package; e.g., Kentucky and Maryland use only the referendum, while Florida and Mississippi have only the initiative [ibid., p. 220]).

By the late 1970s, a number of states that had not yet established the initiative and/or referendum saw major attempts (sometimes successful, sometimes not) to make them available. New Jersey, Hawaii, Texas, and Minnesota all experienced attempts to adopt these measures. States that already made these devices available to voters experienced an upsurge in activity.[4]

There is currently no initiative or referendum available at the national level in the U.S., but there have lately been strenuous efforts to implement such a device. But many other federal systems around the world have these mechanisms in place and there is a movement in the U.S. that promotes an equivalent national system here.

GOOD, BAD, OR INDIFFERENT? THE IMPACT OF DIRECT DEMOCRACY ASSESSED

Controversy swirls around the initiative and referendum, as many writers seem convinced that these devices play a crucial role in the formulation and implementation of public policy. The opponents of direct democracy usually don't challenge the basic claim that these institutional mechanisms have important effects, but maintain that these effects are almost entirely negative.

Probably the source of the greatest opposition involves the non-fiscal implications. For example, consider the critical broadside directed at the initiative process by Miller (1999). She maintains that direct ballot initiatives have been directed against things like affirmative action programs, the rights of homosexuals, and efforts to stem "sexism", and they consequently constitute a "dangerous example of lawmaking" (Miller 1999, p. 2). Like many opponents of these measures, she bases her opposition on two main "problems." First, the power in an initiative campaign is supposedly centralized in a small group of people who are unaccountable to the public at large. In other words, "direct democracy" is fundamentally undemocratic! Second, the party possessing greater wealth might expect to obtain greater media exposure and has a greater ability to "spin" the issues in its favor. That is, in practice the initiative reflects the inequality of the distribution of wealth, and this fact is allegedly relevant despite the apparent absence of any argument to the effect that "direct democracy" *increases* this inequality. "When a select group of well-financed individuals has the power to fashion a campaign to eliminate these programs, fundamental democratic principles of equal representation and majority rule are compromised" (ibid.)

Proponents of initiatives and referendums argue that the employment of these devices imparts a greater sense of *legitimacy* to political decision-making, at least in the eyes of the general citizenry. They argue that while elected officials can be influenced by the pleadings of special interest groups (which may or may not include outright bribery) to make decisions contrary to "the public interest", initiatives and referendums are largely insulated from these kinds of corrupting influences. This is basically the "good-government", Progressive-Era defense of direct democracy.

Most proponents, however, rely on some variation of an "economic" rationalization for utilizing these mechanisms. This approach provides a more plausible and satisfying alternative perspective on direct democracy. An important potential benefit of these devices is that they permit the voters to evade the tendency of organized interest groups to "capture" the Legislature, where they effectively direct the law-making process into directions which favor their members yet (in many cases) are at variance with the general interests of the citizen-voters in the jurisdiction in question.

It is generally conceded that organized interest groups dominate the use of the initiative process (Eagleby 1984; Tots 1990). Although ostensibly intended to open the democratic process to "citizen legislators," the practice of "direct democracy" clearly imposes barriers to entry confronting individuals or groups who might potentially benefit from utilizing these devices in practice. After the requisite valid signatures have been gathered, the sponsors of the ballot measure must begin the often-difficult task of collecting the resources to wage a campaign that successfully markets the initiative in question. The heavy expense required may well dissuade private citizens from using the process at all.

The key element in the economic analysis of direct democracy is the application of the theory of agency. An agent-principal relationship exists whenever one person is responsible for making decisions that affect the wealth position of some other individual. The "agency problem" involves the divergence between the actual behavior of the agent and the interests of the principal. In the political context, the "agency problem" takes the form of the tendency of politician/agents to selfishly pursue their own personal agendas (or simply shirk) instead of devoting their efforts to furthering the goals of their constituents/principals—i.e., do the work they are being paid to do. A major expression of the political agency problem is the tendency of elected officials to serve the interests of economic pressure groups instead of the interests of the majority of voters in cases where the two conflict.

Transaction costs drive the application of the theory of agency. Transaction costs associated with political participation tend to be substantial and the actions of agents (in this case, politicians) will fail to simply mirror the preferences of the principals (the electorate), elected officials tend to pursue their own agendas, either motivated by their individual beliefs or the maximization of their personal wealth. Such pursuit is constrained by the need to secure sufficient voter support to provide for continuing re-election. In actual practice, however, this constraint is weakened due to the familiar phenomenon of the concentration of benefits compared to the diffusion of costs.

Periodic elections offer one constraint on this agency problem; voters will, in theory, have the opportunity to replace elected officials who are viewed as shirking their duties. Because the costs of political participation tend to be relatively high, while the benefit sought tends to be concentrated, the multi-candidate election will likely prove somewhat inefficient as a constraint on the opportunism practiced by politician-agents.

A common feature of modern democratic systems is the notably large role played by unelected officials, regulators, and other civil servants—i.e., the bureaucracy—in public decision-making. These people control access to many public resources, and they nominally serve as the agents of elected officials. In theory, then, this "bureaucracy" is subject to the same electoral constraint as that confronting politicians. In practice, however, this public bureaucracy exercises a considerable level of independence from the elected officials (who are their principals).

These personal agendas reflect the respective maximization function of the public bureaucracy. They consistently imply the pursuit of bigger budgets (assuming that the pecuniary remuneration and/or amenities are closely linked to the organization's budgetary allocation), or the bureau may be used by the official in question to pursue some ideological agenda he personally favors.

Enter the initiative/referendum. The use of the voter initiative in U.S. states began during the Progressive Era, and was openly advocated by those favoring expanded government intervention in the economy as an effective device to achieve such expansion. The alleged corruption in state Legislatures supposedly frustrated the popular support for increased levels of government regulation and general control over resources, and permitted greedy special business interests to achieve their selfish personal designs (bribing government officials as required).

"Direct democracy" in the form of the initiative/referendum may thus be said to function as a kind of "firewall" protecting the interests of voters against the potential opportunism of the politicians they elect to public office. Consider the factors which function to discipline the behavior of elected officials. Bureaucrats (i.e. non-elected, permanent governmental decision-makers), as well as the courts, constrain rent seeking by politicians to a considerable degree, although this constraint is imperfect There are several reasons why. One problem is that these actors are themselves restricted via the constitution from interfering with this rent seeking by politicians, at least to any great extent. This "separation of powers" limits the degree to which different branches of government compete against one another, that is, engage in "poaching" on their fellow branch's jurisdiction. (Of course, these constitutional rules can be amended, but usually only at considerable cost to the politicians' security of tenure.)[5] Also, bureaucrats and jurists typically are rewarded as a function of how effectively they serve the interests of the politicians with whom they have ongoing strategic relationships, and consequently tend to have only a weak incentive to effectively oppose those legislators. The referendum avoids this incentive problem and allows voters to directly express their preferences concerning government activities, thereby providing a more effective constraint on self-interested malfeasance by elected officials (see Frey 1994).

Initiatives, then, basically represent lawmaking independent of the Legislature; these devices grant control of the public-policy agenda to the general electorate. Consider, for example, the determination of the salaries of elected officials. Legislatures typically make a considerable effort to disguise or hide attempts to increase the salaries, pensions, and general perquisites of politicians, rendering rent seeking by those politicians hard to track and, thus, to oppose. The initiative/referendum effectively sidesteps this problem.

Of course, the rent seeking by politicians may not necessarily involve pecuniary considerations, but instead the pursuit of non-cash perquisites, possibly including benefits flowing from the exercise of discretionary power. Such perquisites might include such things as generous sick leave, lax performance of assigned tasks, simple shirking, and so on. Referenda may provide an effective institutional means by which politicians intending to extract rents are frustrated from securing such amenities.

Malfeasance by elected officials may take the form of pursuing an ideological agenda at variance with the preferences of the voters. If government grows faster than the median voter deems appropriate (due perhaps to rational ignorance, or fiscal illusion) the initiative and referendum may provide a check on this tendency as those voters are enabled to forestall the inefficient expansion of government activities and/or spending.

For all of the *Sturm und Drang* over initiatives and referendums, it would be natural to assume that these instruments played a crucial role in the functioning of those political systems which featured them, but in reality this relationship is extremely weak. Indeed, there is much empirical support for the proposition that "direct democracy" doesn't make much difference, at least not in terms of reining in government spending or overall growth.

A body of empirical work examines the issue of exactly how the availability of the initiative process affects the formation of government policy. Most of this research is principally devoted to the exploration of the effects of initiatives on government spending. The empirical results have basically been a wash. First, some studies have found that the initiative process results in higher expenditures (Zax 1989). However, other studies purport to have found government expenditures to be systematically, albeit only slightly, smaller than they would have been in the absence of such institutions (Matsusaka 2000), while still others report that the availability of the initiative makes little difference (Farnham 1990).[6]

The history of direct democracy in the U.S., which has been carefully studied by Matusaka (2000), is very important and illuminating. He shows very clearly that the history of these measures in the U.S. is *not* consistent with the claims of some that they are always oriented towards restraining the growth of government; often the true aim of initiatives and referendums is clearly to *ease* and *accelerate* that growth.

Matsusaka considers the history of initiatives in three states, California, North Dakota, and Oregon, selected because they have been major users of this device, concentrating on the period 1900–1950. He finds that, although in these states the initiative was not always used to *increase* spending, this was in fact the case more often than not. Seven of the nine successful measures in California increased government spending, taxes, or borrowing (four for education, one for veterans, one for the aged and the blind, and one for highways). Of the 11 successful initiatives in North Dakota, three increased spending (for old-age pensions, financially distressed schools, and highways), two increased taxes, and two made it easier to borrow. Of the 14 initiatives passed in Oregon, three increased spending (one for state schools, one for old-age pensions, and one for rural credits), three increased taxes, and one made it easier to borrow. For the three states overall, 21 initiatives were approved that increased spending, taxes, or borrowing compared to 11 initiatives that reduced spending, taxes, or borrowing.

He also notes that the list of initiatives that failed is much longer than the list that passed. Most proposed initiatives either fail to earn a spot on the ballot (perhaps because they failed to garner sufficient valid signatures) or else gained a position on the ballot but went down in defeat at the polls. In particular, several attempts to limit taxes and spending were defeated. California voters rejected limits on the growth of school taxes in 1918 and rejected measures that would have eliminated the income tax in 1936 and 1939. North Dakota rejected property tax limits in 1924, school tax limits in 1934, and repeal of the state income tax in 1944. Oregon voters declined to reduce motor vehicle license fees in 1926, rejected limits on taxes and debt in 1932, and rejected limits on property and school taxes in 1934 and 1936. Interestingly, most of the defeated measures would, Matsusaka explains, have increased state spending or taxes.

The initiative/referendum often takes the form of a fiscal legal edict, and such a measure necessarily has important implications for the distribution of costs and benefits associated with governmental activities. We now turn to a closer examination of these relationships.

CONFISCATION, REDISTRIBUTION, AND LOOPHOLES: WEALTH TRANSFERS AND DIRECT DEMOCRACY

The use of the initiative process to allocate the burden of taxes is extremely widespread in the U.S.; a total of 130 such measures were on the ballot in various states since the passage of Proposition 13 in California (which was the opening wedge in a flood of tax initiatives over the following 20 years).

Over the past forty years, the interest-group theory of government behavior has shown itself to be an empirically rich and powerful explanatory tool. Applications have been extremely wide ranging, including: environmental regulation [Malone and McCormick 1982; Pashigian 1984]; federal trucking regulation [Moore 1978]; the output of state legislatures [McCormick and Tollison 1981]; the organization of Congress [Kroszner and Stratmann 1998]; historical problems such as explaining "mercantilism" [Ekelund and Tollison 1997]; and the recent expansion of the federal government [Holcombe 1999], as well as many other applications.

The interest-group theory holds that spending, taxing, and the host of other policies pursued by government represent the outcome of competition across political markets (e.g., the Legislature) among rent-seeking interest groups for the purpose of maximizing benefits and minimizing costs accruing to their members. According to this model, actual policy outcomes represent equilibria in political markets, across which wealth transfers are provided to interest groups by the "producers" of such transfers, political decision-makers. This presumably operates as an efficient market, in which deadweight costs generated by the transfers are minimized.

This implies that selective tax exemptions (i.e., loopholes) are available to the Legislature as means by which it can eliminate opposition to specific tax increases from particular individuals and/or groups—by rendering them unaffected by the proposed tax increase. That is, by strategic dispersal of loopholes, the legislature can "buy off" opponents of a tax hike who might otherwise effectively block that particular change in the tax code.

When well-organized special interest groups are bought off by the Legislature, the general level of taxation rises as the only opposition to higher taxes will come from the politically unorganized. There is, of course, a limit to the level of tax increases that can occur before individuals are willing to bear the costs of organizing for effective political action.

Organized interest groups tend to dominate the lobbying process for several reasons. For instance, they have a substantial advantage in that they will typically be much better equipped to bear the costs associated with the initiative process. Furthermore, some of this theoretical literature indicates that small interest groups may be able to garner support for policies favored by the majority of potential voters, particularly when ballot proposals are complicated and information is very limited and costly (Lupia 1994). One might also predict that in states where there is relatively little conflict among interest groups, "narrow" interests would be more likely to utilize the initiative mechanism, and with greater success. By contrast, the same kind of "narrow" interests might have less success where there is a countervailing network of opposing groups.[7]

Legislatively brokered wealth transfers differ in their security against modification or repeal. A wealth transfer provided by way of statute is more vulnerable to shifting legislative coalitions than one provided by means of constitutional amendment, for example. A more durable wealth transfer "contract" is, *ceteris paribus*, a more valuable. But achieving greater durability is costly, and other things are *not* equal; hence we would expect to see (and, in fact, do observe) a mix of wealth transfer generating laws in terms of durability. Laws (for example, the parameters of the tax code) enacted via the initiative process are relatively highly durable, given the substantial hurdles a prospective initiative must surmount to succeed.

In other words, the initiative process is available as an alternative to interest groups who are seeking wealth transfers created by government, an alternative that tends to have higher durability than a statutory enactment. Special interest groups frustrated by the cost and difficulty of achieving wealth transfers from the Legislature may experience greater success with the voters.

There has been much interest in the functioning of the constitution as a constraint on government. State constitutions provide the underlying structure regulating the activities of governments within the particular state, and protecting (some of) the rights of individual citizens from the depredations of those governments. But the state constitution is also an alternative means for the provision of wealth transfers to interest groups. Laws enacted by the state Legislature are the way most wealth transfers are organized, but have a serious limitation: they will last only so long as the interest group equilibrium is undisturbed. After the next election, the political coalitions may be completely overturned, and the wealth transfer programs may be substantially altered as a result. New Legislators may not act to ensure the continuing integrity of the contracts between their departed predecessors and the relevant interest groups.

In principle, the initiative process can be used to redistribute either the burden of taxes or the benefits of spending. However, in the U.S. states, there is a pronounced tendency for the initiative to be used largely for the purpose of rearranging the tax burden; few initiatives (or referendums, for that matter) are seldom employed to enact spending programs. ["Direct democracy" is more often used to *bolster existing* spending programs—i.e., strengthening their underlying basis—by providing a constitutional provision that requires the state Legislature to fund those programs.] [8]

There are, then, two key points, which must be adumbrated in connection with the employment of the initiative/referendum process and public finance. First, these institutions of "direct democracy" may not have any particular net effect on the size and growth of government; and second, that these devices are useable in efforts to *raise* taxes as well as those aimed at tax *reduction*.

While the net effect on state revenue of the tax modifications effected via the initiative can go either way, we must acknowledge that the exercise of direct democracy is sometimes possibly going to result in a lowering of taxes. Most attention paid to the results of direct democracy on taxes focuses on this net impact on revenue. But there also exists another effect of these measures which is somewhat less obvious; that is, the burden associated with particular taxes is *redistributed*.

But ballot initiatives have not been confined to merely increasing or decreasing particular tax rates; a number of initiatives have been designed to shift the tax burden around on both the demand-side and on the supply-side. For example, an initiative might cut one tax while increasing another (say, reducing taxes on the poor while increasing taxes on the rich). Oregon voters passed one such "shuffling" measure in 1986, in which a new state sales tax was begun at the same time that property taxes were lowered. However, these initiatives only rarely pass; out of the 15 measures on the ballot since 1978, only 1 (an Idaho home improvement exemption from the state *ad valorem* tax) successfully passed.

Everything government does—*or refrains from doing*—affects the distribution of income. In a basic functional sense, direct government spending and tax subsidies are economically equivalent. A dollar is a dollar is a dollar; rents derived from governmental wealth transfers may take either form. A subsidy is implied whenever taxpayers are allowed to keep value they would otherwise be forced to pay to the government. There are three different forms that this "tax subsidy" may take: exclusions, deductions, and credits. Exclusions subsidize the beneficiary to the extent of the tax foregone, equal to the taxpayer's marginal rate applied to the excluded sources of income. (Examples include the exclusion from reported gross income of housing allowances received by ministers and the exclusion from employee income of the cost of employer-provided health insurance.) Deductions similarly operate as subsidies equal to the beneficiary's marginal rate times the deductible amount. (For instance, the home mortgage interest deduction in the U.S. federal tax code.) Credits are subsidies equal to the full extent of the dollar value of the credit. Although these mechanisms operate differently, all three reduce the tax liability of the beneficiary, and are completely equivalent for all intents and purposes to simple cash transfers.

In one sense, whenever the government declines to impose a tax on a good or service, it is expending resources every bit as much as when it spends money on direct subsidies. Thus, any value retained by the individual producer of that value represents a kind of "wealth transfer" insofar as the fact of its retention bespeaks a successful effort aimed at influencing the government to *not* tax it away! (This point must not be confused with the ridiculous proposition that the government is the ultimate source of all wealth.)

Writers appear to have concluded that a change in the level of available loopholes in the tax code would, other things held equal, have a negative impact on the level of tax revenues. Surrey and McDaniel (1985) argue that tax expenditures are just an alternative form of government spending by means of which selected individuals and/or groups are subsidized, at the expense of government revenue foregone. In other words, a dollar of tax expenditure is equivalent to a dollar lost to the government in potential revenue. Obviously, an individual, *ceteris paribus*, will be indifferent between a dollar of government subsidy and a dollar reduction in his tax burden. Further, it seems plausible that a dollar increase in tax expenditures will have a negative effect on net revenues collected (although probably significantly less than a one dollar loss).

Advocates of "flat tax" reform imply that a given income tax rate structure *with* loopholes will generate less net revenue than would the same rate structure *without* loopholes.[9] In other words, tax exemptions reduce tax revenue, *ceteris paribus*. On the surface, this seems like elementary common sense: as loopholes proliferate, resources which would otherwise be available to government "leak" out of the tax system, and total tax revenue *must* be lower than it would have been, holding everything else constant.

Unfortunately, other things are *not* equal. The production of revenue by the tax system is a dynamic, not a static, process. It is common for estimates of the revenue loss due to "tax expenditures" to assume that taxpayer behavior will remain the same after loopholes are modified. Effective tax rates are simply assumed to have no effect on choice.

Anderson, Martin, and Tollison (1987) examined the problem empirically, using the measured length of the tax codes as a proxy for the extent of loopholes across states, and discovered evidence that *increasing* the number of loopholes apparently *increased* tax revenues, at least within the existing range of tax rates. They suggest that the proliferation of loopholes may effectively diffuse opposition to tax increases from relatively cohesive and well-organized interest groups who then are unwilling to invest resources in efforts to resist via lobbying.

REDISTRIBUTING THE TAX BURDEN VIA DIRECT DEMOCRACY

The initiative is used quite often to alter the tax structure at the state level. For example, tax measures on the ballot in six states (Arkansas, California, Colorado, Georgia, Montana, and Virginia) were voted on in the U.S. in a recent year (1998). Three of these ballot measures would have raised taxes (those in Arkansas, California, and Georgia); the rest would have limited tax increases or actually have lowered taxes. Only one of these tax-raising initiatives passed in the end, the tobacco tax initiative in California. Clearly, the initiative process is actually employed as a means by which taxes are both raised and lowered. (The tax burden imposed by the state and local governments is manipulated up and down.)

Indeed, most initiatives at the state level are ostensibly designed to constrain the growth of government taxing and spending. That is, the investment in resources by interest groups associated with the initiative process is heavily weighted towards defensive rent seeking (or rent avoidance); these efforts tend to involve the attempt to limit governmental confiscation of privately owned assets. Obviously, the argument in favor of initiatives which emphasizes the effect they may have as limits on the excessive growth of government is consistent with the (recent) historical record.

Consider first the measures whose purpose is restricting the tax power of (usually) state governments—those similar to California's Proposition 13, income tax limits, general tax limits, and supermajority/voter approval requirements.

Proposition 13 in California was a major watershed in the history of direct democracy, because it definitively established that direct democracy was capable of imposing meaningful constraints on the fiscal behavior of politicians. The bulk of the current interest in the tax implications of the initiative process dates from the passage of this measure. For this reason we will use the year 1978 as the baseline for the discussion of the recent record of tax initiatives/referenda.

First consider initiative measures similar to Prop 13 in that they would generally reduce existing property tax rates while at the same time implementing a strict time limit on annual tax increases. Since 1978 there have been 23 such measures on the ballot in 11 states. Only nine became law.

The second type of initiative designed to constrain government revenue raising via tax confiscation is the limitation on the personal income tax. However, there was only one measure of this sort since 1978, and it failed.

More common have been initiatives designed to limit the overall tax burden by limiting the overall growth of taxes, revenue, or expenditures, typically to a set formula. Since 1978 there have been 12 of these measures on the ballot, seven of which passed into law.

SUPERMAJORITY REQUIREMENTS AND ANTI-EXEMPTION EXEMPTIONS

Supermajority requirements do not limit the power to tax explicitly, but provide an implicit constraint in the form of the increased difficulty of actually enacting tax increases. Such rules make the redistribution of the tax burden more costly, and to the extent that these rules work in effect "freeze" the existing pattern of the overall tax burden. By limiting the ability of the Legislature to increase particular tax rates, the opportunities for revenue-neutral deals (which may result in redistribution of the tax burden) are limited as well. If, for example, the Legislature wanted to increase property tax rates in exchange for reducing personal income tax rates (while holding government tax revenue constant), the supermajority requirement might prevent any such deal from occurring.

Supermajority rules basically fall into three different types. First, some states restrict legislation that is *intended* to raise revenue. California, for instance, imposes its supermajority requirement on those bills with the purpose of increasing revenue.[10] Oklahoma's constitutional mandate mentions "revenue bills," which the Oklahoma Supreme Court has interpreted to mean those bills with the purpose of raising revenue.[11] Some other states have looked to the *effect* of the bill. Delaware imposes a supermajority on new taxes or increases in the effective rates of old ones.[12] Nevada requires a supermajority on any bill that "creates, generates, or increases any public revenue in any form."[13] Supermajority requirements are the usual means by which local government tax collection is constrained at the state level.[14]

Assuming that the supermajority rule is intended to limit the size of government, unfunded mandates obviously must be included in the restriction, because otherwise government activities may simply be shifted "off-budget" or onto the shoulders of another level of the federal system. State governments can simply shift the burden on to the localities, forcing them to raise tax revenue.[15]

A total of 24 of these requirements have been on the ballots of various states since 1978, eight of which were enacted into law as a result. Twelve states currently have supermajority rules limiting the use by government of the taxing power, and which have been established via the initiative process.[16]

Some initiatives have sought to abolish certain taxes altogether (e.g., eliminating the state sales tax). Seven such measures have been voted on since 1978. Other initiatives have been designed to cut existing taxes. These measures don't place any limits on future tax increases or overall tax and spending levels. There have been 11 of these measures on the ballot since 1978, and five of these have actually passed. Yet another type of initiative is intended to exempt a particular good or service from a specific tax (such as exempting food or clothing from the sales tax). Ten such initiatives have been put before the voters since 1978, and five of these have passed. Only three initiatives to index taxpayers' disposable income to inflation have come before the voters since 1978, but all three have passed. In 1986, Oregon voters defeated a measure that, among other things, barred the state from ever adopting a sales tax (except via initiative). In 1988, voters in Nevada approved an initiative prohibiting the adoption of a state income tax.

A number of initiatives that obtain ballot status (some, but not all, of which eventually pass) effectively *increase* taxes. This amounts to the "dirty little secret" of the history of initiatives, which are sometimes mistakenly portrayed as consistently opposed to the growth of government.[17]

These increases seek to raise revenue, either by raising the rate of a particular tax, raising a tax rate on a specific product (e.g., taxes on cigarettes or gasoline) or else eliminating certain tax deductions (e.g., property tax exemptions for religious organizations). There have been 25 such measures on the ballot since 1978, eight of which have been passed into law.

The type of tax increase initiative that has been by far the most popular since 1978 has been the tax(es) on tobacco. Taxes on various tobacco products have been proposed in the form of initiatives eight times in six states, passing five times. The next most popular object of tax increases has been the category "natural resources" (which includes oil, gasoline, minerals, etc.), on the ballot six times in five states, but passing only once. Coming in third have been sales tax increases, which appeared on the ballot four times in three states, although only passed into law on one occasion.

The next best (or worst) thing to actually *increasing* taxes is extending the life of (supposedly) temporary levies beyond the date they were due to expire. Recently, there have been only two such measures, both in Missouri, in which state voters passed initiatives in both 1988 and 1996 to extend the state "sales and use" tax.

CONCLUSION

The institutions of direct democracy—the initiative and the referendum—have often been promoted as effective limits on the size, scope, and growth of government. Both opponents and proponents basically agree that initiatives are an important institution, although they differ on the matter of whether or not they produce desirable results. But research appears to indicate that these devices have little or no effect on the variables usually of concern to observers, such as the growth of government.

Most scholarly attention in relation to initiatives/referenda has been devoted to the normative assessment of these devices as tools for improving the performance of, and restricting the overexpansion of, government. Much of this literature can be fairly classified as "goo-goo" ("Good Government") fantasy, or sanctimonious boilerplate with little plausibility and less usefulness.

We have argued that the mechanism of the initiative/referendum can be assessed in terms of its actual function in a democratic state. From an economic perspective certain types of initiative (at least) provide a means by which coercive wealth transfers, brokered by the relevant politicians, are "packaged"; a more secure and durable alternative to enacting the same tax reduction or tax exemption via the Legislature. Initiatives provide government with the opportunity to redistribute the burden associated with revenue collection. Explaining and understanding the initiative/referendum process does not require the adoption of the bizarre and unmotivated Public Interest model (in which government acts to maximize the Social Welfare for no apparent reason), but requires only the assumption that the players in the initiative game are examples of *Homo economicus* engaged in ordinary rent-seeking.

ENDNOTES

1. Sixteen of the twenty-two states allow for constitutional ballot initiatives.
2. The five states are Michigan, Nevada, Ohio, Utah, and Washington.
3. Magleby (1984). Referendums placed on the ballot by state legislatures in the U. S. are similar to the facultative referendum in European nations. See Bogdanor (1994).
4. See National Center for Initiative Review (1982).
5. Investing political capital in attempting to modify or overturn rules which have the de facto effect of constraining the misbehavior of elected officials is likely to be interpreted by voters as indication of the rent-seeking motivations of those politicians.
6. However, there may be other effects which might arguably be deemed important. For example, Frey, Kucher, and Stutzer (1999) report that public employees are paid somewhat less when these institution are in place.
7. This relationship is strongly implied in papers by Gray and Lowery (1993, 1994).
8. This may be largely a result of the characteristic features of the organization of responsibilities in state government; in most states, the appropriation of funds is the constitutionally protected province of the Legislature!
9. Commenting on the impact of proposed-but-never-enacted Hall-Rabushka flat tax (which would have closed most if not all existing loopholes in the tax code), Buchanan (1983) comes to the same conclusion, albeit based on an entirely different line of reasoning. He argues that precisely because loopholes in the tax code can be expected to reduce the efficiency of the income tax as a revenue generator, the availability of loopholes function as an important constraint on the growth of government. Therefore, given that tax loopholes act as constraints on the maximization of revenue by the Leviathan state, Buchanan's argument implies that the increased availability of loopholes should have a negative effect on net revenue collected.
10. California Constitution, Article 13A, Section 10.
11. Oklahoma Constitution, Article 5, Section 33.
12. Delaware Constitution, Article 8, Section 10.
13. Nevada Constitution, Article 4, Section 18.
14. Several states have supermajority restrictions in place that limit property tax rates at the local government level. In the St Louis and Kansas City school districts, the state Constitution—which was amended to read this way by means of popular initiative—limits the tax rate to $1.25 per $100 of assessed valuation, but it also provides that the rate may be increased to $3.74 on a majority vote and above $3.75 on a two-thirds majority vote. The state Constitution also limits the total amount of property tax rates, the electorate has imposed (again, by way of initiative) a statutory and a constitutional limit on the total amount of revenue available to school districts under the "authorized" rates.
15. Arizona is the only state with a supermajority provision that specifically regulates the interaction between states and localities It applies its supermajority requirement to "changes in the allocation among the state, countries, or cities of Arizona and transaction privilege, severance, jet fuel and use, rental occupancy, or other taxes" (Arizona Constitution, Article 9, Section 22 B).
16. The states (and dates of enactment of the supermajority rules via initiative) are as follows: Arizona (1992), California (1978 and 1979), Colorado (1992), Florida (1994 and 1996), Hawaii (1978), Massachusetts, (1986), Michigan (1978), Missouri (1980 and 1996), Nevada (1996), Oklahoma (1992), South Dakota (1978), and Washington (1993).
17. The first two statewide initiatives in the U. S. were both measures which *increased* taxes—one imposing a "gross earning tax on telephone and telegraph companies, and the other imposing these taxes on sleeping, refrigerator, and oil-car companies (Piper 1999, pg. 1).

REFERENCES

Anderson, Gary M., Martin, Dolores T., and Tollison, Robert D. (1987), "Do Loopholes Decrease or Increase Tax Revenue?" *Journal of Public Finance and Public Choice* 2 (Fall): pp. 83-95.

Bogdanor, Vernon (1994), "Western Europe," in Burtler, David and Ranney, Austin (eds.) Council of State Governments, *Book of the States, 1992-93*, Lexington, KY.: Council of State Governments.

Dougan, William R. and O'Hara, Erin A. (1998), "Redistribution through Discriminatory Taxes: A Contractarian Explanation of the Role of the Courts," *George Mason Law Review* 6 (Summer): pp. 869-902.

Ekelund, Robert B. and Tollison, Robert D. (1997), *Politicized Economics: Monarchy, Monopoly, and Mercantilism*, College Station, TX.: Texas A&M University Press.

Farnham, Paul G. (1990), "The Impact of Citizen Influence on Local Government Expenditures," *Public Choice* 64: pp. 201-211.

Figlio, David N. and O'Sullivan, Arthur (2001), "The Local Response to Tax Limitation Measures: Do Local Governments Manipulate Voters to Increase Revenue?", *Journal of Law and Economics* 44 (April): pp. 233-251.

Frey, Bruno S. (1994), "Direct Democracy: Politico-Economic Lessons from Swiss Experience," *American Economic Review* 81 (May): pp. 338-342.

Frey, Bruno S., Kucher, Marcel, and Stutzer, Alois (1999), "Outcome, Process, and Power in Direct Democracy: New Econometric Results," Institute for Empirical Research in Economics, University of Zurich, Working Paper #25 (November).

Gray, Virginia, and Lowery, David (1993), "Stability and Change in State Interest-Group Systems , 1975-1990," *State and Local Government Review* 25: pp. 87-96.

Hahn, Harlan and Kamienjecki, Sheldon (1987), *Referendum Voting: Social Status and Policy Performances*, New York, NY.: Greenwood Press.

Holcombe, Randall G. (1999), "Veterans' Interests and the Transition to Government Growth: 1870-1915," *Public Choice* 99 (June): pp. 311-326.

Jost, Kenneth (1990), "Initiatives: True Democracy or Bad Lawmaking?" *Editorial Research Reports* 17 (August): pp. 462-475.

Kroszner, Randall S. and Stratmann, Thomas (1998), "Interest-Group Competition and the Organization of Congress: Theory and Evidence from Financial Services Action Committees," *American Economic Review* 88 (December): pp. 1163-1187.

LaPierre, D. Bruce (1993), "Enforcement of Judgements Against States and Local Government: Judicial Control Over the Power to Tax,: *George Washington Law Review* 61 (January): pp. 301-350.

Lupia, Arthur (1994), "The Effect of Information on Voting Behavior and Electoral Outcomes: An Experimental Study of Direct Legislation," *Public Choice* 78: pp. 65-86.

McCormick, Robert E. and Tollison, Robert D. (1981), *Politicians, Legislation, and the Economy: An Inquiry into the Interest–Group Theory of Government*, Boston, MA.: M. Nijhoff.

Magleby, David B. (1984), "Direct Legislation in the American States," in Butler, David and Ranney, Austin (eds.), *Referendums Around the World: the Growing Use of Direct Democracy*, Washington, D.C.: AEI Press.

Malone, Michael T. and McCormick, Robert E. (1982), "A Positive Theory of Environmental Quality Regulation," *Journal of Law and Economics* 25 (April) : pp. 99-123.

Matsusaka, John G. (2000), "Fiscal Effects of the Voter Initiative in the First Half of the Twentieth Century," *Journal of Law and Economics* 43 (October): pp. 619-638.

Miller, Jody (1999), "Democracy in Free Fall: the Use of Ballot Initiatives to Dismantle State-sponsored Affirmative Action Programs," *New York University School of Law Annual Survey of American Law:* pp. 1-23.

Minzner, Mark (1999), "Entrenching Interests: State Supermajority Requirements to Raise Taxes," *Akron Tax Journal* 14: pp. 43-88.

Moore, Thomas G. (1978), "The Beneficiaries of Trucking Regulation," *Journal of Law and Economics* 21 (October): pp. 327-343.

Pashigian, B. Peter (1984), "The Effect of Environmental Regulation on Optimal Plant Sizes and Factor Shares," *Journal of Law and Economics* 27 (April): pp. 1-28.

Piper, William (1999), *A Brief Analysis of Voter Behavior Regarding Tax Initiatives from 1978 to 1999*, Memphis, TN.: National Council for Initiatives and Referenda.

Price, Charles M. (1975), "The Initiative: A Phenomenon, " *Western Political Quarterly* 28.

Schmidt, David D. (1989), *Citizen Lawmakers: the Ballot Initiative Revolution*, Philadelphia, PA.: Temple University.

Stanley, Harold W. and Niemi, Richard G. (1994), *Vital Statistics on American Politics*, Washington, D.C.: CQ Press.

STATE CONSTITUTIONS may be found at www.limitedgovernment.org.

Surrey, Stanley S. and McDaniel, Paul R. (1985), *Tax Expenditures*, Cambridge, MA.; Harvard University Press.

Verhovek, Sam Howe (1998), "From Same-Sex Marriage to Gambling, Voters Speak," *New York Times*, November 5: p. B1.

Wagner, Richard E. (1997), "Choice, Exchange, and Public Finance," *American Economic Review* 87: pp. 160-163.

Wolfinger, Raymond E., and Greenstein, Fred I. (1968), "The Repeal of Fair Housing in California: An Analysis of Referendum Voting," *American Political Science Review* 62.

Zax, Jeffrey S. (1989), "Initiatives and Government Expenditures," *Public Choice* 63: pp. 267-277.

6 PUBLIC CHOICES AND FISCAL MEANS: ANALYZING TAXES AS COLLECTIVE OUTCOMES

Walter Hettich and Stanley L. Winer

INTRODUCTION

Joseph Schumpeter (1981) argued that a people's spirit is written in its fiscal history, "stripped of all phrases". There is no doubt that fiscal or tax history is central to a nation's development and to its ongoing political and economic life. And Schumpeter was surely correct in directing attention to actual fiscal outcomes, rather than to the political discussion surrounding tax policy, where rhetorical phrases and flourishes abound. Fiscal history provides us with a wealth of information on actual, specific choices made by democratic societies and on the impact of these choices on the economy and on different groups in the country.

Of course, tables of figures, or historical series of numbers, do not explain themselves. To understand the "fiscal spirit", it is necessary to start with an appropriate framework and to use accepted methods of statistical research to test suitable hypotheses.

In this essay, we show how both of these elements can be applied to the study of taxation. We start by surveying two collective choice models that have been used successfully in positive tax analysis, and by discussing the major implications of these and related models for the understanding of taxation.

The theoretical part of the essay is followed by a second one that deals with empirical research. Here, we focus on statistical work that takes its departure from models of collective choice. In the discussion, we draw attention to a variety of interesting questions that have been analyzed in the literature, or that can be asked in future research, while also reviewing important methodological problems that arise in investigations of this nature. We end the discussion with a brief set of concluding remarks.

TAXATION AS AN OUTCOME OF COLLECTIVE DECISION-MAKING

In order to carry out their function, governments need to draw resources from the private sector. In modern democratic societies, taxation is the most common way to accomplish this goal.

Economists have often asked whether taxation can be structured in a way that is analogous to the price system of the private economy. In other words, is it possible to charge each member of the society the true costs of public services that he or she consumes? Taxes that accomplish this purpose are usually called user charges, and they do play a limited role in the financing of public budgets.

In most cases, however, such charges are not a viable policy tool. The reason is the nature of most goods and services provided through the government sector. A majority are "public" to some degree, i.e. consumption of a unit of the good by someone does not prevent enjoyment of the same unit of the good by somebody else. The best-known example of publicness relates to national defense. As is often pointed out, an effective missile defense will protect everyone in a particular territory, with the enhanced security being consumed equally by all. While this is an example of "pure" publicness, there are other goods provided by governments where only a part of the output has a non-exclusionary nature. Nevertheless, it would be difficult to apply user charges even to those goods.

Publicness creates a problem for preference revelation. Individuals who consume public goods do not have the incentive to expose their true preferences through their actions as occurs in private markets. When goods have a public aspect, a free-rider problem arises, since others in society can be expected to pay for provision of the good, even if a particular individual (who cannot be excluded from consumption) does not pay his or her proper share. Most societies use coercive taxes that differ significantly in their incidence from user charges to finance a large portion of their budgets.[1]

A second reason that makes the government sector different from the private economy is the pursuit of distributional aims. Most democratic societies use the provision of public goods to redistribute income in various ways. Achievement of redistributional objectives thus provides a second explanation for the separation of taxation and spending.

Markets serve a central role in the private economy since they provide the mechanism for allocating scarce resources. The interaction of demand and supply determines how much of different inputs is drawn into the production of a particular good, how that good will be produced, and how much of it will become available at what price.

Although the government sector cannot rely on markets, essential allocation decisions must nevertheless be made. In democratic societies, voting mechanisms perform a similar function in the public sector to the one served by markets in the private economy. Ultimately, they determine how much of a particular good is to be provided and by what means it is to be produced and to be made available.

One might object that the decision process is a complex one that may involve bureaucratic choices and legislative decisions in addition to voting choices by individual citizen-taxpayers. No doubt, this is correct; yet it does not negate the essential function of voting mechanisms. Production and allocation of resources in the private sector is also a process of high complexity. Economic analysis tries to cut through the working of the myriad forces that operate in actual circumstances to the essential underlying interactions. For the private economy, this is achieved with the use of highly stylized descriptions of market institutions and of the players that participate in them.

A similar analysis for the public sector must focus on the essential ingredients of underlying voting mechanisms (Winer and Hettich 1998). Much can be explained by the schematic description and study of such mechanisms and the formal modeling of decisions that are made by participants. In the following section, we shall concentrate on two voting models that have been used extensively in the literature to explain the nature and level of taxation in democratic societies.

EQUILIBRIUM TAX RATES, BUDGET SIZE, AND REVENUE COMPOSITION

To understand the essential nature of taxation, it is useful to focus on three crucial types of variables. First, we must explain rates of taxation that emerge in a political equilibrium where voting relates to fiscal issues. Second, we need to determine total budget size as an outcome of the model. Finally, we may want to pay special attention to the shares in total revenues raised from different available tax sources, and to changes in such revenue shares.

A Comparison of Two Models

We shall base our exposition, which relies primarily on diagrammatic comparisons, on a fiscal framework that is characterized by several simplifying assumptions. We shall restrict the analysis to a situation where the public sector provides a single public good, and where decision makers use proportional tax rates on two available bases to finance their budget. Voters have preferences for the public good, as well as for output that is privately produced. This setup allows us to employ diagrams that relate voter utility to tax rates imposed on one or on two tax bases, depending on the voting model that is analyzed. Furthermore, diagrams of this type can be given a helpful intuitive interpretation. We can look at them as representing the indirect utility functions of voters who make choices relating to a variety of tax rates in different fiscal contexts.[2]

When economists first started to explore fiscal issues with the help of voting mechanisms, they relied heavily on the median voter model derived from the work of Duncan Black (1958). The analysis refers to instances of direct democracy, such as the voting in a referendum on school bonds. In the most general version, any voter can propose amendments, and voters act in accordance with their true preferences, that is, they do not behave strategically in making proposals or in casting their votes.[3]

Assume that an existing group must choose a proportional tax rate either on labor or on capital income. Each voter is fully informed about the consequences for herself of any rate that is possible, while having a well-defined, single-peaked preference ordering over all rates. Voting takes place for pairs of proposed tax rates until a winner is found that cannot be defeated in further pair-wise voting. The framework is called the median voter model since the winning rate will equal the most preferred one for the voter having median preferences in the group.

The model is illustrated in Figure 1 for three voters, with preference rankings being represented on the vertical axis and tax rates being shown on the horizontal one.[4] Rate t^*_m, most preferred by the "middle" voter, emerges as the equilibrium tax rate.

Figure 6.1. **A Median Voter Model**

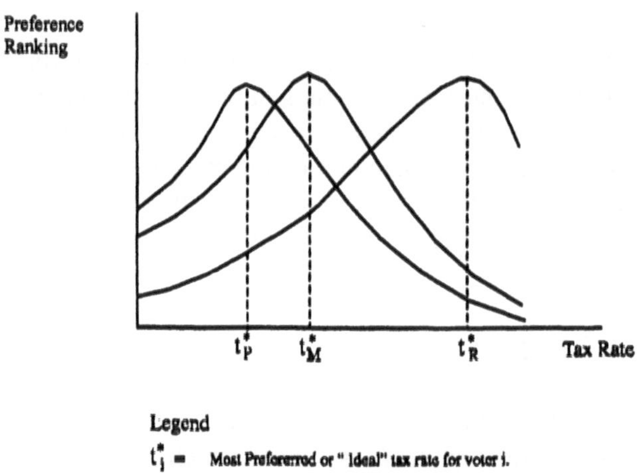

Although the model has an attractive simplicity, it also has several important shortcomings. Theoretical work has shown that outcomes are only stable if voting occurs in one dimension (on a single issue) and if preference orderings of voters have a single peak. It is true that stability can be achieved if alternatives are limited by an agenda setter, but this leaves open the question of how agenda-setting power emerges in such a framework. One should also note that the median voter's most preferred alternative may not be the winner when we have agenda setting.

The shortcomings of the median voter model are particularly significant for tax analysis. Most fiscal choices are multi-dimensional, involving more than one tax rate or tax base. In our example, the group may for instance want to impose taxation on income from both capital and labor. More complex decisions of this type can only be discussed with the help of the median voter model if we assume that given institutional constraints keep voting on the two issues strictly separate, to the extent that voters cannot perceive any meaningful link between the two voting decisions. There is some empirical work on taxation based on the median voter framework where unrelated, sequential voting of this nature has been assumed.

There are other models that are more suited to deal with the complexity of tax systems. Among them, probabilistic voting has been used quite extensively in empirical work in recent years. In this framework, two or more competing parties offer policy platforms to voters who evaluate them by comparing benefits and costs relevant to their own individual situation. Parties (or politicians acting on behalf of parties) are uncertain whether particular voters will give them their support in the next election. However, they are able to estimate the probability of such support. In order to gain office, or to stay in power, parties continually adjust policy platforms so as to maximize the sum of expected votes. The technical literature on the model shows that stable equilibria will emerge under well defined conditions, even when multi-dimensional issues must be decided.[5]

Figure 2 shows preferences by three voters in such a framework when choices relate to proportional tax rates on labor income (t_L) and capital income (t_C).[6] Points P*, M*, and R* are the most desired outcomes by voters P, M and R respectively. For simplicity, we assume indifference curves having a circular shape, with those for the voter with median preferences being shown as circles around point M*. Indifference contours passing through M* are also shown for P and R. The ideal points of the three voters have been connected with straight lines to enclose an area of triangular shape.

Figure 6.2. **Three Voters and Two Issues**

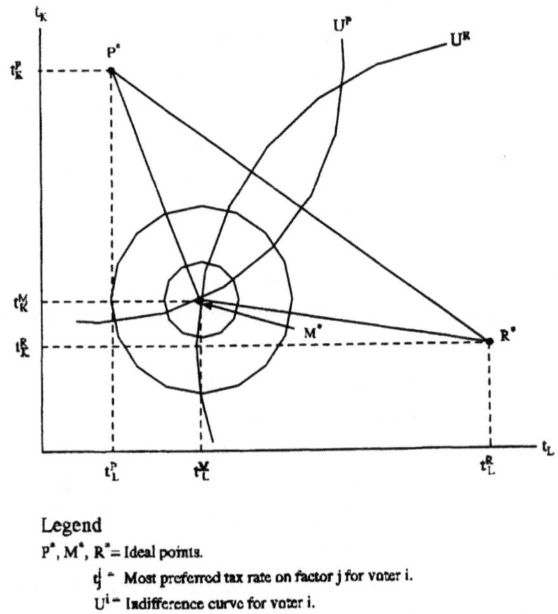

If choices on each tax rate were made in separate and unrelated majority votes, M* would be the result since the median voter would become decisive. Note, however, that in any vote relating to the joint determination of the two tax rates, a majority would favor a different outcome. Points falling in the area bordered by contours U^P and U^R would be preferred over M* by voters P and R. (Since M* lies at the median in each dimension, the nonemptiness of this lens indicates that a generalized median voter theorem does not apply in this case, a result that generally applies whenever there are two or more issue to be decided.)

With probabilistic voting, equilibrium tax rates will fall somewhere into the triangular area P*M*R*. The lines bordering this area represent contract curves between pairs of voters, given the assumption of circular indifference contours. If a party offers a platform corresponding to a point lying outside the area, the competing party can attract more votes by formulating a platform that represents a combination of the two tax rates that falls within the bounded area. As a result of competition among parties, a Nash equilibrium will emerge with a tax rate combination falling in the area enclosed by the three pair-wise contract curves, although the exact location of the equilibrium point cannot be predicted without more information about the factors affecting the parties' calculation of support probabilities.

Figure 2 shows that the choice of model plays an significant role in tax research based on collective choice analysis. Predictions to be tested by empirical research may be model-specific. Furthermore, it is clear that models dealing successfully with multi-dimensional issues provide a better basis or understanding of the complexity of modern tax systems.

The Structure of Taxation

We can start from the probabilistic voting model to construct a graphic analysis throwing light on the structure of taxation, as it emerges in a competitive political system. To achieve this, it will be helpful to view the use of tax instruments from the vantage point of the governing party that adjusts its policies in order to stay in power, rather than from the point of view of individual voters. One may note that a similar analysis of comparative statics could also be developed on the basis of other modeling approaches that allow for the discussion of stable multi-dimensional equilibria.

Let us assume that two tax bases are available to policy makers who have to decide on the amount of public goods to be provided (i.e. the size of the budget), and who must choose tax rates in order to raise the required revenues. Politicians know that greater provision of public output increases the probability of receiving support from voters, while higher taxation has a negative impact on expected support. If we think of loss of support as political costs, we can assign a political cost function to each tax base. The exact nature of such functions will differ from base to base since political reactions to an increase in tax rates depend on the constituency that bears the main burden of a particular tax source. In addition, the degree to which the government already draws on this source will be important.

Figure 3 illustrates the choice of tax rates and budget size by the governing party. Panels A and B relate to two different tax sources, with marginal political costs of raising an additional dollar of revenue being shown on the vertical axis and total revenue collected from that source being marked off on the horizontal axis in the upper portion of each panel. The third panel (C) shows the sum of marginal political costs, as well as the marginal political benefit function created by providing increments in the output of the public good.

Figure 6.3. **Tax Structure in Political Equilibrium**

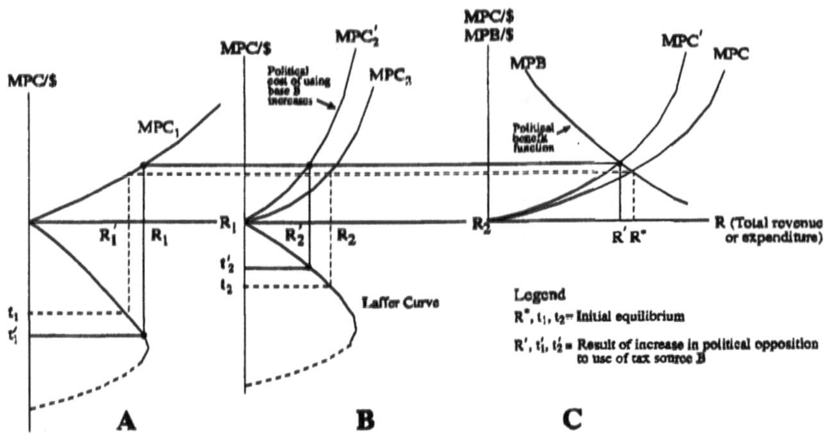

The figure allows us to determine budget size, tax rates and revenue composition, the variables identified at the beginning of Section 3 as crucial to the analysis. Expected political support will be maximized at budget size R*, where total marginal political costs are equal to total marginal benefits. Maximization also requires that marginal political costs on each tax base be equal. We can therefore draw a horizontal line starting from the intersection in panel C and crossing the other two panels to determine the equilibrium combinations of marginal political costs and revenues raised in each case.

In a final step, the lower portion of panels A and B is then used to find equilibrium tax rates t_1 and t_2 using the curves in the lower part that indicate the general equilibrium relationship between tax rates and tax revenues, or so-called Laffer curves[7]. Note that no government in a competitive political system would ever want to be on the backward bending (dotted line) part of any Laffer curve, since then tax revenues could be increased and political opposition reduced by lowering the corresponding tax rate.

The graphic analysis has two important implications for empirical research on taxation. First, it indicates that the tax system in a democratic political environment will have complex features, such as multiple bases and tax rates. In addition, it shows that exogenous shocks affecting any one of the underlying components will lead to changes in all of the crucial variables characterizing the tax system.

In the simple system represented by Figure 3, there will be two different equilibrium tax rates. With more tax sources, the number of rates will grow. In addition, complexity will increase if we go beyond the limitations of the graphic analysis and allow each tax base to have its own rate structure. It will increase further, and markedly so, if we account for the introduction of special provisions attached to each base.

In principle, a support-maximizing governing party would like to vary rates among taxpayers on a given tax base. Such individually tailored treatment would produce the largest total expected support. However, complete differentiation of this nature would entail large administrative costs that would reduce the party's ability to provide public benefits. The result will be a compromise solution where individual taxpayers are grouped into rate bands, with each member of a rate band paying the same tax rate.

Special provisions, such as deductions, exemptions and exclusions, serve a similar function. Decision makers interested in maximizing expected support will use such features to allow additional variation in the tax treatment of individuals at relatively low administrative costs. The end result is a rate structure on each base, and a variety of special provisions for each tax source.

The effects of an external shock on equilibrium values of crucial variables can be seen directly in Figure 3. Let us assume that the marginal political cost function for tax source two (shown in panel B) tilts upward as indicated in Figure 3. A possible cause might be a change in the political costs of gasoline taxation when gasoline prices undergo a sudden and substantial rise. A change of this nature will reduce budget size (panel C) and will alter equilibrium values in the remaining panels. As indicated in the graph, t_2 will fall to t'_2, while t_1 will increase to t'_1. Revenue shares will also assume new values, with the second base now contributing a lower proportion of total revenues.

Figure 3 suggests a strategy for empirical research that has proven quite successful in past work. If we can identify exogenous factors that influence the position of marginal political cost functions, we can use observations on such factors to explain differences in the structure of tax systems in various jurisdictions. Such an approach allows us, for example, to throw light on why some state governments in the U.S. rely heavily on personal income taxation, while others make little use of it. In addition, it can serve to explain variations in the design of international tax systems. We shall expand on this approach to empirical research in a later section.

Other Models As A Basis For Theoretical Work

There are several models not discussed so far which have also been used as a basis for empirical research. We shall briefly mention them, although space limitations prevent us from giving a detailed exposition of each model. [8]

The median voter framework has been combined with extensive assumptions about institutional arrangements that govern the context and sequence of votes, and that limit the range of available alternatives, an approach often called structure-induced equilibrium analysis. Although predictions based on models of this kind depend heavily on the institutional context that is postulated, they can yield interesting results if the political environment is carefully specified. The drawback of the approach relates to the fact that the institutions themselves, although a determining factor, remain exogenous and are not explained as part of the analysis.

While structure-induced equilibrium analysis assumes democratic decision making, an alternative model, called Leviathan, starts from the premise that the governing elite is not subject to effective political constraints.[9] In this view, policy makers attempt to maximize resources taken from the private sector when fashioning the tax system. While the model was originally proposed as a way to explore the limits of governmental power and the nature of tax constitutions, it has also been used in empirical work that attempts to throw light on the growth of total tax revenues over time and on other questions related to the relative size of the public sector. Drawbacks of the model, when used as a basis of statistical research, arise from the rather special nature of the underlying behavioral assumptions, and from the incomplete application of equilibrium concepts to the overall framework.

A final model that should be mentioned assumes that policy makers maximize the utility of a representative taxpayer when making fiscal choices. Since no elective process is specified, this approach does not fall into the collective choice literature. It is mainly useful as a reference point when empirical work is compared to research representing the social welfare tradition of analysis, where policy makers are assumed to maximize some index of social welfare, rather than to pursue their own self-interest, and where decisions by voter-taxpayers play no explicit role in the analysis.

FROM THEORY TO EMPIRICAL RESEARCH

How can the theoretical observations and models introduced above be used as a starting point for empirical research on the structure and evolution of tax systems? To discuss the transition from theory to statistical research, it is useful to return to Figure 3, adopting the voting model illustrated there as a basis for studying the evolution of a tax system. In addition to choosing a model, we must also adopt a precise definition of the term "tax system".

There are several ways to do this, mainly differentiated by the degree of detail with respect to the three major features of all tax systems: tax bases, rate structures, and special provisions. Here we shall consider only the choice of tax bases, and concentrate on modeling the relative reliance on different types of tax sources such as personal income taxes, domestic consumption taxes, taxes on trade, the issue of debt, and so on. The dependent variables in our empirical model, then, will be the shares of each source in total revenue, or revenues from each source relative to GDP, in some well-defined set of political jurisdictions. Since tax systems are just that—a set of interrelated components—we must formulate a *system* of equations explaining the extent to which each tax source is relied upon.

The next step is to figure out what set of explanatory variables should appear on the right side of the equation for each revenue share. Here the choice of the underlying model is crucial. Careful inspection of the probabilistic voting equilibrium illustrated in Figure 3 suggests that there are at least five types of variables that will be significant determinants of the relative reliance on any tax base or source, and which all must be somehow measured and used as explanatory variables on the right side of estimating equations. Our discussion of these types of explanatory variables will be heuristic, and will be summarized later on using a simple system of equations.[10]

The comparative static experiment illustrated in Figure 3 points towards a first set of factors that can be used to explain the relative reliance upon any tax source. This is the set of political factors that determine how the economic consequences (for the welfare of voters) of taxation levied on any base are translated into political opposition. (In Figure 3, these factors determine the shape of each marginal political cost function.) For later use, we denote such factors by the vector ***P***. The costs of organizing opposition by those most directly affected by each tax source would be one example of such a political variable. One may note that collecting data on such a set of political factors is likely to be a challenging exercise in its own right.

The next three sets of factors can be identified by looking carefully at the Laffer curves in the bottom part of the panels in Figure 3 and in Figure 4 below. The position of each Laffer curve is likely to depend on the determinants of the size of potential tax bases, denoted by the vector ***B***. A good example of such a determinant is the size of natural resource deposits in the case of taxes on natural resources.

Figure 6.4. **Comparative Statistics in a Model of Political Equilibrium**

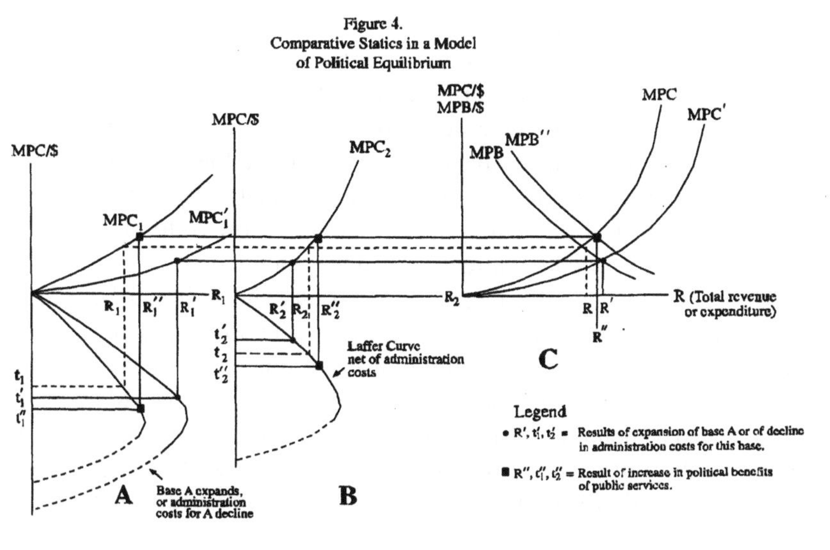

Figure 4 illustrates the role of factors of type ***B*** by showing what happens when the size of the potential base for tax source 1 expands at each tax rate. As indicated in the figure, as the Laffer curve for base 1 shifts out, the corresponding marginal political cost function tilts downwards (with ***P*** given). The expansion of a tax base, for whatever purpose, is likely to reduce political costs of relying on this revenue source for at least two reasons: (i) because a larger base allows the same revenue to be raised with a lower rate, thus reducing excess burdens and the full costs of taxation; and (ii) since the same revenue can be spread more widely across taxpayers which, given the fixed costs of organizing, will lead to less effective political opposition to taxation. As illustrated in Figure 4, the new equilibrium involves greater reliance on tax base 1, and reduced reliance on base 2. [11]

Another set of factors that may be used as explanatory variables are those that determine the administrative costs of collecting revenue from any source, denoted ***A***. Administrative costs place a wedge between revenues collected and public services that can be delivered and thereby reduce any political party's ability to generate votes. If the administrative costs associated with a particular tax source decline, for example, political competition will force the government to increase the relative reliance on that source in order to make the quantity of public services that can be provided to voters as large as possible for any given total tax revenue.

If we interpret the Laffer curves in Figure 4 as being net of administration costs, it can be seen in the figure that a decline in the cost of collecting revenue from, say, tax source 1, will be generally equivalent in its effects to an increase in the potential size of tax base 1, the result of which we discussed earlier. Again, the Laffer curve for base 1 shifts to the right as shown, and in the new equilibrium, the reliance on tax source1 is increased relative to the use of the other tax source.

So far we have only considered the effect on tax structure of the general position of each Laffer curve. But the precise shape of each curve, and particularly how quickly each one turns backwards, will affect equilibrium tax structures. The factors that determine the shape of each rate-revenue relationship will include all those factors that determine the elasticity of each tax base with respect to tax rates, denoted ***E***. For a relatively elastic base, the Laffer curve will turn backwards at a relatively low rate, making the corresponding revenue base less attractive as a tax source.

Finally, we must consider the factors determining the political benefits of providing public goods and services. The reason for including this type of explanatory variable can be seen in Figure 4 if we imagine an increase in the scale of the public sector as the marginal political benefit curve (MPB) shifts to the right because benefits derived from public sector activity are valued more highly. In the figure it can be seen that this exogenous change leads to an increase in the scale of the public sector, and to increased reliance on all (both) revenue sources.[12]

A SIMPLE SET OF ESTIMATING EQUATIONS

It is useful to summarize the above discussion by writing down the following system of equations to be estimated:

$$R_{jt} = f(P,B,A,E,G) + E_{jt}; \qquad j=1,2,...,J \text{ and } t=1,2,..., T$$

where
R_{jt} = revenue from tax base or revenue source j at time t
P = a vector of factors determining how the full economic burden of any tax is translated into political opposition
B = a vector of factors determining the size of potential tax bases
A = a vector of determinants of administrative costs of raising revenue from each source.
E = a vector of factors determining the shape of Laffer curves (i.e., factors determining the elasticities of tax bases with respect to tax rates)
G = a vectors of determinants of the perceived benefits of public services
E_{it} = a stochastic error term, possibly serially correlated and heteroscedastic

An alternative system could be formed by using revenues from each source relative to GDP, R_{jt}/GDP, on the left side of each of the equations.

Several features of this system are worthy of further comment. First, as a set of equations that represents the equilibrium outcome of a political process, it is a reduced form system in which every explanatory variable that affects any tax source enters into the estimating equation for each relationship. Thus, for example, the variable representing the base for the personal income tax will also appear in the equation for the share of revenue raised from domestic consumption taxes, since we should expect that the reliance on other bases such as consumption will also be altered when the income-tax base expands. Second, since the revenue shares always sum to one, the sum across equations of the coefficients on any particular explanatory variable must be zero: if an increase in this variable increases reliance on one source, it must also reduce reliance on some other source(s). For the same reason, the stochastic errors must sum to zero across equations at each point in time, which means that the system of equations is "seemingly unrelated".

Third, if we want to consider the effect of an increase in the size of the public sector on the extent to which any tax base is used relative to GDP, it will be necessary to estimate the system in which R_{jt}/GDP is used as the dependent variable in each equation.

What sort of results might emerge from estimation of systems of estimating equations explaining tax shares or tax revenues relative to GDP? At least two empirical regularities appear to be coming out of this kind of empirical work (see for example, Hettich and Winer 1984, 1991 and Kenny and Winer 2001):

(1) There is robust evidence that as the size of a potential tax base increases, revenue structures are adjusted to rely more on the larger or growing base and less on other tax sources. Political jurisdictions where natural resources are plentiful, for example, usually rely more heavily on natural resource revenues. This is especially so for oil-producing countries, but also applies to provinces and states within the U.S. and Canada.

(2) As the scale of the public sector increases, all tax sources tend to be relied upon more heavily relative to GDP, although not to the same extent. It does not appear to be the case that some tax sources decline in relative importance while others grow to make up for the loss.

OTHER INTERESTING APPLICATIONS AND AREAS OF RESEARCH

The empirical model discussed in the preceding section provides just one example of empirical work on the formation and evolution of tax systems using positive models of political equilibrium. In this section we briefly outline five additional areas of empirical application. The discussion remains illustrative. Extensive references to the literature are found in Hettich and Winer (1999, chapter 8), Kenny and Winer (2001), and Baker and Gould (2001).

(1) *The evolution of the tax skeleton.* It was pointed out earlier that all tax systems can be thought of as having three basic elements: tax bases, rate structures, and special provisions. The empirical application illustrated in the previous section concerns only the first of these elements. There is as yet only a small literature that attempts to model the relationship between the different parts of the skeleton.

Consider the following situation. A jurisdiction is considering increasing its reliance on the personal income tax. As the income-tax rates increase, so does overall opposition to the government. The increase in opposition can be attenuated, though not eliminated, if at the same time, some special provisions are opened up for taxpayers who are likely to offer especially strong resistance. Special provisions arising for this reason might include a tax credit or deduction for a specific class of taxpayers. Of course these special provisions have a cost in terms of reduced tax revenue. But it is likely that overall, total revenues will be higher than if no special provisions were opened up; to paraphrase Eric Lindahl (1959), the majority can tax the minority more if the minority can find some justice in the injustice.

The example suggests that the construction of simultaneous equation models that include more than one element of the complete tax skeleton ought to be on the research agenda. One should also note that in most cases, it will as a practical matter be necessary to estimate a system that is not complete in all aspects, and that this raises interesting questions of choice for the applied econometrician, as well as questions of interpretation.

(2) *Unusual trade-offs: taxation versus regulation:* Governments that seek re-election are forced to use all available policy instruments. Although we have so far only discussed relationships between different parts of the tax skeleton, political parties will also trade off the consequences of taxation with those of other government instruments.

One interesting example of such a trade-off concerns tax reductions and restrictions on the entry of new firms into a market as ways of generating votes and campaign contributions. Tax reductions for large groups of unorganized voters will generate votes directly. Restrictions on, or 'regulation' of entry into an industry, the first order of business for an industry that seeks political favors, may also be used to generate votes directly (from affected workers), as well as indirectly via increased campaign contributions. Entry restriction will also raise prices for the average voter. So the party involved has to weigh the benefits and costs (in terms of votes) attached to the different policy instruments in deciding how to proceed.

The investigation of the resulting substitutability of taxation and other policy instruments such as regulation in the process of political competition deserves more attention than it has received.[13]

(3) *Political regime and revenue composition*: Another fruitful area of research in positive tax analysis is the comparative analysis of revenue systems in various types of democratic and non- democratic regimes. Examples of work on this topic include Musgrave (1969), Steinmo (1993), Levi (1988) and Kenny and Winer (2001). It should be noted that even in repressive regimes, tax data are often quite good. All regimes need to raise revenue, and must be concerned with the heightened ability of tax collectors to steal when the size of tax collections are kept secret. Moreover, some public data on tax revenues are often required, or revealed, in the process of receiving international aid.

A difficulty faced in pooling data from all types of regimes is that at present there are no models allowing us to include both democratic and non-democratic political systems within the same conceptual framework. On the other hand, uncovering the basic stylized facts concerning differences in tax systems across types of political regimes is likely to be of help in constructing more encompassing theories and should be pursued more extensively for this reason.

An intriguing question that arises in the context of a search for such stylized facts is whether consent of the people matters for the level or structure of taxation. (One hopes the answer is yes.) Another related question that also deserves empirical investigation is whether repression that is often used in non-democratic regimes as a policy instrument (see Wintrobe 1996) can ever be a substitute for voluntary compliance in collecting revenue from hard-to-tax sources such as personal income?

> (4) *Identification problems concerning the appropriate model of revenue structure in competitive political systems:* We noted in section four that some authors have argued that even in competitive political systems there are Leviathan—like tendencies in the political system. A model of taxation in a democratic system in which principal-agent problems are of central importance stands in contrast to other frameworks, such as the probabilistic voting model, in which constraints on political agents are assumed to be strong.

It is interesting to point out that distinguishing empirically between these two sorts of approaches is much harder than one might imagine. Figure 5 can be used to illustrate the difficulty. The figure shows the Laffer curves associated with one particular tax base, before and after economic growth has occurred. A simple Leviathan-type model predicts that the government will always be at the inflection point of the Laffer curves, expanding its use of this tax source as shown in the figure. It can also be seen that a government that is constrained by democratic institutions to operate on the upward sloping parts of the curves would also follow a path of adjustment that is similar to Leviathan. Thus in a model of revenue structure such as that outlined in the previous section, estimating equations for each type of model would generally be the same, except that the exact values of the coefficients on each explanatory variable would be different. The one key difference between the two models would relate to the political factors, denoted by $\boldsymbol{P}$ in the earlier discussion. These would appear in a framework based on democratic choices, but be absent in a test of the Leviathan model.

Figure 6.5. **Identifying the Role of Principal Agent Problems in Shaping Tax Systems**

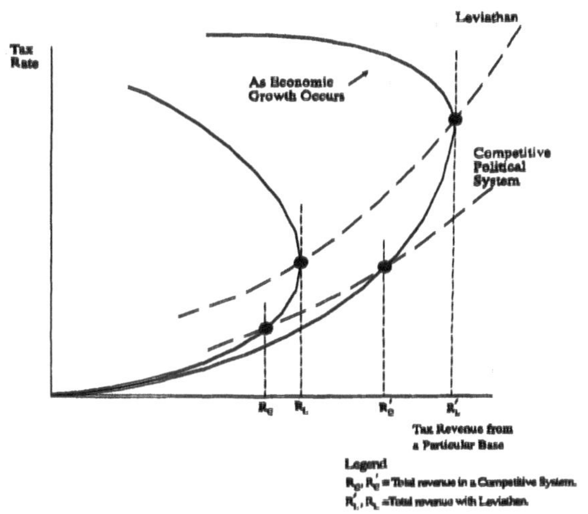

(5) *Governance and structural features of revenue systems*: The last area of research that we shall introduce concerns the role of governance, as distinct from the study of elections. The study of government ought not to be limited to the study of electoral competition. The nature of political institutions—Parliamentary and Congressional forms of government, for example—may also play important roles in shaping policy outcomes. Put differently, one could say that the organization of the supply side of government also matters, and not just because there are problems in controlling public servants.

How do political institutions affect tax structure? Answers to this important question may be found by studying tax systems in democratic countries with differing institutions. For example Hettich and Winer (1999, Chapter 11) compare tax systems in the Congressional system of the United States and the Parliamentary system of Canada. They argue that transaction costs of responding to economic shocks are higher in the Congressional system since agreement is required among the three branches of government, a problem not encountered in a parliamentary system where the government, by definition, controls parliament. Hence one should expect that tax systems are less frequently adjusted in the U.S. than in Canada, a prediction that seems to be borne out by their work. A similar result appears to hold with respect to responses in overall size of government. Persson and Tabellini (2001) investigate a sample of 61 democracies from 1960 onwards, and find that the size of government is less responsive to shocks in Presidential regimes, where centers of powers compete for influence and control.

CONCLUSION

The study of taxation is of special interest to economists concerned with the public sector. Fiscal history provides a record of important choices made by the collectivity and shows the changing relationship between citizens and the state. In addition, tax history provides a wealth of data that can be used to test hypotheses about the nature and consequences of policy actions.

It is important to understand that voting mechanisms play a role in the allocation of public sector resources that is analogous to the one played by markets in the private economy. For this reason, the study of such mechanisms lies at the heart of research on taxation. Voting models provide the basis for a theoretical understanding of fiscal decisions and fiscal structures. In addition, they serve as the starting point for the derivation of estimating equations in empirical research on the nature of tax systems and on a number of related policy questions.

This chapter reviews the use of voting models and shows how they are linked to empirical work on fiscal systems. A wide range of research questions dealing with taxation can be approached with a framework based on collective-choice analysis. They include the investigation of how revenue composition is determined, why particular revenue sources play a more significant role in public budgets than do others, and why and how special tax provisions are used in the design of fiscal policy. In addition, there is scope for comparative research that explains the different fiscal patterns observed across local jurisdictions, across states or provinces, and across different countries. Finally, we can ask questions related to the trade-off between taxation and other policy instruments, such as regulation, and about the influence of constitutional structure and of political regime on actual fiscal outcomes.

Although the study of taxation has a long history in economics, the analysis of fiscal decisions and fiscal systems based on collective-choice models is a relatively recent phenomenon. This makes it a challenging area of research where new and creative solutions in research design are needed, and where empirical results can significantly enhance our understanding. More than a century ago, the Scandinavian Economists Knut Wicksell and Eric Lindahl created a new way of looking at public sector analysis. While recent research discussed in this paper falls into this tradition, and while much progress has been made in understanding the working of public-sector choices, we still fall short of a full implementation of the original vision suggested by Wicksell and Lindahl. Creative work on taxation that is based systematically on voting models can contribute significantly to the achievement of a new and more complete synthesis of theoretical and empirical research on the public sector.

ENDNOTES

1. Wicksell (1896) first raised the question in a systematic way of how a collective choice approach can be applied to both sides of the budget if goods provided by the government have an aspect of publicness. Lindahl (1919) made a further contribution to the analysis. See also Lindhal (1959) for some of his later views. Downs (1957) provided the classic treatment of political parties as mechanisms for collective action on public sector issues, although he did not deal with tax or expenditure structure.
2. A more detailed treatment of different collective choice models is found in Hettich and Winer (1999), chapter 2.
3. An excellent overview of the median voter model is given by Mueller (1989).
4. See Hettich and Winer (1999, p. 14)
5. See Coughlin and Nitzan (1981), Coughlin (1992), Enelow and Hinich (1984, 1990) and Merrill and Grofman (2001) for a technical discussion of the probabilistic voting framework.
6. See Hettich and Winer (1999, p. 17).
7. The graphic analysis assumes that Laffer curves depend only on one tax rate, not on both. In a more general mathematical analysis, this restriction can be dropped.
8. For a more detailed review of these models and for an inclusive comparison of model predictions, see Hettich and Winer (1999), chapter 2.
9. The classic presentation of the Leviathan framework is found in Brennan and Buchanan (1980)
10. For more extensive discussion of a similar approach to modeling tax system, see Hettich and Winer (1991) and Kenny and Winer (2001).
11. The prediction that an expansion of the potential size of any base will lead to increased relative reliance on that base can be empirically tested once the complete empirical model has been constructed.
12. For further discussion and examples of the sort of explanatory variables discussed above, see for example Kau and Rubin (1980) and Kenny and Winer (2001).
13. A recent exception is Kelman (1999).

REFERENCES:

Black, Duncan (1958). *The Theory of Committees and Elections.* Cambridge, MA.: Cambridge University Press.

Baker, Peter J. and Gould, Andrew C. (2001). "Democracy and Taxation". University of Notre Dame, Unpublished, 2001.

Brennan, Geoffrey and Buchanan, James (1980). *The Power to Tax: Analytical Foundations of a Fiscal Constitution.* Cambridge, MA.: Cambridge University Press.

Coughlin, Peter (1992), *Probabilistic Voting Theory*, Cambridge, MA.: Cambridge University Press.

Coughlin, Peter and Nitzan, Shmuel (1981). "Electoral Outcomes with Probabilistic Voting and Nash Social-Welfare Maxima", *Journal of Public Economics* 15, pp. 113-121.

Downs, Anthony (1957). *An Economic Theory of Democracy*, New York: Harper and Row.

Enelow, J. and Hinich, M. (1984). *The Spatial Theory of Voting.* Cambridge, MA.: Cambridge University Press.

Enelow, J. and Hinich M. (1990). *Advances in the Spatial Theory of Voting.* Cambridge, MA.: Cambridge University Press.

Ferris, J. Stephen and West, Edwin G. (1996). "Testing Theories of Real Government Size: U.S. Experience, 1959-89". *Southern Economic Journal* 62(3), pp. 537-553.

Hettich, Walter and Winer, Stanley L. (1988), "Economic and Political Foundations of Tax Structure", *American Economic Review* 78, September, pp. 701-713.

Hettich, Walter and Winer, Stanley L. (1999). *Democratic Choice and Taxation.* Cambridge, MA.: Cambridge University Press.

Hettich, Walter and Winer, Stanley L. (2000), "Rules, Politics and the Normative Analysis ofTaxation", unpublished manuscript, p.39.

Kau, James B. and Rubin, Paul H. (1981). "The Size of Government," *Public Choice*, 37(2), pp. 261-74.

Kelman, Mark (2001). *Strategy or Principle?: The Choice Between Regulation and Taxation.* Ann Arbor, MI. : University of Michigan Press.

Kenny, Lawrence and Winer, Stanley L. (2001). "Tax Systems in the World: An Empirical Investigation into the Importance of Tax Bases, Collection Costs, and Political Regime," *Carleton Economic Papers.*

Levi, Margaret (1988). *Of Rule and Revenue.* Berkeley, CA.: University of California Press.

Lindahl, E. (1958). "Just Taxation: A Positive Solution." R.A. Musgrave and A. Peacock, (eds.), *Classics in the Theory of Public Finance*, New York, NY.: Macmillan, pp. 168-177.

Lindahl, E. (1959), "Om Skatteprinciper och Skattepolitik," in *Ekonomi Politik Samhalle*, Festschrift for Bertil Ohlins, Stockholm, 1959. Translated by T..L. Johnston as "Tax Principles and Tax Policy," in A. Peacock, R. Turvey, W. Stolper, and H. Liesner (eds.), *International Economic*, No 10. London, UK.: Macmillan, pp. 7-23.

Mueller, Dennis (1989). *Public Choice II.* Cambridge, MA.: Cambridge University Press.

Musgrave, Richard (1969). *Fiscal Systems*, New Haven, CT.: Yale University Press.

Persson, Torsten and Tabellini, Guido (2001). "Political Institutions and Policy Outcomes: What are the Stylized Facts?" Center for Economic Studies and IFO Institute for Economic Research, Munich Germany, Working Paper 459, April.

Schumpeter, Joseph A. (1981). "The Crisis of the Tax State". Translated in A. Peacock et. al., (eds.), *International Economic Papers* 4, London, UK. : Macmillan & Co., pp. 29-68.

Wicksell, Knut (1896), "A New Principle of Just Taxation," in Musgrave, Richard and Peacock, Alan (eds.), *Classics in the Theory of Public Finance*, New York, NY.: Macmillan & Co.

Winer, Stanley L. (2002). *Political Economy in Federal States: Selected Essays of Stanley L. Winer.* Cheltenham, U.K.: Edward Elgar Publishing.

Winer, Stanley L. and Hettich, Walter (1998), "What is Missed if We Leave Out Collective Choice in the Analysis of Taxation", *National Tax Journal* 51(2), pp. 373-389.

Wintrobe, Ronald (1996), The Political Economy of Dictatorship, Cambridge, MA.: Cambridge University Press.

7 EXCISE TAXATION AND INTEREST GROUP POLITICS

Randall G. Holcombe

Excise taxes represent a small, but not insignificant, source of tax revenue in the United States. Federal excise taxes make up about 6.6 percent of all federal taxes, state excise taxes make up about 16 percent of all state taxes, and local excise taxes are about three percent of all local taxes. Aggregating across governments, excise taxes are about eight percent of total taxes in the United States.[1] Public finance theory offers several justifications for relying on excise taxes, and this chapter offers a critical assessment of the standard public finance analysis of excise tax policy. One fundamental problem with the standard public finance approach to excise taxation is that it does not consider the political environment within which excise taxes are created. This is a problem with the economic analysis of taxation in general, but the political environment creates more problems for excise taxation than for other types of taxes, for several reasons. After considering the problems that interest group politics raises for the application of excise taxes, the chapter then discusses optimal excise tax policy in light of the political environment of excise taxation. The chapter concludes that in general, excise taxes should be avoided, but that they may be justified in certain narrow cases where the revenues from the tax clearly finance a benefit targeted to those who pay the tax.

This chapter focuses on three main problems that interest group politics create for excise taxes more than for other types of taxes. First, while public-finance theory offers many justifications for the use of excise taxes, it does not offer any method for determining when each justification applies, or if several apply, how each relates to the others. This opens the door for interest groups to argue for or against excise taxes based on conflicting criteria, and economic theory offers no way of sorting out the claims of various interests. Second, even if it was clear which of the many criteria justifying excise taxes was applicable in a particular case, all of the criteria offered by public-finance theory require information that is unobservable. As a result, the information must be generated through the political process if excise taxes are to be used according to the rationales of standard public-finance theory. Again, this opens the door to interest group politics, as interest groups enter the political process to try to manipulate the information that is used to make decisions about the tax structure. Third, excise taxes are inherently redistributional, meaning that by their very nature they pit the interests of some against the interests of others.

THE MANY JUSTIFICATIONS FOR EXCISE TAXATION

The standard public-finance justifications for excise taxation fall into three main categories: they are a source of revenue, they can act to discourage the purchase of goods that impose costs on others, and they can be used as a tool of industrial policy to encourage some industries relative to others. These three main justifications for excise taxation can be subdivided into a number of others.

A primary justification for any tax is that it raises revenue for the state. In this vein, excise-taxes are justified as a method of minimizing the excess burden of raising general revenues, and as a method of implementing the benefit principle of taxation. Ramsey (1927) notes that when many goods are to be taxed, then subject to certain conditions, the excess burden of taxation will be minimized when excise-tax rates are levied in inverse proportion to the goods' elasticities of demand.[2] This Ramsey rule of optimal excise taxation is one of the most enduring principles of tax policy, and suggests the way in which excise taxes should be structured to minimize the welfare loss of taxation. Buchanan (1976) criticizes this concept of optimal taxation because it fails to take into account how the revenues from the tax are to be used.[3] Buchanan recommends designing the tax structure to implement the benefit principle of taxation, which is the second way in which excise taxes are justified as a revenue source. Thus, the general justification of excise taxation as a source of government revenues offers two specific recommendations for the design of excise taxes—they should conform to the Ramsey rule, and they should conform to the benefit principle of taxation—and as Buchanan (1976) argues, in at least some cases the two imply different tax structures.

The second major justification for excise taxation is that excise taxes discourage the purchase of certain goods. Following this line of reasoning, they can be supported as a method of controlling negative externalities, using an argument dating at least as far back as Pigou (1924), and as a method of discouraging the purchase of what Musgrave (1959) has called demerit goods. Demerit goods and goods that generate negative externalities are not necessarily the same things, so again, these two sub-justifications do not necessarily point to the same structure of excise taxation. For example, luxury taxes are sometimes justified along these lines (Frank 1999), but the purchase of luxuries does not necessarily generate negative externalities.

Even if one agrees that excise taxes should be employed to discourage the purchase of certain goods, there are conflicting criteria for determining which goods should be taxed.

Third, excise taxes have been justified as a method of improving resource allocation by supporting some industries or discouraging others. If tariffs are viewed as excise taxes, in a modern economy they raise little revenue (only 2.3 percent of federal tax revenues, and 1.1 percent of total tax revenues), but are used to protect domestic industries from foreign competitors. More generally, excise taxes can be used as a tool of industrial policy to encourage some industries at the expense of others (Thurow 1985).

This brief review of justifications economists offer for excise taxation shows at least five distinct justifications:

(1) to implement the Ramsey rule for minimizing the excess burden of excise taxes
(2) to implement the benefit principle of taxation
(3) to internalize the production of externalities
(4) to discourage the consumption of demerit goods
(5) to encourage some industries or discourage others as a component of industrial policy.

These justifications are not fringe concepts in economics: all are a part of mainstream public-finance theory, but each justification implies a different structure of excise taxation. The theories that offer these justifications offer no clear way for judging which of them should be applied under which circumstances, and if many of them might apply, how they should be weighted.

The ambiguity created by the many potentially inconsistent justifications for excise taxation has implications for the standard theory of excise taxation, and further implications when one considers the role of interest-group politics. From a purely theoretical standpoint, it shows that while public-finance theory does have many different theories of excise taxation, they are not consistent with each other, so while each individual justification survives relatively unquestioned, public-finance theory in fact does not offer a clear theory of optimal excise taxation. These various approaches to excise taxation show that public-finance theory offers no single way to determine what constitutes an optimal excise tax.

How did economics come to have many generally-accepted theories of excise taxation, yet no one generally applicable theory of excise taxation? The answer is that each of the above-listed theories of optimal excise taxation was developed not to try to try to identify an optimal tax structure, but rather as a response to other types of problems. Ramsey (1927) probably comes the closest to trying to define an optimal tax structure, but the problem he addressed was the more narrow one of how excise taxes could be structured to minimize the excess burden of excise taxes for a given amount of tax revenue. But, if one wants to implement the benefit principle, then excise taxes could be used to do so; if one wants those who generate externalities to take account of the costs they impose on others, then excise taxes could be used to do so; if one wants to discourage the consumption of demerit goods, then excise taxes could be used to do so. This same logic applies to each justification, but no justification is related to the others. None of these justifications (with the possible exception of Ramsey's) was intended to offer a general theory of optimal excise taxation. Rather, each offered excise taxation as a mechanism for accomplishing some other goal. The result is a set of generally accepted theories of excise taxation that are potentially inconsistent with each other. Because of this, interest-group politics is potentially more problematic with excise taxes than with other types of taxes.

Because economic theory offers many conflicting justifications for excise taxes, interest groups can use the justification that suits their group the best to argue for or against a particular excise tax. There is no one correct answer in theory, so various theories become supporting arguments for various interest groups. This is a theoretical problem for public finance. Considering the many justifications for excise taxation, what structure of excise taxes would be optimal if the tax system were designed by an omniscient and benevolent government? This also generates a political problem, because with no clear right answer in theory, the structure of taxation will be designed based on the strength of various interests rather than on objective criteria. One might raise the same issue with any political decision, but the problem is exacerbated for excise taxes because there are so many generally accepted but potentially conflicting justifications for excise tax policy.

INFORMATION AND OPTIMAL EXCISE TAXATION

Of the many approaches to optimal excise taxation offered by standard economic theory, all require information that is not readily observable. To see that this is true, consider the several justifications for excise taxes listed in the previous section. Probably the best-established justification for excise taxation is that different rates of taxation on different goods can minimize the excess burden of taxation. The Ramsey rule says that when many goods are to be taxed, then subject to certain conditions, the excess burden of taxation will be minimized when excise tax rates are levied in inverse proportion to the goods' elasticities of demand. However, while the price of a good is clearly observable as market data, the elasticity of demand for a good is not, and must somehow be estimated. Furthermore, just as prices can change, so can elasticities of demand, so there is no guarantee that the elasticity that was estimated for a good last month still applies to that good today. To implement the Ramsey rule, information is required that is not actually observable, so that information will have to be generated within the political process. The political process has no way to verify that any elasticities it uses are accurate, raising the question about how political decision-making actually will work to produce elasticities of demand. This leaves the process of determining the appropriate elasticities open to potential manipulation by special interests. Because elasticities are not observable, political decision-makers do not have sufficient information to implement the Ramsey rule even if they want to.

The next justification for excise taxes noted in the previous section is that they can be used to implement the benefit principle of taxation. The advantages of the benefit principle were articulated by Adam Smith (1776: 777) and have remained a part of standard public finance, but like the demand elasticities just discussed, the benefits that people receive from government output are not readily observable. When Samuelson (1954, 1955) argued for the public provision of what he defined as public goods, he did so because he claimed there was no good way to identify people's preferences for public goods. Subsequently, Tiebout (1956), Minasian (1964), and others identified ways in which market mechanisms could reveal people's preferences, but Samuelson's point, applied to the benefit principle of taxation, still holds, as Samuelson (1964) himself vehemently argued. When goods are financed through taxation rather than being sold to consumers, there is no way to measure the benefit that consumers get from consuming the good. If excise taxes are to be applied following the justification that they charge for the benefits received, the state has no good way to actually measure these benefits. If an estimate of benefits from the consumption of government output is determined through the political process, again there is the potential for distortion in their measurement. The key point is that if excise taxes are justified based on their being an application of the benefit principle of taxation, the state does not have sufficient information to measure the actual benefits taxpayers receive.

The exception to this is certain instances where excise taxes are applied as user charges. With user charges, excise taxes more closely resemble market prices. If fees cannot be charged directly, then excise taxes can be earmarked for specific expenditures that benefit the taxpayers. Taxpayers who believed those specific expenditures were cost-effective would agree to be taxed more to finance those expenditures. Thus, the political process can provide a revealed-preference mechanism when excise taxes are earmarked and designed to correspond to the benefit principle. This is the one case—discussed further below—in which excise taxes may make sense when taking account of the political process through which the tax system is designed.

Excise taxes are also justified as corrective taxes on negative externalities. This idea goes back at least to Pigou (1924), and remains a part of the economist's public-policy toolbox. But here again, because externalities exist where there is no market for some scarce and valuable resource, there is no objectively correct measurement of the actual cost of the externality, so it will have to be estimated. As with other justifications for excise taxation, the information needed to apply excise taxes to correct for a resource misallocation due to a negative externality will have to be determined through the political process, where special interests have an incentive to try to alter government estimates in a way that benefits them. Those who generate externalities have an incentive to argue that the costs they impose on others are small, while competitors to the externality-generators have an incentive to argue they are large. Without objective measurements of external costs, the ultimate determination of the appropriate tax will be through politics rather than based on any objective criterion.

Excise taxes are also justified as "sin taxes," or "luxury taxes," which tax goods such as tobacco and alcohol, or yachts and personal aircraft, because consumption of those goods is considered by many to be undesirable or unnecessary. Once again, this cannot be objectively measured, and what some people consider to be undesirable consumption may be desirable to others. Smoking, a generally-accepted custom at mid-20th century, was viewed as an undesirable and nearly socially-unacceptable addiction at the end of the 20th century. Gasoline has also moved regularly from one end of the spectrum to the other. Conservationists have argued for higher excise taxes on gasoline, viewing it as wasteful consumption of resources and a source of pollution, while in response to energy shortfalls and higher prices in 2001 there was a call for lower excise taxes because the high price of this necessity was harming poor people and slowing economic growth. Once again, the point is that there can be no objective measure of whether a good should be taxed as a demerit good, so if this rationale is used for excise taxes, the level of taxation will be determined by the political clout of those for and against consumption of those goods.

The argument that excise taxes should be used as a method of supporting some industries or discouraging others also does not lend itself to objective measurement. History has shown that government is has a poor track record of differentiating those industries that should be protected for the good of the economy from those that should be discouraged. The invisible hand of the market does a much better job. This rationale especially lends itself to political manipulation. Industries always have an incentive to engage in rent-seeking to try to have taxes placed on their competitors, and to keep from being taxed themselves. Again, the main point is that there is no objective measure of the extent to which economic benefits accrue to supporting or discouraging firms or industries through tax policy.

This section has considered the information problems involved in the many justifications for applying excise taxation. For every justification of excise taxes found in standard public finance, there is no objective source of information available to determine how excise taxes should be set to achieve that goal. Standard public finance makes public-policy recommendations as if they would be implemented by an omniscient and benevolent government. Even if the government is benevolent, always implementing the best policy it can within its ability, but is not omniscient, government decision-makers cannot obtain the information necessary to implement policies consistent with the recommendations of standard public finance. Government could not design an optimal system of excise taxes with the information available to it, even if it wanted to. This opens the door to interest-group politics, as different groups try to manipulate the information political decision-makers will use to design excise taxes.

THE INHERENTLY REDISTRIBUTIVE NATURE OF EXCISE TAXATION

Taxes with broad bases, like income taxes, general sales taxes, and property taxes, are inherently less redistributive than narrowly based excise taxes. Taxes with broad bases limit differences among interest groups, because many interest groups are affected the same way by the tax. Taxes with narrow bases pit the interests of those who pay the tax against those who do not. Broadly based taxes can pit one group against another regarding the groups' tax shares; determining the progressivity of income taxes or exemptions to sales taxation are examples. However, there are fewer differences among interest groups with broadly based than with narrowly based taxes, because with narrowly based taxes, by definition the tax is paid by only a small segment of the population. Even if excise taxes are used to implement the benefit principle, they are potentially redistributive because they target a small group, making it attractive from a political perspective to expand the tax to finance benefits for groups other than the taxpayers.

There is a line of reasoning, following Becker (1983), Wittman (1989) and Hettich and Winer (1988) arguing that the Legislature acts as a political marketplace, and although the tax structure is determined by interest-group politics, the political marketplace will produce an efficient equilibrium tax structure. The political marketplace weighs the political demands of various interest-groups, leading political markets to be as efficient as economic markets, and to equilibrate in the same way. There is a different line of reasoning, based on rent-seeking (Tullock 1967; Kreuger 1974), and on interest-group politics (Weingast, Shepsle, and Johnsesn 1981; Holcombe 1985), arguing that the political marketplace does not operate in a manner analogous to economic markets. However one views this debate, the arguments that the political marketplace generates optimal taxes are less applicable to very distributional taxes like excise taxes, for two reasons. First, there is not necessarily an equilibrium outcome with redistributional taxes. Second, because of the coercive nature of taxation, resources will be inefficiently used in rent-seeking.

REDISTRIBUTIVE TAXATION

The issue of whether the political process leads to an equilibrium structure of excise taxation is closely tied to the redistributive nature of excise taxes. Arrow (1951) begins his famous treatise with a discussion of cyclical majorities, and McKelvey (1976) suggests that cycles should be the rule rather than the exception in political decision-making. Regardless of how general these conclusions are, they are more applicable to excise taxation because of the redistributive nature of excise taxes. To illustrate the point, assume that three taxpayers are going to decide by majority rule how to divide the tax burden. Each group will favor excise taxes that will push the burden onto other groups. The divisions (2/3, 1/3, 0), (1/3, 0, 2/3), and (0, 2/3, 1/3) create a cyclical majority. The second division is preferred to the first by a majority, the third division is preferred to the second by a majority, and the first division is preferred to the third by a majority. There is no outcome that is more highly valued than any other, so even of the logic of Becker (1983) and others is applied, because of the purely distributive nature of this issue, there is no unique majority-rule equilibrium outcome. Once a tax structure is determined, there is always another that would be preferred by majority rule, because of the distributional nature of the tax structure.

Compare this situation with a broadly-based tax, which, within the context of the previous paragraph, can be represented as (1/3, 1/3, 1/3). Using this broadly based tax, everybody's taxes rise and fall together, in contrast with the example in the previous paragraph where some can gain at the expense of others. One can see that if government revenues are constitutionally limited to come from broadly based taxes, there will be fewer interest-group conflicts over taxes because changes in taxes affect everyone the same way. Conflicts can still remain over how revenues are spent, but broadly based taxes eliminate one source of conflict. If there is a constitutional mandate requiring broadly based taxation, represented by (1/3, 1/3, 1/3), any interest group lobbying for higher taxes would see its taxes going up along with everyone else's, placing a limit on interest-group pressures for tax increases. With narrowly based taxes, interest groups not paying the taxes have much weaker reasons to oppose taxes, pitting the interests of taxpayers (a small group with narrowly based taxes) against non-taxpayers (a large group).

Excise taxes, as narrowly based taxes, give interest groups the incentive to argue for lowering excise taxes on their group, financing that reduction with an increase in excise taxes placed on others. With distributive taxes like excise taxes, the cyclical majority example shows why there is never a majority-rule equilibrium tax structure. For any given tax structure, there is always another one the majority would prefer. If a constitutional rule mandated a particular tax structure, like (1/3, 1/3, 1/3), this source of conflict would be eliminated, making it more likely that there would be an equilibrium. Excise taxes invite political instability by pitting one interest group against another.

Constitutional restrictions on the use of excise taxes are probably necessary to secure the political benefits of broadly based taxes. A more narrowly based outcome like (0, 1/2, 1/2) dominates the broadly based (1/3, 1/3, 1/3) by majority rule, which in turn is dominated by (2/3, 1/3, 0), which can lead to a cyclical majority. Majority-rule politics creates an incentive structure that pushes interest groups to favor more narrowly based taxes like excise taxes over broadly based taxes so that they can use the political process to push the costs of government to others. Without restrictions in the fiscal constitution, interest groups will always favor narrowly based taxes (that tax others) to broadly based taxes (that tax everyone). In principle, everyone may favor broadly based taxes, but without restrictions on the use of narrowly based taxes, interest groups always have the incentive to try to use excise taxes to lower their tax burdens and place the costs of government on others.

Excise taxes, as narrowly based taxes, are more susceptible to interest-group politics because by their nature they pit the interests of some against the interests of others. Because of the distributive nature of excise taxes, efficiency considerations will be largely irrelevant, because any efficiency losses will be swamped by the possible distributional gains and losses. Interest groups (or the Legislators working to support particular interest groups) will not look for the most efficient type of tax, but rather will look for the politically most-vulnerable taxpayers. When trying to fund more spending, the Legislature will not use the logic that if this tax is used, it will minimize the excess burden of taxation. Rather, it will use the logic that if that tax is used, the groups opposing it probably do not have enough political power to prevent the tax from being implemented.

Wittman (1989) would argue that economic efficiency and political power should be the same, because the greater the economic burden, the greater the incentive an interest group has to oppose a tax. Essentially, this is an application of the Coase (1960) theorem to politics. However, Coase's point was not that economic outcomes are always efficient, but that transactions costs prevent them from being so. Political decision-making brings with it much more in the way of transaction costs than market exchange. As Olson (1965) argues in his classic book, all interest groups do not have the same ability to organize. Smaller groups will tend to be more cohesive than larger groups because there is less of a free-rider problem, and groups that have other reasons to organize independent of any proposed taxes (such as trade associations) will have an advantage over groups that must organize specifically to oppose the government's taxing them. Wittman's argument would hold in a world of no transactions costs, and would approximate reality more closely if the transactions costs of all groups were approximately the same. However, in the real world, where there are vastly different costs of organizing and lobbying among various groups that could be taxed, the argument is not valid.

The distributional nature of excise taxation means that any tax structure can be defeated by some alternative tax structure by majority rule. The idea that the political process will produce an efficient equilibrium system of excise taxes does not hold up under scrutiny. These arguments could be applied to any type of tax, but they apply more strongly to excise taxes because excise taxes are by their nature more redistributive than more broadly based taxes. By design they tax a narrow base, creating the potential for some interests to enter the political process to obtain resources through excise taxes placed on others. As a result, interest-group politics will be especially active on excise tax issues.

THE COERCIVE NATURE OF TAXATION

All taxes are coercive. However, the distributive nature of excise taxes makes the coercive nature of taxation more pernicious. If the fiscal constitution required broadly based general taxation, the ability of interest groups to use the political process to impose taxes on some for the benefit of others would be limited. Excise taxes allow interest groups to lobby for taxes that will be placed on others. The coercive nature of the tax system has several implications. First, it means that taxes are not the result of a political exchange that is analogous to market exchange. Rather, they are a result of some people being able to use the political process to take resources away from others. The analogy to private markets does not hold up; if one wanted an analogy, it would be more accurate to say that taxation is theft. This is true no matter how patriotic people are, and no matter how much they might agree in principle with the tax policies of their governments. As shown by a wide variety of authors, from Tullock (1967) to Usher (1992), resources are not allocated the same way when they are allocated by predation as when they are allocated by exchange.

A second implication of the coercive nature of taxation is that people must always be on their guard against others trying to transfer resources away from them. The choice is not to engage in rent-seeking to try to get benefits from government or to ignore the political process and forego any rents. Those who ignore the political process become targets for rent-seeking predation, and have resources transferred away from them. In private markets, to avoid dealing in a market means that the individual will gain no benefits and incur no costs in that market. In the "political marketplace," those who choose to avoid it set themselves up as targets for predation.

While all taxes are coercive, excise taxes are especially prone to predatory politics because they are narrowly based, allowing some to use the political process to impose costs on others. Taxation, generally, can be used to fund transfers, but broadly based taxes impose their costs broadly to do so. In the three-group example above, consider a constitutional requirement that the tax burden be divided as (1/3, 1/3, 1/3). In this case, if one group's taxes go up, every group's taxes will go up the same amount. If one pays an extra dollar, everyone must do the same. Now consider an unrestricted environment which allows (0, 2/3, 1/3). Now, groups can use the political process to reduce their contributions at the expense of others. Everyone wants the 0 share, and wants to avoid being stuck with the 2/3 share. Because excise taxes can target narrow groups of taxpayers, their coercive nature pits the interests of some against the interests of others.

THE POLITICS OF EXCISE TAXATION

Taxes are a product of the political system, so any type of tax will be subject to interest-group politics. The foregoing analysis suggests that excise taxes will be more susceptible to interest-group politics than other types of taxes, for several reasons. Many problems would prevent government from being able to design an optimal system of excise taxes if that was its goal, but the government's goal is not to create optimal excise taxes anyway. The justifications for excise taxation from standard public-finance theory imply that "government" is the decision-maker, but governments do not make decisions: people do. When "government" makes a decision, that is a shorthand way of referring to the collective decision-making process in which citizens interact with their government through voting, lobbying, and other political activities, and Legislators weigh the inputs of citizens and interest groups along with their own preferences to make their own decisions. The process then continues as the preferences of individual Legislators are aggregated through a collective decision-making process to produce the government's policy. One cannot understand the government's excise-tax policies without understanding the political process through which they are produced.

All government policies, including its tax policies, are a product of politics, not a product of a benevolent dictator always trying to act in the public interest. An alternative to an excise tax is some type of general tax, like a sales tax or income tax. When looking at the alternatives, the detached economic analyst might place herself in the position of a benevolent dictator and consider when it would be in the public interest to use excise taxation rather than a more broadly based tax. This is not how democratic politics weighs the alternatives. If one wants to understand why excise taxes actually are used, the general answer is that they are used when the political forces in favor of them are stronger than those opposed.

Assume that Legislators agree that they want a set of excise taxes to conform to the Ramsey rule by taxing goods in inverse proportion to their demand. Because Legislators cannot observe elasticities of demand, these elasticities must be estimated, and there is an incentive for potential taxpayers to hire their own experts to calculate elasticities and lobby Legislators to accept them. Sellers in particular markets will look for "experts" to persuade the Legislature that the goods they sell have very elastic demands, and that other sellers have inelastic demands. Other interest groups will hire experts to show the opposite. The Legislature will not be in a good position to assess the economic analysis presented by various interest groups, with the result that the political process will become dominated by "junk science," as various interest groups line up experts to present their cases.[4] Each interest group will have its own set of elasticities that it will try to promote to the Legislature, so the actual determination of tax rates will pit one interest group against another.

Legislators are not necessarily good economists, and even if they were, are not necessarily interested in accurate estimates of elasticities. The nature of the political process suggests that the actual set of excise taxes that will be implemented will be determined more by the political power of various interest-groups than by the actual demand elasticities of the goods, which earlier analysis showed can never be determined with complete accuracy anyway. In such an environment of imperfect information and distributive issues, interest-group politics will have more clout than normal.

If, rather than implementing the Ramsey rule, Legislators instead agree that they want excise taxes to impose costs on certain specific taxpayers (smokers, for example), then again there is no objectively measurable indicator of the appropriate tax, so again politics will pit one interest group against another. The political problem of designing excise taxes is more serious than it appears when considering only one motivation for excise taxes because there are many possible motivations. Not only are tax rates subject to interest group politics, but so is the very nature of the tax. One group can argue that an excise tax should be placed on car rentals, because the demand for rental cars is inelastic, while another can argue that an excise tax should be placed on cigarettes because of the negative aspects of consuming the product, and yet another group can argue for a tax on cars powered by gasoline engines to help promote the development of vehicles that run on alternative fuels.

Even the most public-spirited government could not have enough information to actually determine a system of optimal excise taxes, and in response to the possibilities of lobbying from various interests, any actual system of excise taxes will be determined by the political power of interest groups rather than on the underlying merits of the taxes using the criteria of abstract economic theory. In reality—and in contrast to the goals of public finance theory—the use of excise taxes allows the politically powerful to tax the politically weak. When the political process that produces tax policy is taken into account, an economic analysis of excise taxes must be modified substantially.

THE POLITICAL COSTS OF THE TAX SYSTEM

The tax system imposes costs on the taxpayer and the economy in addition to just the revenues collected. Students of economics will be most familiar with the excess burden of taxation, which is the cost borne by taxpayers because a tax causes them to alter their behavior to avoid the tax. But as Slemrod and Sorum (1984) note, there are also substantial compliance costs associated with the tax system, which are the costs taxpayers must incur to comply with tax law. These costs include such things as keeping tax records, filling out forms, and meeting with government auditors. In addition, there are enforcement costs, which are the costs the government incurs to try to make sure that taxpayers are complying. These excess burden, compliance, and enforcement costs have been recognized by public-finance economists, but economists have barely mentioned the political costs associated with the tax system.

These political costs are the costs that taxpayers and potential taxpayers incur in lobbying and rent-seeking to try to lower their tax burdens or increase someone else's, and the costs incurred by the government in designing and altering the tax structure. That these costs exist and can be substantial is well-established by a large literature on rent-seeking going back to Tullock (1967) and Kreuger (1974), but as Holcombe (1998) notes, public-finance economists have done little to apply these insights to the tax system and to recognize the substantial political costs the tax system generates. As a rough estimate, Holcombe (1997) suggests that they are in the range of about 10 percent of the total amount of taxes collected each year, so if this estimate is in the ballpark, the political costs of taxation are substantial.

Political costs are incurred for two reasons: because it is possible for interests to engage in political activity to have the tax system altered to benefit them, and because people must engage in political activity to try to protect themselves from changes in the tax system that might be harmful to them. If the tax system is subject to change, then interest groups have an incentive to engage in lobbying activity to try to get favorable changes. This is the straightforward rent-seeking for benefits through taxation, as described by Tullock (1967) and Kreuger (1973). People are willing to incur rent-seeking costs up to the expected value of the benefits they can expect to receive from rent seeking.

Now consider the second reason the tax system generates political costs. If the tax system is subject to change, it is possible that the Legislature could impose a tax on a taxpayer and make the taxpayer worse off. Citizens and interest groups who isolate themselves from the political process run the risk of having costs placed on them, so they are forced to engage in lobbying activities—even if they would prefer to remain apolitical—as a defensive measure to try to protect themselves from being harmed by changes in the tax code. In this case, political costs are incurred not because interests are rent-seeking to try to get benefits through predatory taxation, but because they are trying to protect themselves from the predation of others. The less constrained government is in its policies, the more danger there is that people will be made worse off by the interest group activities of others.

Excise taxes have a greater potential to create political costs than more general and broadly based types of taxes. Broadly based taxes affect most people similarly, so changes will have less of a predatory aspect to them. Excise taxes are targeted to a particular subset of taxpayers, meaning that potential recipients of tax revenues have an incentive to seek revenues that impose costs on others but not themselves, and potential payers of the excise tax face a greater threat of predation and have the incentive to incur political costs to try to protect themselves from predation. The potential for predation is increased with more narrowly based taxes like excise taxes, increasing the potential for political costs incurred by both predators and prey.

The standard literature on taxation almost completely neglects political costs, even though these costs are well-recognized by public-choice theory. The political costs of taxation can be substantial, and will be larger for narrowly based excise taxes than for more broadly based taxes. These political costs can be minimized by creating a tax system that is relatively inflexible and difficult to change.

There is another advantage to making the tax structure comprehensive and inflexible: predictability. Taxpayers make many economic decisions based on the tax consequences, and if the tax system is flexible and subject to change, taxpayers cannot be certain that they are making appropriate business decisions. Changes in the tax code can turn profits into losses for some, while generating windfall profits for others. A predictable tax structure has substantial economic advantages, which is another reason for the fiscal constitution to be relatively inflexible. Excise taxes invite political predation, so a tax structure that allows them will tend to be less predictable. There are strong arguments for specifying the structure of excise taxes in a relatively inflexible fiscal constitution. This points directly to the question of what characteristics the fiscal constitution should specify about excise taxes.

OPTIMAL EXCISE TAXATION

Because of the politics involved in determining excise taxes, and because adequate information is not available to political decision-makers to design optimal excise taxes along the lines recommended by economic theory, there are substantial arguments against incorporating excise taxes into the tax structure. Information problems mean that the goals of traditional public finance cannot be accomplished, and the political environment within which excise taxes are created implies that excise taxes are likely to generate more in political costs than broadly based taxes. Excise taxes are narrowly targeted, inviting political costs from rent-seekers who see them as a source of special-interest revenue paid by others, which in turn pushes potential taxpayers to incur political costs to try to protect themselves from predation.

When taxing transactions, a retail sales tax has much to recommend it over excise taxation. In its ideal form, a retail sales tax clearly distinguishes between taxed and untaxed transactions: retail transactions are taxed; other transactions are not. Ideally, all transactions are taxed at the same rate, so there are no political costs incurred in trying to gain a differentially low tax rate, or trying to tax some other group differentially higher. Because the tax is general, there is more likely to be a congruence of interests among different interest groups. If people want more government spending, everyone will have to pay more in taxes; if people want lower taxes, government spending will have to be cut. Of course, most sales taxes are far from ideal in these respects, because they do not define the tax base carefully enough, and sometimes have differential rates on different transactions. These faults with real-world sales taxes merely suggest ways that sales taxes can be improved. The general point is that in most cases, a retail sales tax is a better tax instrument than a system of excise taxes.

There may some justification for selective excise taxation when the tax is clearly associated with some government-produced benefit to the taxpayers. For example, an excise tax on motor fuels, earmarked for the construction and maintenance of roads, makes sense. In this case, as Buchanan (1976) argues, the fiscal exchange model of taxation clearly applies, and the excise taxes are clearly associated with a specific benefit targeted to the taxpayers. If the tax really is earmarked for benefits to the taxpayers, then the distributional aspect of the excise tax is eliminated. Taxpayers would favor a higher excise tax if they valued the additional benefits more than the additional tax payments, and would favor a tax cut only if they also would favor a cut in those earmarked expenditures. Those who were not paying the tax would have no incentive to involve themselves in the issue because any changes in the tax would not affect them, again minimizing political costs.

This is the best case for excise taxation: a tax with revenues earmarked for expenditures that benefit the taxpayers. Even with the best case, if excise taxes are admitted into the fiscal constitution under these terms, many of the problems outlined above still remain. There remains the danger that another interest group could lobby the Legislature to use the excise tax for their benefit, at the expense of the taxpayers. For example, proponents of mass transit might favor using gasoline taxes to build rail lines. They might even claim that these expenditures would benefit the taxpayers (by lowering traffic congestion, or pollution, for example), referencing the benefit principle. Claims could even be more indirect. For example, proponents of public financing of a major league baseball stadium could argue for a tax on cruise ships, claiming that the tourism industry benefits from a major league baseball team.[5] As noted earlier, there is no objective source of information to design taxes that correspond to the benefit principle, so even though in theory using excise taxation to implement the benefit principle looks good when one abstracts from the political process, once interest-group politics are taken into account, even this best case for excise taxation rests on shaky ground.

Even under the most ideal circumstances, the political costs and information problems make it difficult to create a system of excise taxes that would be superior to a general retail sales tax. One could argue that in theory the excess burden could be lower with a set of excise taxes conforming to the Ramsey rule than with a general sales tax with only one rate, or that in theory resources could be allocated more efficiently with an optimal corrective tax on the producer of a negative externality. Once one considers the political environment within which taxes are created, however, the argument for broadly based taxes that impose uniform rates on all taxpayers become stronger.

EXCISE TAXES AND THE FISCAL CONSTITUTION

The fiscal constitution is the framework within which the tax structure is designed. The above analysis shows that if the fiscal constitution allows excise taxation, there is inadequate information to design them according to the ideals of economic theory, and that by their nature, excise taxes generate more in political costs than more broadly based taxes. A complete prohibition of excise taxes in the fiscal constitution may be reasonable, recognizing that with real-world information theoretically ideal excise taxes are not possible. The political costs and inefficiencies caused by interest group politics may outweigh any movement toward efficiency and equity that excise taxation would allow.

One might argue for excise taxes only when the taxpayers themselves approve, but even if taxpayer approval is required, other potential problems arise. Taxpayers may be rationally ignorant (Downs 1957), and taxpayers may vote expressively rather than instrumentally (Brennan and Lomasky 1993). Voters' opinions at the ballot box may not reflect their true interests. Furthermore, the political process may not be able to identify taxpayers ahead of time. For example, if an excise tax is to be placed on airline tickets for airport improvements, how would the political process actually identify the future taxpayers and ask their approval? Voter approval, while desirable, may be difficult to implement.

There are strong arguments against any use of selective excise taxes, and only when there is a direct correspondence between taxes paid and benefits received should they even be considered. Even then, when one considers the nature of the political process that designs the tax structure, there is a strong argument for prohibiting excise taxation and allowing only broadly based taxes that tax all taxpayers at uniform rates.

CONCLUSION

Economic analysis of excise taxation almost always ignores the political process that creates taxes, and as a result has derived policies of optimal excise taxation whose logic applies to an abstract theoretical world of perfect information, and devoid of politics. Standard public-finance theory has little guidance to offer for the design of optimal excise taxation, for a number of reasons:

(1) Economic analysis offers a multiplicity of potentially conflicting goals for excise taxation, but offers no way to choose one over another, or to weight them. Thus, one tax structure might be appropriate to further one goal, but another might be appropriate for another, and there is no way to determine how these different goals should be taken into account. This invites interest groups to engage in political activity to try to influence the Legislature to favor excise taxes that push the costs of taxation onto other groups.

(2) Even if policymakers are clear on their goals, and even if they act in the best possible way to achieve them, the information required to implement theoretically optimal excise taxes is not available to those who design the taxes. Again, this invites interest-group politics as each group tries to push information on the Legislature that favors that group's agenda over others.

(3) Excise taxes are inherently redistributive. While all taxes have redistributive elements, excise taxes are more redistributive because by design they are narrowly based, imposing their costs on only a subset of the population. Redistributive policies are more prone to interest-group activity because interest groups can gain from engaging in predatory politics to have resources transferred from others to them, and because interest groups must engage in political activity to protect themselves from the predatory politics of others.

(4) Taxes are a product of the political system, and the incentives in democratic decision-making are at odds with those required for any of the goals of excise taxation offered by economic analysis. Actual excise taxes will be determined by the political power of those who support and oppose them, not by the recommendations of economic analysis.

(5) Economic analysis has completely ignored the political costs of the tax system, which are the costs borne by those outside government to try to influence political decisions, and by government itself to weigh various interests and make public policy. These political costs have been recognized more generally in the literature on rent-seeking, but this general rent-seeking framework has not been applied directly to tax policy. Because excise taxes are by design narrowly based and more redistributive than broadly based taxes, they generate more in political costs than broadly based taxes.

When the political institutions that produce taxes are incorporated into the economic analysis of taxation, the optimal structure of excise taxes is significantly different from that suggested by standard economic analysis. The political costs of taxation can be minimized by designing a fiscal constitution that severely limits the use of narrowly based taxes like excise taxes. As a source of general revenue, excise taxes are inferior to broadly based taxes. To the extent that excise taxes are used, they should be embedded in a relatively inflexible fiscal constitution that requires them to be approved by taxpayers, that makes tax increases difficult, and that allows the taxpayers the option of reducing the tax if they believe the benefits of its expenditures are not worth the cost imposed by the tax. In the current political environment, despite many economic justifications for excise taxes, excise taxation is actually a device that allows the politically powerful to benefit themselves by imposing costs on the politically weak.

ENDNOTES

1. The source for these statistics is the *Statistical Abstract of the United States,* 120th edition (2000), p. 302.
2. See Holcombe (1996: 221-223) for a more complete explanation of the Ramsey rule.
3. Buchanan (1976) targets his criticism more toward the optimal tax literature spawned by Diamond and Mirrlees (1971), but his criticisms also apply to use of the Ramsey rule as a method of determining optimal tax policy.
4. Holcombe (1997) documents this process with regard to excise taxes on soft drinks and cigarettes.
5. The Miami Marlins baseball team wanted such a tax to finance a new stadium for them in 2000, but lobbying efforts failed, and at the time of this writing it appears that the cruise-ship operators have defeated the Marlins. This is an example not only of the misuse of the benefit principle, but also of the political costs of excise taxation. Both the Marlins organization and the cruise-ship operators incurred substantial lobbying costs, and the Legislature incurred costs in considering the issue before deciding against it. These political costs could have been completely avoided if such a tax was constitutionally prohibited. For example, Florida's Constitution prohibits income taxation, and there are almost no political costs incurred either for or against income taxation in Florida.

REFERENCES

Arrow, Kenneth J. (1951) *Social Choice and Individual Values.* New Haven: Yale University Press.

Becker, Gary. (1983) "A Theory of Competition Among Pressure Groups for Political Influence." *Quarterly Journal of Economics* 98, No. 3: pp. 371-400.

Buchanan, James M. (1976) "Taxation in Fiscal Exchange." *Journal of Public Economics* 6: pp. 17-29.

Coase, Ronald H. (1960) "The Problem of Social Cost." *Journal of Law & Economics* 3: pp. 1-44.

Diamond, Peter A., and James A. Mirrlees (1971) "Optimal Taxation and Public Production: I and II." *American Economic Review* 81 (March): pp. 8-27, (June): pp. 261-278.

Downs, Anthony (1957) *An Economic Theory of Democracy.* New York: Harper & Row.

Frank, Robert H. (1999) *Luxury Fever: Why Money Fails to Satisfy in an Era of Excess.* New York: Free Press.

Hettich, Walter, and Stanley L. Winer. (1988) "Economic and Political Foundations of Tax Structure." *American Economic Review* 78, No. 4: pp. 701-112.

Holcombe, Randall G. (1985) *An Economic Analysis of Democracy.* Carbondale: Southern Illinois University Press.

Holcombe, Randall G. (1996) *Public Finance: Government Revenues and Expenditures in the United States Economy.* St. Paul: West Publishing Company.

Holcombe, Randall G. (1997) "Selective Excise Taxes from an Interest-Group Perspective." In William F. Shughart II (ed.) *Taxing Choice: The Predatory Politics of Fiscal Discrimination,* New Brunswick: Transaction: pp. 81-103

Holcombe, Randall G. (1998) "Tax Policy from a Public Choice Perspective." *National Tax Journal* 51, No. 2: pp. 359-371.

Kreuger, Anne O. (1974) "The Political Economy of the Rent-Seeking Society." *American Economic Review* 64, No. 3: pp. 291-303.

McKelvey, R.D. (1976) "Intransitivities in Multi-Dimensional Voting Models and Some Implications for Agenda Control." *Journal of Economic Theory* 12, No. 2: pp. 472-482.

Minasian, Jora. (1964) "Television Pricing and the Theory of Public Goods." *Journal of Law & Economics* 7: pp. 71-80.

Musgrave, Richard A. (1959) *The Theory of Public Finance.* New York: McGraw-Hill.

Olson, Mancur, Jr. (1965) *The Logic of Collective Action.* Cambridge, MA: Harvard University Press.

Pigou, A.C. (1924) *The Economics of Welfare,* 2nd ed. London: Macmillan.

Ramsey, Frank P. (1927) "A Contribution to the Theory of Taxation." *Economic Journal* 37: pp. 47-61.

Samuelson, Paul A. (1954) "The Pure Theory of Public Expenditure." *Review of Economics and Statistics* 36: pp. 387-389.

Samuelson, Paul A. (1955) "A Diagrammatic Exposition of a Theory of Public Expenditure." *Review of Economics and Statistics* 37: pp. 350-356.

Samuelson, Paul A. (1964) "Public Goods and Subscription TV: A Correction of the Record." *Journal of Law & Economics* 7: pp. 81-83.

Shughart II, William F., ed. (1997) *Taxing Choice: The Predatory Politics of Fiscal Discrimination.* New Brunswick: Transaction.

Slemrod, Joel, and Nikki Sorum. (1984) "The Compliance Cost of the U.S. Individual Income Tax System." *National Tax Journal* 37, No. 4: pp. 461-474.

Smith, Adam. (1937 [orig. 1776]) *An Inquiry into the Nature and Causes of the Wealth of Nations.* Indianapolis, IN.: Liberty Fund.

Thurow, Lester, ed. (1985) *The Management Challenge: Japanese Views.* Cambridge: MIT Press.

Tiebout, Charles M. (1956) "A Pure Theory of Local Expenditures." *Journal of Political Economy* 64: pp. 416-424.

Tullock, Gordon. (1967) "The Welfare Cost of Tariffs, Monopolies, and Theft." *Western Economic Journal* 5, No. 3: pp. 224-232.

Usher, Dan (1992) *The Welfare Economics of Markets, Voting, and Predation.* Ann Arbor: University of Michigan Press.

Weingast, Barry R., Kenneth A. Shepsle, and Christopher Johnsen (1981) "The Political Economy of Benefits and Costs: A Neoclassical Approach to Distributive Politics." *Journal of Political Economy* 89, No. 4: pp. 642-664.

Winer, Stanley L., and Walter Hettich. (1998) "What is Missed if We Leave Out Collective Choice in the Analysis of Taxation." *National Tax Journal* 51, No. 2: pp. 373-389.

Wittman, Donald. (1989) "Why Democracies Produce Efficient Results." *Journal of Political Economy* 97, No. 6: pp. 1395-1424.

8 TAXATION THROUGH LITIGATION

Robert A. Levy

Three dozen states, faced with ballooning Medicaid costs, decided that litigation against the tobacco industry would be a relatively painless path to fiscal fitness. Couching their legal claims in the lofty cant of public health, they sought to recover tax-funded Medicaid expenditures for tobacco-related injuries. The states could have raised taxes on cigarettes, of course. That option would have been simpler, less expensive, and quicker; and the parties who would have paid the tax—smokers and tobacco companies—would have been the same parties that would ultimately pick up any bill for court-awarded damages. Why then were lawsuits substituted for taxation?

Here's the principled answer—although not the real answer, as we shall see: Even though it may be more efficient to raise revenue by legislation than by litigation, when particular parties are subject to sanctions for wrongdoing, the courtroom and not the Legislature is where they have an opportunity to defend themselves. The court is the proper forum for evidence, fact-finding, and verdict following a trial before a jury of peers. As a just society, we cannot suffer our Legislature to embark upon a punitive crusade against a disfavored industry without guaranteeing due process of law.

Unhappily, in the real world, the reason that the states opted for Medicaid recovery suits instead of tax hikes had everything to do with politics and nothing to do with due process. Both taxes and tobacco companies were (and still are) immensely unpopular; so the states took the politically safe course by avoiding the first and attacking the second. To affect that scheme, the states came up with a quasi tax, camouflaged as litigation damages. It was far easier to sue a baneful industry than to attach yet another users' fee to a product already bloated with government exactions. But there was one large fly in the ointment.

TOBACCO WARS: EXTORTION PARADING AS LAW

Until March 2001, there had not been a single final adjudication of damages against a tobacco company in more than four decades of litigation (Rabin). Industry defendants invariably prevailed, first, by disputing that tobacco was the cause of a particular person's ailment and, second, by demonstrating that the plaintiffs knowingly and voluntarily assumed the risk of smoking, in which case they were responsible for the adverse health effects.

That set the stage for some legal legerdemain—a fresh wave of litigation by state attorneys general, beginning in 1994, grounded in a new claim that gave the states more legal rights than any aggrieved cigarette smoker. Florida became the first state to codify the new claim—by amending its Medicaid Third-Party Liability Act in 1990 and 1994 (Fla. Stat. Ann. § 409.910 (1995)). In two essential respects the Florida statute tilted the playing field hopelessly against the tobacco industry. The express language of the statute left little room for doubt.

- First, "causation and damages ... may be proven by use of statistical analysis" without showing any link between a particular smoker's illness and his use of tobacco products.

- Second, "assumption of risk and all other affirmative defenses normally available to a liable third party are to be abrogated to the extent necessary to ensure full recovery by Medicaid from third-party resources."

Before the new dispensation, the state could assert only those theories of recovery against cigarette makers that an injured patient could assert. That is, under a process called subrogation, if an insurer—like Medicaid—sues to recoup its outlays for a patient, the insurer must step into the shoes of the patient and convince a jury that the patient's claim is valid. Thus, the same rules of evidence, the same standards of responsibility, and the same burden of proof would apply to the state Medicaid system, suing under subrogation, as to the patient if he had sued on his own behalf. A tobacco company that would not have been liable in a direct suit by a smoker would not be liable in a similar suit by a state standing in the smoker's shoes.

That principle of law was cavalierly dismissed to pick the deep pockets of the tobacco industry. Not surprisingly, when self-interested politicians determine the legal regime under which a few friendless corporations will be fleeced, there is great potential for mischief. As of early June 1997, 35 states[1] and several cities had filed Medicaid recovery suits against the industry. Each state raised much the same claims that the Florida case raised, but only in Vermont and Maryland was there, like in Florida, a supporting statute. The other states and cities argued that judges, as a matter of fairness and equity, should adopt legal rules corresponding to those in Florida, even without a law similar to that state's Medicaid Third-Party Liability Act.

The irony—or outrage, depending upon your perspective—is that the Medicaid recovery suits were instigated by states to recover costs that they voluntarily incurred by participating in the federal Medicaid program—costs supposedly attributable to a product that the states refused to declare illegal.

As University of Chicago law professor Richard Epstein (transcript, 200-01) put it: "The government can decide that it's not going to provide ... this kind of insurance.... It might even ... decide that it's going to ban tobacco.... But the one alternative that is absolutely unacceptable is ... retroactively [to] impose a system of liability which nobody dreamed of."

LIABILITY WITHOUT CAUSATION

Yet that is precisely what 35 states and assorted other governmental units did; they retroactively embraced a legal regime that nobody dreamed of. First, they ignored the rules of causation. In mass tort cases, statistical evidence combined with other corroborating evidence can "supply a useful link in the process of proof" (Tribe, 1350). But statistics alone are not enough. "An essential element of the plaintiff's cause of action for negligence, or for that matter for any other tort, is that there be some reasonable connection between the act or omission of the defendant and the damage which the plaintiff has suffered" (Prosser § 41, 263).[2]

Florida, however, substituted its own rendition of the law of causation (Fla. Stat. Ann. § 409.910(9)-(9)(a) (1995)).

> In any action brought under this subsection, the evidence code shall be liberally construed regarding the issues of causation and of aggregate damages. The issue of causation and damages in any such action may be proven by use of statistical analysis.... [If] the number of recipients for which medical assistance has been provided by Medicaid is so large as to cause it to be impractical to join or identify each claim, the agency shall not be required to so identify the individual recipients for which payment has been made, but rather can proceed to seek recovery based upon payments made on behalf of an entire class of recipients.

In other words, under the Third-Party Liability Act, the state could sue the tobacco industry for health expenditures attributable to smoking by Medicaid recipients without disclosing (1) the names of recipients, (2) whether recipients actually smoked, or (3) whether smokers had illnesses that could be traced to tobacco use. All that had to be disclosed were aggregate statistics for Florida Medicaid recipients as a group.

In response to a due-process challenge, the Florida Supreme Court upheld the part of the Act that authorized statistical proof, but excised the provision permitting non-disclosure of Medicaid recipients. The Court could "find no way in which this subsection would allow a defendant to challenge improper payments made to individual recipients [or prove] that its product was never used by the recipient.... It is illogical and unreasonable to call this a fair process" (*Agency for Health Care Admin. v. Associated Inds. of Fla. Inc.*, 1254). As a result, trial judge Harold J. Cohen instructed the states to provide the names of 400,000 Medicaid patients, from which lawyers for the tobacco companies could select 25 persons. The state would then make available the medical records for those persons and the industry could investigate the 25 cases, and no others, in order to confirm that the aggregate data proffered by the state were reliable (Connor).

That process was fundamentally flawed. If an insurance company were filing subrogation actions, each claimant would be required to disclose his medical record. Likewise, tobacco company defendants should have been able to investigate the legitimacy of each plaintiff's claims[3] and explore such questions as whether and how much each claimant smoked. Yet unlike any other tort action by any other plaintiff, Florida's showing of causation didn't have to be injury-specific. Instead, the state could show generalized causation based upon no more than aggregate epidemiological data—notwithstanding authoritative and near-universal acknowledgment that "[e]pidemiology cannot prove causation" (Federal Judicial Center, 157).

ASSUMPTION OF RISK

There's more. To eliminate any possibility that the tobacco companies could mount a successful defense, the states abolished the assumption-of-risk doctrine, which had immunized the industry from liability for 40 years. That doctrine says: "If the user or consumer...is aware of the danger, and nevertheless proceeds unreasonably to make use of the product and is injured by it, he is barred from recovery" (American Law Institute § 402A, cmt. n).

Thus, under a traditional tort regime if a consumer knows about the risks of smoking, yet still smokes and thereby contracts a tobacco-related illness, he has no more claim against the tobacco manufacturer than would a non-smoker who suffers the same illness from another source. A state may thereafter provide no financial assistance, some assistance, or complete assistance to the victim, but the amount of assistance has no effect on the responsibility of the tobacco manufacturer to the individual or to the state (Van Alstyne, 576).

No matter. The states simply wiped that rule off the books and, for good measure, made the new rule retroactive so that it would apply to illnesses allegedly caused by cigarettes sold decades earlier. As the President of the Maryland Senate blurted to the *Washington Post* in an unguarded moment, "We agreed to change tort law, which was no small feat. We changed centuries of precedent in order to assure a win in this case" (Cherry).

Even without recourse to its usual assumption-of-risk defense, the tobacco companies thought they could rely upon an analogous defense known as "unclean hands." That doctrine says simply that the plaintiff's own fault is relevant to what if any remedy he is entitled to (*Black's*, 1058). In other words, if Florida engaged in activities that had the effect of exacerbating any harms attributable to tobacco, the state might not be able to recover for those harms. Like assumption of risk, unclean hands takes into account the extent to which alleged damages may have arisen or increased as a result of the plaintiff's behavior. Also like assumption of risk, the doctrine of unclean hands is rooted in the principle that holds parties accountable for the consequences of their own conduct.

Let's see if Florida's hands were unclean. For starters, why did it take 30 years after the Surgeon General's initial warnings for the state to press its claims? Why didn't Florida opt out of the Medicaid program, or ask the federal government to exclude smoking-related illnesses from its list of covered treatments? Why didn't the state mandate lower nicotine content, or raise their tax rate on cigarettes, or ban their sale outright?

State officials could not have been unaware of the criticism heaped upon the tobacco industry, dating from nearly four hundred years ago. In his authoritative history of the industry, Richard Kluger reports that King James I, in 1604, castigated smoking as "a custom loathsome to the eye, hateful to the nose, harmful to the brain, dangerous to the lung, and the black stinking fume thereof, nearest resembling the horribly Stygian smoke of the pit that is bottomless" (Kluger, 15). By the early 1900s, goaded by the National Anti-Cigarette League, 14 states had prohibited the sale of cigarettes (Kluger, 37-40). When Tennessee's ban was challenged on constitutional grounds (*Austin v. State*, 566), the state Supreme Court minced no words in upholding the statute, railing against cigarettes as

> wholly noxious and deleterious to health. Their use is always harmful; never beneficial. They possess no virtue, but are inherently bad, and bad only. They find no true commendation for merit or usefulness in any sphere. On the contrary, they are widely condemned as pernicious altogether. Beyond question, their every tendency is toward the impairment of physical health and mental vigor. There is no proof in the record as to the character of cigarettes, yet their character is so well and so generally known to be that stated above, that the Courts are authorized to take judicial cognizance of the fact. No particular proof is required in regard to those facts, which, by human observation and experience, have become well and generally known to be true.

In the 1950s, epidemiologists Doll and Hill published a series of articles documenting the increased risk of lung cancer among smokers. They found that death from lung cancer was ten times more likely for persons who smoked ten to twenty cigarettes daily than for those who did not smoke at all (Doll and Hill).

Without doubt, Florida officials were mindful of the dangers of smoking. The state's case, supposedly based on fairness and equity, should have been fatally compromised, just as a smoker's case would have been compromised under traditional common law if the smoker had assumed the risk. Whenever the plaintiff is at fault, unclean hands frustrate relief. One of the states' hired guns, attorney Richard Scruggs (transcript, 188), recounted the law:

> [A]ll of the states have, as the basis of their cases against the tobacco industry, these equitable theories. It doesn't mean that the tobacco industry is defenseless. They can show that the state has unclean hands, that the state has participated in the activity somehow, licensed it, or received tax revenues from it.

Predictably, however, Scrugg's recitation of the law was one thing, but Florida's adherence to the rules was quite another.

Starting in 1972, the Florida prison system manufactured unfiltered cigarettes and distributed them at no cost to the state's inmates. In order to generate income, the state also sold some of its cigarettes to local governments. Those activities continued for roughly a decade despite widespread discussion in the Legislature about the health hazards of smoking and the addictive power of nicotine (Geyelin, January 27, 1997). Unclean hands? You bet. But when Philip Morris filed a pre-trial motion to assure that the evidence would be admissible, Florida successfully opposed the motion and persuaded Judge Cohen that evidence of the state's shared responsibility for tobacco-related illness was just another "affirmative defense," forbidden by the Medicaid Third-Party Liability Act (Rothman). So much for Scruggs' pledge that the doctrine of unclean hands was still alive and well.

Florida pulled out all the stops. Governor Lawton Chiles, his attorney general, and the Legislature, without much resistance from the judiciary, exploited the laws they liked, repealed the ones they didn't, and concocted novel theories of liability whenever necessary to stack the deck. Yet the state's hands were worse than unclean; they were downright filthy. Roughly \$825 million of Florida's pension assets were invested in tobacco stocks.[4] Ten of Florida's 23 Congressmen guaranteed that federal subsidies for the industry would survive. Their votes were more than enough to defeat the Durbin amendment, which would have prohibited the use of federal funds for certain tobacco programs. On June 12, 1996, the House of Representatives rejected that amendment by a two-vote margin (*Congressional Quarterly*).

Perhaps most appalling of all, Florida relied on the assumption-of-risk doctrine in defending against a lawsuit brought by a prisoner seeking access to nicotine patches and other treatment for an alleged addiction to smoking (*Waugh v. Singletary*). In its October 1995 motion to dismiss that case, the state shamelessly asserted that "any future harm which Plaintiff may potentially suffer ... is a direct result of Plaintiff himself choosing to buy and smoke cigarettes. Defendants are not responsible for Plaintiff's decision to purchase cigarettes any more than they would be responsible for Plaintiff buying a candy bar at the canteen." Continuing in the same vein: "Plaintiff is in no way entitled to medical intervention to 'cure' a habit which Plaintiff himself continues to indulge, and over which Plaintiff has ultimate control." Florida, it seems, had no compunction summoning the principle of personal responsibility whenever its own money was at stake.

Even the federal government, which pursued an aggressive anti-smoking campaign under President Clinton, acknowledged the role of personal responsibility. In 1993, senior lawyers in the Department of Veterans Affairs decided that the federal government might be liable for tobacco-linked illnesses contracted by millions of military personnel who smoked while on active duty. Sounding much like a tobacco executive, VA Secretary Jesse Brown declared that it would be a "borderline absurdity" for the government to pay "for death or disability resulting from veterans' personal choice to engage in conduct damaging to their health" (McAllister).

The military plainly encouraged its employees to smoke. Not only were cigarettes sold on bases at a huge discount, but soldiers in combat zones were given free cigarettes as part of their rations. That is surely more of an inducement than tobacco companies ever offered their customers. And no one has ever accused the tobacco industry of preying on young military recruits under enormous stress by plying them with free cigarettes. "We know there's a dichotomy," rationalized a Pentagon spokeswoman, "but you have to balance the need for a healthy fighting force and an individual's right to use tobacco" (Ingersoll). Rather than blame the government, Secretary Brown volunteered this controlling principle: "If you choose to smoke, you are responsible for the consequences of your act" (McAllister). Clearly, if that principle was sufficient to render the government immune from liability, it should have been sufficient to inoculate private companies as well. But it was not.

With tobacco companies unable to assert their principal defense, and states exempted from having to prove causation, the industry finally capitulated in November 1998. The result, the multi-state tobacco settlement, is nothing but a shakedown—no better than extortion, based on a repugnant rule of law: States need money; tobacco companies have money; ergo, the companies pay, the states collect. Predictably, that financial windfall spawned a new round of lawsuits—this time against gun makers.

GOVERNMENT'S ASSAULT ON THE GUN INDUSTRY

Engulfed by a torrent of litigation from dozens of cities, gun makers were threatened by the Clinton administration during the summer of 1999 with additional claims from more than three thousand public housing authorities coordinated by the U.S. Department of Housing and Urban Development (HUD) (Barrett, July 28, 1999). Under President Bush, further action by HUD will almost certainly be shelved. Still, ongoing city- and state-sponsored lawsuits could destroy the firearms industry, with profound implications for the rule of law and the Constitution. The government's resort to litigation as a tactic of intimidation and extortion will have destructive consequences extending far beyond a single industry.

In bullying gun makers, the plaintiffs have included three corrosive ingredients, carried over from the tobacco wars, in their litigation formula: First, they have sued in multiple jurisdictions, thereby escalating the industry's legal costs. Second, they have employed contingency-fee lawyers, many of whom are major political donors. Third, they have tried to use the judicial branch in order to bypass the Legislature.

NEW LITIGATION MODEL

When public officials prosecute lawbreakers, those officials are fulfilling a legitimate role of government. Most of the time, that prosecutorial role is unobjectionable, often commendable. But the latest rounds of litigation—tobacco, then guns—are different in three respects, each of which threatens the rule of law.

First, coordinated actions by multiple government entities can impose enormous legal fees on defendants. As a result, those actions have been used to extort money notwithstanding that the underlying case is without merit. Just listen to former Philadelphia Mayor Edward G. Rendell (D) calling for dozens of cities to file concurrent suits against gun makers: They "don't have the deep pockets of the tobacco industry," Rendell explained, and multiple lawsuits "could bring them to the negotiating table a lot sooner" (Butterfield). Never mind that the suits are baseless. We're not dealing with law, but with extortion parading as law.

One effective way to stop that thievery is by implementing a "government pays" rule for legal fees when a governmental unit is the losing plaintiff in a civil case. In the criminal sphere, defendants are already entitled to court-appointed counsel if needed; they're also protected by the requirement for proof beyond reasonable doubt and by the Fifth and Sixth Amendments to the Constitution. No corresponding safeguards against abusive public-sector litigation exist in civil cases. By limiting the rule to cases involving government plaintiffs, access to the courts is preserved for less affluent, private plaintiffs seeking redress of legitimate grievances. But defendants in government suits will be able to resist meritless cases that are brought by the state solely to ratchet up the pressure for a large financial settlement.

"Government pays" becomes ever more urgent with the recent emergence of an insidious relationship between the plaintiffs' bar and some government officials. That relationship—common to tobacco and gun litigation—is a second major threat to the rule of law.

Lawsuits against both industries were concocted by a handful of private attorneys who entered into contingency fee contracts with the government. In effect, members of the private bar were hired as government subcontractors, but with a huge financial share in the outcome. That's not a problem, says Rendell. He announced that cities were suing gun makers only for improved safety features and changes in distribution practices, not monetary damages. Yet one day after Rendell's disclaimer, Miami and Bridgeport filed their suits, seeking hundreds of millions of dollars in damages (Appleson). New Orleans asked for damages (Butterfield) and so did Chicago (in fact, $433 million) (Daley). The claims include not only medical costs associated with gun violence, but also the costs of police protection, emergency services, police overtime and pensions, courts, prisons, loss of population, cleaning the streets of blood, lower property values, even lost tax revenue from reduced worker productivity (Kimmelman)—plus punitive damages. And nearly all of the cities have solicited private lawyers to work for a contingency fee based on those damages.

So if money isn't the primary goal, there will be a lot of attorneys working for free. Maybe that's what they deserve. After all, the gun suits aren't intended to go to trial. In fact, HUD's threat, on top of the city and county claims, was meant to force a settlement, not a trial. No doubt, with a piddling $1.5 billion in annual revenues, gun makers are not going to yield the same treasure trove as the tobacco behemoths whose worldwide sales are $300 billion. But that's not fatal, because the real goal of the trial lawyers is to chalk up one more victory, thus demonstrating to future fatter-cat defendants that groundless legal theories are good enough when the coercive power of multiple government entities is arrayed against an unpopular industry.

When a private lawyer subcontracts his services to the government, he bears the same responsibility as a government lawyer. He is a public servant beholden to all citizens, including the defendant, and his overriding objective is to seek justice. Imagine a state attorney paid a contingency fee for each indictment that he secures, or state troopers paid per speeding ticket. The potential for corruption is enormous. Still, the states in their tobacco suits doled out multi-billion-dollar contracts to private counsel–not per-hour fee agreements, which might occasionally be justified to acquire unique outside competence or experience, but contingency fees, a sure-fire catalyst for abuse of power. And those contracts were awarded without competitive bidding to lawyers who often bankrolled state political campaigns (Lochhead).

Government is the single entity authorized, in narrowly defined circumstances, to wield coercive power against private citizens. When that government functions as prosecutor or plaintiff in a legal proceeding in which it also dispenses punishment, adequate safeguards against state misbehavior are essential. That is why in civil litigation we rely primarily upon private remedies with redress sought by, and for the benefit of, the injured party and not the state. As the Supreme Court cautioned more than 60 years ago, an attorney for the state "is the representative not of an ordinary party to a controversy, but of a sovereignty whose obligation to govern impartially is as compelling as its obligation to govern at all" (*Berger v. United States*, 88).

Put bluntly, contingency fee contracts between government and a private attorney should be illegal. We cannot in a free society condone private lawyers enforcing public law with an incentive kicker to increase the penalties.

Third, and perhaps most important, laws are supposed to be enacted by Legislatures, not by the executive or judicial branches. In too many instances, government-sponsored litigation has been a substitute for failed legislation. That process violates the principle of separation of powers—a centerpiece of the federal and many state constitutions. Evidently, none of that matters to many of the attorneys general, mayors, and their allies in the private bar. In an attempt to circumvent the legislative process, they intend to pursue through litigation what was rejected by the Legislature.

It's interesting to contrast the legal perspective on product prohibition that prevails today with the view that prevailed in 1919—more than eight decades ago. In 1919, we understood that Congress did not have the power to prohibit the sale of alcohol, so prohibition was accomplished by a constitutional amendment (the 18th). Today, the drug war is entirely statutory with little thought of its constitutional implications. When it comes to tobacco, the Clinton administration argued not only didn't we need a constitutional amendment; we also didn't need a statute—just a delegation of some sort to an unelected and unaccountable administrative agency (the Food and Drug Administration) with authority to ban nicotine.[5] And in the case of guns, it seems we don't need a constitutional amendment, or a statute, or a delegation, just multiple lawsuits by means of which the executive branch uses the judicial branch to bypass the Legislature and effectuate a variety of gun prohibitions. So much for limited government and separation of powers. We're left with the executive state; the return of the king. That's the regime under which dozens of cities, aided by the Clinton administration, took the gun battle to the courts—suing gun makers for "negligently marketing" a "defective product."

FEDERAL CLAIMS

At the federal level, Clinton's HUD secretary, Andrew Cuomo, had a plan to change the way the nation's gun makers do business. Already smothered by litigation from dozens of cities and counties, the gun industry would have been crushed under the weight of legal action from a horde of 3,200 housing authorities synchronized by HUD. The government wanted to hold gun makers responsible for defraying the cost of security guards and for alarm systems installed to curb violence in public housing (Barrett, July 28, 1999).

Like the cities, HUD said it was not interested in money damages. Maybe so, but Cuomo and his acolytes understood very well that the small gun industry couldn't afford to defend itself—even against unfounded suits—in the face of such overwhelming firepower. A *Wall Street Journal* story emphasized that very point:

> As with the municipal suits, one filed on behalf of housing authorities would be groundbreaking and certainly not a sure bet to succeed in court. But a suit by a large group of housing authorities could [exhaust] gun companies' resources in pretrial maneuvering—by making demands for documents concerning industry distribution practices in hundreds or thousands of localities (Barrett, July 28, 1999).

That's no better than thinly veiled blackmail.

In justifying HUD's litigation plans, Cuomo contended, "only one percent of the dealers are selling over 50 percent of the guns used in crimes" (Gearan). But if crimes were linked to guns sold by particular dealers, why weren't the underlying data turned over to authorities whose duty it is to shut down dealers who break laws against those sales—laws that are on the books in all 50 states? Instead, Cuomo sought to compel gun makers to become police, judge, and jury—to ferret out "bad" dealers, some of whom were entirely innocent, and deny to those dealers, without due process of law, the merchandise that they sell for a living.

That was just the beginning. Cuomo also demanded safer guns. "We have safety caps on aspirin," he says, so why not safety locks on guns (Gearan)? Well, let's see, there are a couple of relevant differences between guns and aspirin. The requirement for safety caps on aspirin arose out of legislation, not judicial mandate. Aspirin is legally accessible to kids; guns aren't. Furthermore, not many people when confronted with an emergency will turn to a bottle of aspirin for protection. Use of a gun for self-defense could be dangerously compromised if the gun is locked. Listen to Sammy "The Bull" Gravano, the Mafia turncoat, quoted in *Vanity Fair*: "Safety locks? You ...

pull the trigger with a lock on, and I'll pull the trigger [without one]. We'll see who wins" (Blum, 165).

Actually, if Cuomo was concerned about unsafe public housing, he should have sued his own agency (Epstein, December 9, 1999). HUD is responsible for housing authorities—including their location, selection of tenants, eviction policies, even inadequate policing. But rather than admit to the abject failure of public housing, Cuomo instructed his minions to plan lawsuits, modeled after those filed by cities and counties from coast to coast. Here are the two principal legal theories.

NEGLIGENT MARKETING

The city of Chicago, and other cities following its example, accused gun makers of "negligent marketing"—flooding the suburbs, where gun laws are relaxed, with more guns than suburban residents will buy, knowing that the excess will find its way to the inner city, where gun laws are more restrictive.

Simple economic logic puts the lie to Chicago's negligent marketing claim. If gun makers reduce the supply of firearms sold to suburban dealers, the market price of guns will rise. Consumers with the most "elastic" demand—that is, consumers who are most sensitive to price changes—will reduce or eliminate their purchases. The evidence is clear: Those price-sensitive consumers are typically law-abiding citizens. By contrast, criminals' demand for guns is highly "inelastic." They operate in a "survival at any price" environment—which is why crooks are willing to pay inflated black-market prices for firearms. Perversely, by restricting the legal supply of guns and raising price, manufacturers will put relatively more weapons in criminals' hands and relatively fewer in the hands of honest citizens.

Besides, any coordinated industry response to a negligent marketing claim would surely run afoul of the antitrust laws. Manufacturers that supposedly overproduce would have to collude in order to reduce production jointly. Yes, Smith & Wesson knows how many of its guns are going to, say, Maryland. But those guns, by themselves, don't come close to saturating the Maryland market. And Smith & Wesson has no idea how many Maryland guns are shipped by Colt, Beretta, Glock, Ruger, or any other manufacturer. Because brands are more or less interchangeable, no single gun maker would agree to cut back production for fear that other manufacturers would simply take up the slack. An antitrust suit is sure to follow.

Compare the gun model with dram shop laws, which hold bartenders liable when they continue to ply obviously drunk patrons with liquor knowing full well that the customer could kill himself or others when he drives home. Whatever the merit of those laws, the analogy in the gun context is not to hold the bartender responsible or even the bar owner. Instead, it's the equivalent of holding Seagrams or Anheuser Busch accountable for the ensuing drunk driving fatality.

An obvious solution to Chicago's problem, said the judge who dismissed the city's case this past September, would be for the police to enforce laws that already prohibit sales to minors, felons, the mentally incompetent, and anyone else without a state-issued firearm owners ID card (Stern). Instead, Chicago sued gun makers—who lawfully sell to wholesalers who, in turn, sell to licensed retailers. The city wants to hold gun makers liable for the violent acts of criminals, most of whom did not buy from licensed retailers and over whom the manufacturers have no control. As the Seventh Circuit held in a 1989 case, *City of Bloomington v. Westinghouse Electric Corp.*, a manufacturer is not liable for creation of a nuisance by the buyer unless the manufacturer participated in the conduct.

The chain of causation is broken when a criminal act intervenes between a gun maker's original sale and an injury arising out of the gun's violent use. That time-honored principle of law, by itself, is sufficient to dismiss these cases. A gun maker is liable only if the risk of injury was foreseeable. And when the law says "foreseeable," it doesn't mean merely possible; it means that the intervening criminal act was the natural and probable outcome of the gun maker's sale.[6] Yes, Americans own roughly 250 million guns and commit about 500,000 gun-related crimes each year (Lott). But even if a different gun is used in each of those crimes, only 2/10 of 1 percent of all guns are involved in criminal activity in any given year. That negligible chance of criminal conduct surely doesn't cross the "natural and probable outcome" threshold.

Interestingly, the legislative unit in the Chicago suburbs is Cook County, which could have enacted more restrictive gun laws. For whatever reasons, it chose not to do so. Instead, Cook County signed on as co-plaintiff in Chicago's lawsuit. It wanted the judicial branch to do what the county elected not to do. Think about it: Cook County's complaint to the court, quite literally, is that the county has itself failed to pass appropriate legislation. In effect, Cook County's plea is "Stop me before I don't legislate again," which must be a first in American jurisprudence.[7]

DEFECTIVE PRODUCT

Apart from negligent marketing, the second major claim among cities suing the gun industry is that firearms are "defective and unreasonably dangerous" as they are currently manufactured. How are the firearms defective? Do they misfire, or fire inaccurately? Not at all. Even the *Washington Post* has editorialized: "As a legal matter, it is hard to see how companies making lawful products can be held liable when those products perform precisely as intended." No matter. First New Orleans, then other cities, insisted that guns are defective if they are sold without devices that prevent discharge by unauthorized users. On that ground, the cities hope to drag gun makers to the settlement table—turning the law of product liability on its head.

In order to hold gun makers liable for selling an unsafe product, tort law requires a true *defect*, not merely that a product is dangerous when it does what it is designed to do. True enough, some guns have features that are particularly attractive to criminals. But that may be because criminals value many of the same features that appeal to law enforcement officers. Legislatures across the nation have regulated virtually every aspect of gun design and distribution. If a determination is to be made that guns are unreasonably dangerous, the Legislature, constrained by the Constitution, must make that determination, not the courts. Here's how a federal judge in Massachusetts put it in a 1996 case, *Wasylow v. Glock* (381): "Frustration at the failure of Legislatures to enact laws sufficient to curb handgun injuries is not adequate reason to engage the judicial forum in efforts to implement a broad policy change."

Even Brooklyn's Jack Weinstein, the favorite federal judge of the plaintiffs' bar, had this comment about the safety of guns:

> Whether or not ... products liability law would require an anti-theft safety mechanism as part of the design of handguns requires a balancing of the risk and utility.... Plaintiffs have not shown that such a device is available, nor have they asserted the possibility of showing at trial that such a device would satisfy the ... risk-utility test.

Weinstein added, "The mere act of manufacturing and selling a handgun does not give rise to liability absent a defect in the manufacture or design of the product itself" (*Hamilton v. Accu-Tek*, 1323).

Whether the claim is a defective product, negligent marketing, or public nuisance, these lawsuits are rubbish. Five of them have reached final judgement and all five were fully or partially dismissed.[8] In October 1999, an Ohio state judge threw out Cincinnati's claims. He wrote that gun makers are not responsible for the criminal misconduct of customers. "The city's complaint is an improper attempt to have this court substitute its judgment for that of the Legislature" (Reuters, October 7, 1999). The "design, manufacturer and distribution of a lawful product" is not a public nuisance (Barrett, October 8, 1999).

Bridgeport's and Miami's suits were also dismissed in December 1999. Miami's judge observed that the city couldn't use the courts to regulate; that's the job of the Legislature (Barrett, December 14, 1999). A Florida appeals court upheld the Miami ruling, calling the lawsuit "an attempt to regulate firearms ... through the ... judiciary." "Clearly this round-about attempt is being made because of the County's frustration at its inability to regulate firearms," the appeals court wrote. "The County's frustration cannot be alleviated through litigation" (Reuters, February 23, 2001).

In Chicago on September 15, 2000, a judge threw out that city's negligent marketing claim saying that statistical evidence of causation wasn't good enough, and that individual instances of illegal sales were a matter for the police to counter (Stern). Most recently, on December 21, 2000, a federal judge dismissed Philadelphia's claims, describing the city's charge of public nuisance as "a theory in search of a case," and rejecting the negligence claim "for lack of proximate cause" (Duffy).

Nevertheless, the trial lawyers press forward. Sooner or later they're likely to find, somewhere, a sympathetic judge who's willing to ignore the law in order to effectuate his personal policy preferences. It's called forum shopping, and it's a favorite tactic of the plaintiffs' bar. In fact, the major reason each city has sued local dealers as well as gun manufacturers is so the plaintiff and at least one defendant reside in the same jurisdiction. That way the case cannot be removed to federal court, where the rule of law generally prevails—outweighing provincial prejudices.

The implications for other industries should not be taken lightly. If gun manufacturers are responsible for violence, why not the makers of the steel used in the guns? Indeed, Ohio's appellate judge, upholding the dismissal of Cincinnati's gun suit, warned that allowing such suits to proceed could "open a Pandora's box. The city could sue the manufacturers of matches for arson, or automobile manufacturers for traffic accidents, or breweries for drunken driving" (Barrett, October 8, 1999).

NEXT TO BE GOUGED: LEAD PAINT

Until recently, speculation about the next industry to be gouged had centered on the makers of beer, booze, and fatty foods. But prominent tobacco attorney John Coale assured us that he and his pals are "not going after alcohol and hamburgers. We like 'em too much" (Van Voris). Lamentably, there's no shortage of other candidates to target, including pharmaceuticals, chemicals, sporting equipment, even automobiles. It looks like the guessing game can end, however. According to the *Washington Post*, "trial lawyers and politicians locally and across the nation are gearing up to mount a major assault on the former makers of lead paint, which was banned in residences in 1978 but still poisons children in older buildings" (Torry).

Rhode Island's attorney general, Sheldon Whitehouse (D), is pursuing litigation that aims to set the national pattern. He admits that the multi-state tobacco settlement inspired him to file suit (Zoll). In fact, Rhode Island is being represented by Ness, Motley, Loadholt, Richardson & Poole, one of the law firms that was pivotal in rounding up states to sue cigarette makers (Geyelin, October 13, 1999). Whitehouse hopes to replenish his state's coffers, supposedly depleted by medical outlays for lead-related illnesses, and by expenditures to remove lead from housing that hasn't been properly maintained. His sights are set on an industry that has never paid a cent in damages. For years, trial lawyers have sued landlords over lead poisoning and, in some cases, have won large judgments. But unlike landlords, the paint and pigment companies remain unscathed.

The industry has successfully argued: (1) lead was a useful component of paint, helping to hide the prior color of surfaces to be re-covered; (2) paint makers voluntarily stopped using lead in interior paints in the 1950s, once it was known to be harmful; (3) the industry supported a 1978 federal ban; (4) recurring problems are the result of poor maintenance by homeowners (well-maintained surfaces covered with lead paint are not a danger); (5) lead poisoning arises from many products besides paint; and (6) it is impossible in any event to prove whose paint was on which wall.

Here are the facts, as related in an editorial from the *Providence Journal-Bulletin*:

> [I]n 1955, the American paint industry voluntarily removed lead from its interior wall coverings in response to concerns expressed by the American Academy of Pediatrics. That was 23 years before Congress instituted a ban [supported by the industry] on lead in all paints. Lead was most commonly used in housepaint in the 1920s, and for many years, the federal government recommended its use because of lead's superior pigmentation. In other words, the paint industry sought to provide the best possible product to customers, and when the health hazards of lead became known, it took lead out of the paint–on its own initiative.

Despite those facts, Rhode Island will be arguing in its upcoming lawsuit, not that the owners or landlords of aging, substandard homes should have maintained them more diligently, but that lead poisoning in the 1990s should be blamed on the makers of paint that was used in the 1920s through the mid-1950s. That's bad logic, bad law, and bad public policy. Rhode Island will be pursuing innocent companies that produce useful products, employ thousands of people, and haven't used lead for more than four decades.

If it could be proven that a particular manufacturer knew of the harmful effects of lead paint and failed to notify its customers, there might be an argument for liability. But to hold an entire industry accountable without such proof is unconscionable. Therein lies the fundamental problem with these lawsuits: Specific causation—when a defendant's conduct results in a plaintiff's injury—has not been, and cannot be, demonstrated. That's why the plaintiffs want to use a theory known as "market share liability," to circumvent conventional notions of cause and effect.

Essentially, juries will be asked to presume that the companies being sued caused the alleged harm in proportion to their sales of lead paint. The market share liability theory was originally applied in *Sindell v. Abbott Laboratories*. A woman with a rare form of cancer sued the manufacturers of diethylstilbestrol (DES), which was administered to her mother during pregnancy to prevent miscarriage. Many daughters of women who took DES later contracted the same cancer. Because DES was sold by multiple manufacturers as a generic drug, and because of the long lead time between the use of DES and the onset of cancer, it was virtually impossible to determine precisely which company caused the disease in which women. Therefore, said the California Supreme Court, the apportionment of damages based on market share would assure that culpable defendants could not evade liability.

Whatever the validity of market share liability in the DES case, its application to lead paint is plainly inappropriate. On December 30, 1999, in dismissing a private lawsuit against pigment makers, a New York appellate court offered this cogent summary (*Brenner v. American Cyanamid*, 854):

> [L]ead pigments other than white lead carbonate are used in lead-based paint; white lead carbonate is used for products other than interior residential paint; plaintiffs assert that they cannot determine when the lead-based paint was applied to their apartment; lead pigments are found in products other than lead-based paint; lead-based paint is not fungible; the manufacturers of white lead carbonate were not in exclusive control of the risk posed by lead-based paint; there is no signature injury associated with lead poisoning; and there is no indication by the Legislature that there should be a remedy for lead poisoning.

Nonetheless, enticed by the prospect of colossal fees like those looted from the tobacco companies, trial lawyers have fanned out in a frenzied search for attorneys general who are less concerned about the rule of law than about advancing their political aspirations at the expense of another hapless industry.

LESSONS FOR THE FUTURE

There are lessons to be learned from all of this. If we do nothing to rein in baseless, state-sponsored lawsuits, private attorneys and their accomplices in the public sector will continue to invent legal theories to exact tribute from friendless industries. That outcome will likely entice government officials who are eager to avoid the political risk that attaches to higher taxes. It's far easier to swap litigation for taxation, then pay gobs of money to private contingency fee lawyers to do the dirty work. But there can be no pretense that litigation of that sort has any basis in the rule of law.

When the politicians misbehave, the courts are the final bulwark in safeguarding our rights. But voters and jurors must be warned that our tort system is rapidly becoming a tool for extortion by a cabal of public officials and trial lawyers. Sometimes they seek money; sometimes they pursue policy goals; often they abuse their power. Take it from former labor secretary Robert Reich, certainly not renowned for his opposition to imperious government. Reich tells us that his ex-boss in the White House, President Clinton, launched "lawsuits to succeed where legislation failed. The strategy may work," Reich adds, "but at the cost of making our frail democracy even weaker.... This is nothing short of faux legislation, which sacrifices democracy to the discretion of administration officials operating in utter secrecy."

Reich has it just about right. But the problem outlives the Clinton White House. It infests many of the state houses and city halls. Like most infestations, this one can be fumigated. When we condone the selective and retroactive application of extraordinary legal principles, intended specifically to transfer resources from disfavored defendants to favored plaintiffs—or even worse, to the public sector—we substitute political cronyism for fundamental fairness, profane the rule of law, and debase personal freedom.

ENDNOTES

1. In order of filing date: Mississippi 5/94, Minnesota 8/94, West Virginia 9/94, Florida 2/95, Massachusetts 12/95, Louisiana 3/96, Texas 3/96, Maryland 5/96, Washington 6/96, Connecticut 7/96, Kansas 8/96, Arizona 8/96, Michigan 8/96, Oklahoma 8/96, New Jersey 9/96, Utah 9/96, Illinois 11/96, Iowa 11/96, New York 1/97, Hawaii 1/97, Wisconsin 2/97, Indiana 2/97, Alaska 4/97, Pennsylvania 4/97, Montana 5/97, Arkansas 5/97, Ohio 5/97, South Carolina 5/97, Missouri 5/97, New Mexico 5/97, Nevada 5/97, Vermont 5/97, New ampshire 6/97, Colorado 6/97, Oregon 6/97. Source: State Tobacco Information Center, Internet site www.stic.neu.edu, June 11, 1997.

2. See also *Washington v. Davis* and *Arlington Heights v. Metropolitan Housing Development Corp.* (statistical proof alone cannot establish discrimination for Equal Protection Clause challenge).

3. According to the tobacco industry, claims-fraud is rampant in Florida's Medicaid system (Gold).

4. In late May 1997, for what may have been tactical rather than philosophic reasons, Florida's pension trustees ordered the state's portfolio managers to liquidate tobacco stockholdings (Reuters, May 28, 1997).

5. The Clinton administration supported the tobacco bill introduced by Sen. John McCain (R-Ariz). See S. 1414, 105th Cong. (1997) ("a bill to reform and restructure the processes by which tobacco products are manufactured, marketed, and distributed, to prevent the use of tobacco products by minors, to redress the adverse health effects of tobacco use, and for other purposes").

6. The general test for liability in Pennsylvania, for example, is whether a person of ordinary intelligence would have foreseen the injury as the natural and probable outcome of his conduct (*New York Eskimo Pie Corp. v. Rataj*, 185).

7. My thanks for this insight to George Mason University law professor Dan Polsby.

8. Other suits have been allowed to proceed in part, but none has prevailed on final judgment. In 1999, Atlanta survived a motion to dismiss its design defect claim. The following year, New Orleans also survived full dismissal, as did Cleveland, Wayne County, and San Diego. In April 2001, however, the Louisiana Supreme Court threw out the New Orleans claim, citing state law that bans litigation by cities against the gun industry (Associated Press).

CASES

Agency for Health Care Admin. v. Associated Inds. of Fla. Inc., 678 So.)2d 1239 (Fla. 1996.
Arlington Heights v. Metropolitan Housing Development Corp., 429 U.S. 252 (1977).
Austin v. State, 101 Tenn. 562 (1898).
Berger v. United States, 295 U.S. 78 (1935).
Brenner v. American Cyanamid, 699 N.Y.S.2d 848 (N.Y. App. Div. 1999).
City of Bloomington v. Westinghouse Electric Corp., 891 F.2d 611 (7th Cir. 1989).
Hamilton v. Accu-Tek, 935 F. Supp. 1307 (E.D.N.Y. August 12, 1996).
New York Eskimo Pie Corp. v. Rataj, 73 F.2d 184 (3d Cir. 1934).
Sindell v. Abbott Laboratories, 607 P.2d 924 (Cal. 1980).
Washington v. Davis, 426 U.S. 229 (1976).
Wasylow v. Glock, Inc., 975 F. Supp. 370 (D. Mass. 1996).
Waugh v. Singletary, Defendants' Motion to Dismiss (D. Fla. 1995) (No. 95-CVC-J-20).

REFERENCES

American Law Institute (1965) *Restatement (Second) of Torts*. St. Paul, MN.: American Law Institute.

Appleson, Gail (January 28, 1999) "Two More Cities Sue Gun Makers." *Washington Post*, p. A6.

Associated Press (April 3, 2001) "Supreme Court: State Can Block New Orleans from Suing Gun Makers."

Barrett, Paul M. (July 28, 1999) "HUD May Join Assault on Gun Makers." *Wall Street Journal*,p. A3.

Barrett, Paul M. (October 8, 1999) "Judge Dismisses Cincinnati's Gun-Industry Suit." *Wall Street Journal*, p. B11.

Barrett, Paul M. (December 14, 1999) "Florida Judge Dismisses Suit Against Gun Makers." *Wall Street Journal*, p. B15.

Black's Law Dictionary, abridged 6th ed. (1991). St. Paul, MN.: West Publishing Co.

Blum, Howard (September 1999) "Reluctant Don." *Vanity Fair*, p. 148.

Butterfield, Fox (November 4, 1998) "New Orleans Takes on Gun Manufacturers in Lawsuit." *New York Times of the Web.*

Cherry, Sheila R. (April 3, 2000) "Litigation Lotto." *Insight on the News*, p. 10.

Congressional Quarterly (1996) CQ House Vote 233, Item Key 11734.

Connor, Michael (February 28, 1997) "Tobacco Cos. Win Access to Medicaid Patients." Reuters.

Daley, Richard M. (November 12, 1998) "Remarks of Mayor Richard M. Daley—Gun Lawsuit Press Conference," www.ci.chi.il.us/Mayor/Speeches/GunLawSuit.html.

Doll, Richard and A. Bradford Hill (1956) "Lung Cancer and Other Causes of Death in Relation to Smoking." *British Medical Journal* 2: 1071-81.

Duffy, Shannon P. (January 8, 2001) "Philly Loses Its Gun Maker Suit." *National Law Journal*, p. A4.

Epstein, Richard A. (September 12, 1996) "Do the Merits and the Search for Truth Matter Any More?" Federalist Society National Conference on Civil Justice and the Litigation Process

Epstein, Richard A. (December 9, 1999) "Lawsuits Aimed at Guns Probably Won't Hit Crime." *Wall Street Journal*, p. A26

Federal Judicial Center (1994) *Reference Manual on Scientific Evidence*. Washington, D.C.: United States Government Printing Office.

Gearan, Anne (December 8, 1999) "White House Preparing Gun Suit," Associated Press.

Geyelin, Milo (January 27, 1997) "Florida Made, Gave Out Prison Cigarettes." *Wall Street.Journal*, p. B12

Geyelin, Milo (October 13, 1999) "Former Makers of Lead Paint Are Sued by Rhode Island for Health Costs." *Wall Street Journal*, p. A3.

Gold, Scott (May 28, 1997) "Judge Refuses to Limit Liability; Tobacco Claimed Medicaid Fraud." *South Florida Sun-Sentinel*, p. 1B.

Ingersoll, Bruce (April 25, 1997) "Battle over Federal Aid for Tobacco Heats Up as Lawmakers Debate Issue." *Wall Street Journal*, p. A16.

Kimmelman, Susan (July 26, 1998) "Stick 'Em Up; Suing Gun makers for the Cost of Urban Violence." *In These Times*, p. 13.

Kluger, Richard (1996) *Ashes to Ashes: America's Hundred-Year Cigarette War, the Public Health, and the Unabashed Triumph of Philip Morris*. New York: Alfred A. Knopf

Levy, Robert A. (June 20, 1997) "Tobacco Medicaid Litigation: Snuffing Out the Rule ofLaw." Cato Institute Policy Analysis no. 275.

Levy, Robert A. (August 23, 1999) "Turning Lead into Gold." *Legal Times*, p. 21.

Levy, Robert A. (May 9, 2001) "Pistol Whipped: Baseless Lawsuits, Foolish Laws." Cato Institute Policy Analysis no. 400

Lochhead, Carolyn (September 23, 1996) "The Growing Power of Trial Lawyers." *Weekly Standard*, p. 21.

Lott, John R., Jr. (March 2, 1999) "Suits Targeting Gun Makers Are off the Mark." *Wall Street Journal*, p. A18.

McAllister, Bill (April 24, 1997) "Smoking by GIs Raises Liability Issue at the VA." *Washington Post*, p. A1.

Prosser, William L. (ed.) (1984) *Prosser and Keeton on Torts*, 5th ed. St. Paul, MN.: West Publishing Co

Providence Journal-Bulletin (June 21, 1999) "Suing the Wrong People." Editorial, p. 4B.

Rabin, Robert L. (1992) "A Sociolegal History of the Tobacco Tort Litigation." *Stanford Law Review* 44: pp. 853-78.

Reich, Robert B. (January 17, 2000) "Smoking Guns." *American Prospect*, p. 64. Reuters.

Reich, Robert. B. (May 28, 1997) "B.A.T. Plays Down Florida Fund Decision."

Reich, Robert B. (October 7, 1999) "Court Rejects Cincinnati Suit Against Gun Industry."

Reich, Robert B. (February 23, 2001) "Florida Appeals Court Rejects Gun Suit."

Reich, Robert B. (March 8, 2001) "Brown & Williamson Pays Florida Smoker $1.1 Million."

Rothman, Stephen (February 3, 1997) "Tobacco Industry Defense Move Curbed by Fla. Judge." Reuters.

Scruggs, Richard (September 12, 1996) "Do the Merits and the Search for Truth Matter Any More?" Federalist Society National Conference on Civil Justice and the Litigation Process.

Stern, Andrew (September 15, 2000) "Judge Dismisses Chicago Suit Against Gun Industry." Reuters.

Torry, Saundra (June 10, 1999) "Lead Paint Could Be Next Big Legal Target." *Washington Post*, p. A1.

Tribe, Laurence (1971) "Trial by Mathematics: Precision and Ritual in the Legal Process." *Harvard Law Review* 84: pp. 1329-93.

Van Alstyne, William W. (1995) "Denying Due Process in the Florida Courts: A Commentary on the 1994 Medicaid Third-Party Liability Act of Florida." *Florida Law Review* 46: pp. 563-87.

Van Voris, Bob (December 7, 1998) "Gun Cases Use Tobacco Know-How; The Sequel." *National Law Journal*, p. A1.

Washington Post (October 12, 1999) "Guns in Court." Editorial, p. A18.

Zoll, Rachell (April 2, 2001) "Judge Allows State to Sue Lead Paint Industry." Associated Press.

9 EXPLAINING THE PERSISTENT GROWTH IN TAX COMPLEXITY

James L. Payne

"The United States," says law professor Richard Doernberg, "now has the most complex tax laws in the history of civilization" (Doernberg, 1988). The federal Internal Revenue Code, with its thousands of pages, is daunting enough, but it is only the tip of the iceberg. Each and every year, Treasury officials create thousands of pages of regulations interpreting this code. And every year adds to the number of court decisions which further expand the meaning of laws and regulations. The upshot is that no one—no matter how thick his glasses or emphatic his speech—truly knows what is legal, valid, or correct in the federal tax system.

A good demonstration of this point has been provided by *Money* magazine which for many years challenged tax professionals with a tax return test. Beginning in 1987, the magazine recruited several dozen certified public accountants and IRS enrolled agents to calculate the tax owed by a hypothetical family with a moderately complex tax situation. In each of the eight tests conducted between 1987 and 1998 the tax professionals came up with wildly different figures for the amount of tax due. In general, the disparity between the highest and lowest figure was over 100%. For example, in 1998, the lowest tax computed was $34,240 and the highest was a tax of $68,912. None of the tax professionals got the answer of $37,105 which the editors considered to be the correct tax for this family.

Even more significant than the results of the tests is the changing attitude toward them. When *Money* first presented its tax test in 1987, it did so with great fanfare, and the results attracted nationwide media attention. To demonstrate that enormous discrepancies could exist in honest and careful tax calculations was a shocking and newsworthy finding. A decade later, the novelty of this truth has worn off. *Money* presented its 1998 test briefly, almost perfunctorily, and the magazine has not repeated the exercise since. In other words, it is now a boring, established fact that there is no such thing as a demonstrably correct and legal tax under the federal tax system—at least for taxpayers with rather extensive economic affairs.

For most observers, the complexity of the modern federal tax system is thought to be merely a nuisance, something we can live with. This complacency is hardly justified. In a modern tax system, complexity is like an acid, a corrosive agent that progressively weakens the entire institution. In a democratic age, a tax system has to be defensible in order to thrive. People need to feel that tax burdens are the product of rational, consistent rules about who pays how much. In a highly complicated system, this certitude is lacking. Taxes become a function of inside knowledge, tax breaks, and even bad luck. In such a system, everyone is encouraged to conclude that the tax system is unfair, that he is paying more taxes than he "should," and that others—especially envied others—are not paying their "fair share." Once the tax system is perceived to be without rectitude, no one—not taxpayers, nor tax officials, nor lawmakers—will be disposed to uphold it.

ECONOMIC COSTS OF TAX COMPLEXITY

In order to gauge the full impact of tax complexity, it is useful to review the different ways it undermines the institution of taxation. The first is the economic burden that a complex tax system places on individuals, and on the economy in general. Writers on the subject of taxation have noted that in addition to the actual burden of any tax there is also a burden associated with administering it and complying with it. The money collected in taxes does not fly unnoticed from the pockets of taxpayers into the coffers of government. It has to be extracted through an elaborate tussle, and this tussle consumes time and money. The more complicated the tax regulations, the more time-consuming the process of attempting to comply with them.

Although the costs of tax compliance were first noted centuries ago—at least since Adam Smith—it is only recently that scholars have actually got around to measuring them. Apparently the first effort of this kind was made by a Montana economics professor in 1966 who sent his students home with a questionnaire for their parents to fill out about the time it took them to prepare their individual tax returns. As the tax system became more complicated and compliance burdens rose, the U. S. Congress took an interest in this issue and required, in the 1980 Paperwork Reduction Act, that the IRS assess the private sector burden of keeping tax records and filling out tax forms. To carry out this mandate, the IRS turned to the Arthur D. Little consulting firm to design and implement an appropriate survey.

The resulting study, which was published in 1988, is the most comprehensive account of tax compliance costs available. It employed a nationwide sample of individuals (3,831 responses) and businesses (1,474 responses) drawn from the IRS's own masterfile of taxpayers. The questionnaires asked taxpayers about the time they spent in learning about tax requirements, keeping records, preparing forms, and copying and sending them. The study found that in 1985, the nation spent 5.4 billion man-hours on tax compliance work (Little 1988, 17). To put this figure in perspective, it was the equivalent of the entire labor force of the state of Indiana working all year.

Large as this figure is, it greatly understated the actual private-sector compliance burden. To begin with, the A. D. Little study was not independent: it was supervised by the IRS. IRS officials have an understandable interest in downplaying the costs that their activities impose on the American people: no one, after all, likes to be portrayed as the bad guy. This orientation created a bias toward understating tax compliance burdens in the A. D. Little study. For example, researchers followed the practice of arbitrarily lowering seemingly "high" numbers which some taxpayers reported as their compliance times. In another major methodological decision, study writers lowered the figures by 22% by averaging in the results of an obviously defective diary study. Another problem was that the A. D. Little study deliberately excluded two burdens which are an important part of the tax compliance cost: the time consumed by paid preparers, and the time which taxpayers and their consultants devote to tax planning activities (Payne 1993, 22-23). Taken together, these distortions meant that the 5.4 billion man-hour figure was a serious understatement of the true burden of private-sector tax compliance even in the year 1985. The true figure was probably in the order of 7-10 billion hours.

Since that time, this burden has increased still further. Practically every year there is another spate of tax legislation, and—for reasons we shall discuss below—this legislation inevitably adds to complexity. One indicator of the increasing burden of tax compliance is the number of tax returns being filed. In the period 1980-2000, the number of individual income tax returns has increased 37 percent, from 93 million to 127 million. This is nearly double the increase in population. One reason for the increase in individual returns is the growth of the labor force: more people, especially women, are earning taxable income. Another factor is the growing number of children who are holding savings in one form or another and who therefore must file returns to report interest and dividends.

Perhaps even more significant from the point of view of wasted labor is the increase in the number of tax returns of commercial organizations, the trends for which are shown in Figure 1. As the figure shows, the number of corporate tax returns has doubled since 1980, going from 2.7 million to 5.3 million. Since these returns are many inches—and sometimes many feet—thick, the preparation of these 5.3 million returns represents an enormous expenditure of time, money, and high-quality brainpower. A similar pattern of growth is seen in the number of returns for partnerships and non-profit organizations.

Figure 9.1. **Growth in the Number of Commercial Tax Returns Filed**

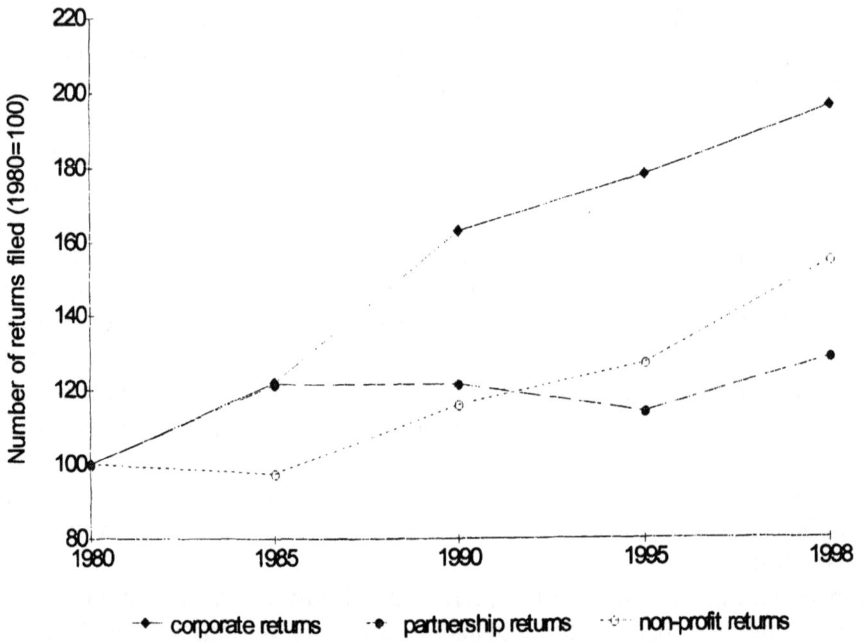

Source: Internal Revenue Service, Data Book, *selected years.*

In addition to the increase in tax returns, there has been a rapidly growing number of additional forms. For example, the number of supplemental documents filed with the IRS (chiefly amended tax returns and requests for extensions) has gone from from 6.0 million in 1980 to 14.7 million in 1998.

Another indicator of the growing complexity of tax requirements is the increase in the use of paid preparers. In 1981, 41 percent of individual taxpayers were using the services of paid professionals; in 1999, the corresponding figure was 56 per cent. The need for preparers has grown so obvious that even officials in charge of the tax system are turning to them for help with their personal returns. IRS Commissioners used to make it a point of pride that they filled out their own tax return—since it would be embarrassing to admit, by their own example, that the tax system was too complicated and too time-consuming for citizens to handle without professional help. This custom has apparently died. In 2001, IRS Commissioner Charles O. Rossotti told the press that he was using a paid preparer.

The economic waste caused by tax complexity is spread all across the economy, from individuals who pay H&R Block to fill out their returns to giant corporations that spend millions of dollars every year on tax compliance chores. As the nation grows increasingly aware of this waste, its impatience with the tax system grows.

A NATION OF TAX CHEATERS

Simple, well-defined problems in arithmetic have a right answer, and therefore a morally-enforceable answer. If the customer buys a $15 shirt and a $20 hat, how much does he owe the cashier? Since we can see the answer is $35, we can point a finger of reproach at the customer who hands the cashier $34. And that customer is embarrassed by his mistake—be it honest or otherwise—because the proof of his transgression is so obvious.

Imagine what would happen to this simple, effective morality if the prices were the product of complex and ambiguous calculations. Suppose the price of a shirt was the square root of the customer's body temperature when he woke up that morning, and the price of a hat was 2.05 percent of the number of friends that he has. The complexity of such a pricing system would undermine its moral force. The customer who offered the cashier $34 would no longer feel the eyes of other customers upon him, because they could have no way of knowing whether he was trying to cheat. And even if he knowingly fudged the truth of his calculations to get his answer, he wouldn't feel very guilty doing so because he knew there was no obviously correct answer to begin with.

This same lowering of moral standards occurs in tax systems as they grow more complex. A simple tax creates a moral imperative: everyone knows the right answer. The best example of such a simple system is a head tax, where each person owes, let us say, $1,000 a year. Under such a system, there could be little cheating because everyone knows what his tax is—and he knows that everyone else knows it, too. An income tax moves away from this simplicity, because the definition of "income" quickly becomes a complex and ambiguous matter. Humorist Will Rogers put his finger on this problem when he commented that "the income tax has made more liars out of the American people than golf has."

If the income tax is inherently "cheatable" even in its simplest form, it has become vastly more so in recent decades as more twists and turns have been added. The *Money* magazine experiments abundantly demonstrated the point that today, for individuals or organizations with anything more than the simplest economic arrangements, there is no such thing as a correct tax. Even IRS officials openly concede that tax calculations have become subjective. As one top official put it—writing, in this case, about tax violations involving international tax havens—"The lines become murky because the law is murky and the information is incomplete. In truth, often the question of whether a tax haven transaction is legitimate or illegitimate, whether it is tax avoidance or tax evasion, is in the eyes of the beholder."

The Office of Management and Budget has made a list of the major tax exemptions and deductions now forming a part of the income-tax code, a total of 146 areas of special exceptions. These include depletion allowances for minerals, tax reductions for the blind, deductions for small life insurance companies, credits for alternative fuel production, income averaging for farmers, accelerated depreciation on rental housing, a work-opportunity tax credit, a Lifetime-Learning tax credit, empowerment zones, new-markets tax credits, and so forth.

The surging complexity of the federal tax system has, quite predictably, given rise to increasing evasion. One indicator of the level of cheating is provided by the result from the IRS Taxpayer Compliance Measurement Program (TCMP). These are intense audits that examine all claims made on the tax return, and determine whether the taxpayer has understated or overstated his tax liability. Over the years, the proportion of taxpayers who have understated their tax (i. e. "cheaters") has increased significantly. In a 1949 audit, the proportion of understaters was 23 per cent. In 1985 it was 47 percent, and in the 1988 audit it was 60 percent. (Since 1988 there have been no further TCMP audits; Congress has banned them as being too grueling for taxpayers.)

Another sign that taxpayers increasingly view tax obligations as "fudgeable" is the growing popularity of the "aggressive" posture toward filing tax returns. Because one's tax liability is no longer taken as given, set by clear, simple rules, taxpayers are increasingly counseled to bend rules in their favor. They are told to view their relationship with the IRS as a contest, a competitive event in which their performance—the amount of tax paid—is the result of how vigorously and how cleverly they play the "game." The authors of a 1987 college textbook for would-be accountants explicitly makes this point: "Your federal tax life is like a hockey game, with the IRS guarding the goal while you try to score with your tax planning decisions. . . . Planning what happens is the taxpayer's competitive edge" (Raby 1987, ix)

The same idea is embraced in many recent books on tax advice for the general public. Their titles reflect the combative stance now being recommended. They include *Fight the IRS and Win!*, *Protecting Your Business from the IRS*, *Stand Up to the IRS*, *How to Survive an IRS Attack*, *How to Settle with the IRS—for Pennies on the Dollar*, *How to Screw the IRS*, *The IRS and You: How to Play the Game and Win*, and two different books both with the title *How to Beat the IRS*. Long gone is the idea that paying taxes is a civic duty which citizens ought to carry out cheerfully and willingly.

The March 2001 issue of *Forbes* documented how pronounced the tendency toward tax cheating has become. The cover of the magazine was entirely taken up by the headline of that month's feature story: "How to Cheat on Your Taxes." The article described the "push-the-edge and over-the-edge" tax shelters that are now being marketed to the masses (even in advertisements in *Forbes* itself). "It isn't just the promotion of outrageous shelters that is tearing this country's tax system apart," the report observed. "It is also the proliferation of conventional cheating—padded deductions, omitted income, inflated costs for assets sold at a gain." The article traced the growth in cheating to the increasing complexity of the tax code with its 15,100 pages of regulations and 9,500 tax-code changes since 1986. "It is choked with exemptions, preferences, credits, subsidies, special-interest favors, phase-ins, phase-outs, and grandfather clauses. It is a big joke. There is not much shame, it seems, in dodging it."

A tax system permeated by evasion is mistrusted by everyone, even the left-wing devotees of taxation. Traditionally, socialists favor a vast and potent system of taxation because, according to their beliefs, it makes the world fairer, transferring wealth from rich to poor. But when the system is riddled with cheating, it no longer performs this function very well. This is the thesis of the recent book *The Cheating of America* by Charles Lewis and Bill Allison (Lewis, 2001). The subtitle explains their point of view: *How Tax Avoidance and Evasion by the Super Rich are Costing the Country Billions—and What You Can Do about It.* Significantly, the book does not deliver on its promise to tell readers what they "can do about it." The authors do not recommend an IRS crackdown because they know this would be unpopular with everyone. "Many people at all levels subtly cheat on their taxes, from dubious deductions to underreporting cash earnings to. . . you name it." This, they feel "explains why no one is really protesting the tepid enforcement of tax laws for certain individuals and corporations."

In an age of tax cheating, the redistribution of wealth becomes an increasingly unworkable goal. The rich reduce their taxes through fiddles and tax dodges, but one can't crack down on them because everyone else, including the poor, is also cheating—and wants to keep the system permeable.

DECLINING SUPPORT FOR THE TAX SYSTEM

Tax complexity, then, represents a triple threat to the tax system. First, it increases compliance burdens, adding to waste and frustration. Second, it makes for an increasingly subjective tax system, a system where right or wrong lose their meaning. Third, complexity encourages cheating—which undermines public trust and confidence in the system. In the long run, a complex tax system loses support of all segments of society: rich and poor, right and left.

This is not just theory. As the U. S. tax system has grown increasingly complex in recent decades, support for it has been steadily declining. Since World War II, the Gallup poll has asked a key question about attitudes toward the tax system: "Do you regard the income tax which you have to pay this year as fair?" In the four surveys taken during the war, an average of 87 percent of the respondents said, "Yes." In the two surveys taken after the war, in 1946, the proportion saying taxes were fair fell to an average of 61 percent. When the question was asked in 1997, the "yes" proportion had fallen to 51 percent, and in 1999, it was 45 percent: for the first time in the history of the poll, only a minority agreed that their tax was fair.

Another question which Gallup has used quite frequently since 1947 asks whether respondents "consider the amount of federal income tax you have to pay as too high, about right, or too low?" In the eight surveys conducted in the 1947-1953 period, an average of 57.0 percent said "too high." The ten surveys conducted in 1990-1999 indicate that dissatisfaction has grown somewhat: an average of 60.1 percent said their taxes were "too high."

The public attitude toward the Internal Revenue Service itself has been undergoing a dramatic shift. Since 1983, the Roper organization has been asking respondents to express their opinion toward various government agencies. The trend in the proportion of respondents with an "unfavorable" opinion of the IRS, shown in Figure 2, indicates a rather clear increase in disapproval. The slope of the trend in the figure indicates that by around the year 2030, the entire population will have a negative view of the agency.

Figure 9.2. **Trend in Negative Rating of the IRS, 1983-1998**

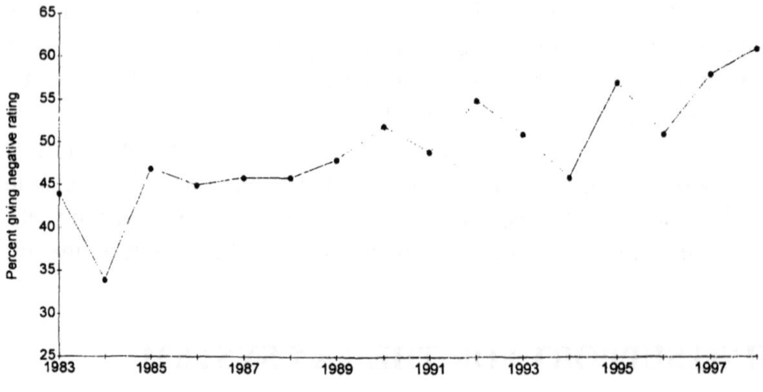

Data courtesy of Roper Starch Worldwide. The Roper question gives respondents four choices in rating the agency: highly favorable, moderately favorable, not too favorable, and unfavorable. The negative rating is the sum of the respondents answering in the last two categories.

Another perspective on public attitudes comes from the trend in taxpayer support for the presidential election fund. In the early 1970s, Congress set up a fund to provide for the public financing of presidential elections. Money for this purpose is raised by having taxpayers check a box on their income tax returns, indicating that they would like $3 of their tax monies to be deposited to this fund. As Figure 3 indicates, the willingness of taxpayers to participate in this program has been falling markedly, going from around 27 percent when the program began to less than 12 percent today.

Figure 9.3. **Taxpayer Support for the Presidential Election Campaign Fund, 1976-1998**

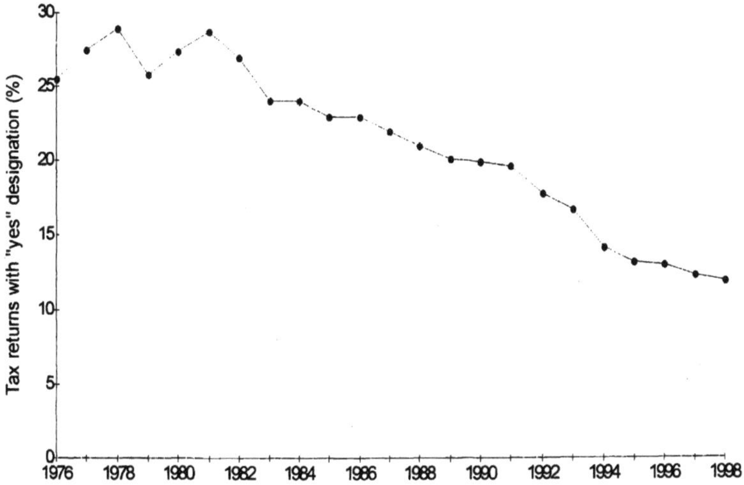

Source: Internal Revenue Service, Data Book, selected years.

This decline probably reflects a number of trends. To some degree it reflects the general decline in the public's confidence in government, its politicians, and its spending programs. But it also seems to be a vote against the tax system, too. After all, the choice to support the fund is being given on the tax return in connection with paying taxes. In other words, it is the tax system which is petitioning the taxpayer to make the "donation." The high and growing level of rejection of this request would therefore seem to reflect an increasingly negative view of the petitioner.

Another sign of growing disapproval is the number of critical books about the Internal Revenue Service. Before about 1980, writings on the IRS were mainly historical and generally adopted a stance of approval. The tax revolt of the late 1970s changed the pattern, and marked the beginning of a flood of highly critical volumes. An early example was *To Harass Our People: The IRS and Government Abuse of Power*, written by Idaho congressman George Hansen in 1980. Another scathing critique of the IRS was *The Big Tax Lie* by William A. Kilpatrick, published in 1986. In 1989, Random House brought out David Burnham's critique, *A Law Unto Itself: Power, Politics and the IRS.* Even tax historians have adopted a critical stance: Charles Adams entitled his 1998 history of taxation in America *Those Dirty Rotten Taxes.* The IRS's own historian, Shelley Davis, wrote a highly critical volume (after resigning), *Unbridled Power; Inside the Secret Culture of the IRS* (1997).

Perhaps the most significant sign that the tax system is losing public respect is seen in the pattern of recent legislative actions. Traditionally, Congressmen have been highly supportive of the tax system, and have reinforced the IRS in its battles against the taxpaying public. About 15 years ago, however, this pattern of rather blind support began to change. One of the first signs that Congress was beginning to switch sides were the 1987 and 1988 hearings critical of IRS practices that led to the enactment of the 1988 Taxpayers' Bill of Rights.

In the mid-1990s, Congress revisited the tax system, with more hearings on the harsh and arbitrary treatment still being meted out to taxpayers in enforcement actions. Even IRS workers came forth to expose co-workers for their anti-taxpayer attitudes and practices—and these "informers" were given Congressional protection against reprisals from IRS managers. Three more laws were passed—in 1996, 1997, and 1998—which further restricted the IRS and gave taxpayers more rights. A few tax officials pointed out that these reforms would endanger the IRS's ability to collect the vast sums needed by modern government, but the measures were too politically popular to be resisted, even by die-hard supporters of the welfare state. "This is a very big freight train," said a Democrat political strategist in 1997. He advised that if liberals in Congress, or the Clinton administration, tried to stand in front of it, "they're just going to get run over." No one did: the reform measures were approved by overwhelming majorities in both houses of Congress, and were quickly signed by the President.

In 1998, the Congressional antagonism toward the tax system ratcheted up a notch with the debate and passage—in the House of Representatives—of the Tax-Code Termination Act. This bill mandated that the entire federal tax code be abolished on December 31, 2002. The purpose of the bill was not to do away with taxation altogether. Proponents of the measure assumed that once termination of the present system was certain, a new tax code would be devised to take its place. Nevertheless, there was a risk that the United States would be left without any tax system at all if Legislators didn't get around to providing for a replacement. As it happens, the Tax-Code Termination Act died in the Senate, so it did not become law. But the fact that the popular chamber was willing to pass it shows the depth of frustration with the current federal tax system.

At the center of this frustration was the complaint that the existing tax code is extremely burdensome, illogical, and complex. "So complex," as Representative Jim Bunning of Kentucky put it, "that no one can understand it." Proponents of the bill argued that all past efforts to simplify the tax code had failed to "clean up this mess," as Representative Dick Armey put it, so that the only alternative was "to cut the cancer out altogether and start afresh."

"WE MADE IT WORSE"

In general, when people agree about the need to fix a certain problem, remedies follow. It is significant that this rule does not apply to the problem of tax complexity. For decades, everyone—Democrats, Republicans, businessmen, accountants, professors of taxation, and IRS administrators—has agreed that the tax system is too complex. And everyone has agreed that this complexity is causing a host of problems which are undermining respect for the tax system. Yet no solution is in sight.

This point was made by Representative Collin Peterson of Minnesota in the debate on the Tax-Code Termination Act.

> I have been in favor of scrapping this code and starting over for a long time. I am one of the few Members of this body that is a certified public accountant that has actually done tax returns for a living and have lived with this code for a long time. . . . I have been for reforming this system ever since 1986 when, under the guise of tax simplification, we passed a bill which I think was arguably the worst piece of legislation that has ever been passed in this Congress. We made it worse in 1990, and we made it worse last year when they passed the 1997 tax act to the point where my partner, who is still doing tax returns, told me this weekend that this is so complicated that he does not think he can any longer do a tax return by hand. The only way he can do a tax return is if he has a computer to be able to make all these computations and go back and forth. Mr. Speaker, this code has gotten completely out of hand. It needs to be simplified. It is not happening under the current process (Tax-Code Termination Act Debate, 1998, H4660).

Representative Peterson's observation was quite correct. Since the 1970s Congress has been holding hearings on—and passing laws entitled—"Tax Simplification," without succeeding in simplifying the system. Occasionally, one or another burden is set aside, but at the same time five or ten new complexities and compliance burdens emerge. In spite of all the concern and all the efforts at simplification, the tax system has been getting more complicated as years go by. What makes this problem so intractable? To answer this question, we need to examine the pressures that are working to cause tax complexity. There appear to be two forces at work.

Civilizing the Tax System

The first is the modern desire to make taxation non-arbitrary and humane. The point is seldom appreciated, but the fact is that the most efficient approach, in terms of minimal complexity, is a tax system run by thugs. If IRS officials could simply go to businesses and individuals and demand any sum they liked—and seize the funds at gunpoint if they weren't handed over—there would be very little complexity in the U. S. tax system. There would be no rules and regulations to read, no calculations to make, no returns to file, no audits to participate in, no appeals to prepare for. The working premise would be that tax officials are always right—no matter how painful or seemingly unjustified their actions.

Ancient tax systems were very much like this: soldiers came to towns and farms and demanded sums, or simply took what they wanted. Protests and complaints were answered with the sword. As civilization evolved, this vicious process was gradually tamed. Lawmakers put down on paper the rules which stipulated the amount of tax owed. With these rules it was no longer possible for a tax collector to demand anything he took a fancy to: he had to show where it said that he was justified in making his demand. This rule-based system makes taxation less arbitrary, but it has come at a stiff price: massive paperwork. This paperwork includes not only the thousands of pages of tax code and billions of pages of tax forms that citizens file. It also includes the systems for adjudicating disputes over how much tax is legally owed—and all the work and frustration these systems involve. In 1998, for example, there were 65,434 audit appeals, and 32,082 cases submitted to the tax court.

As part of the process of humanizing taxation, lawmakers also developed rules and regulations that limited what tax collectors could do in enforcing the tax system. Taxation, after all, means taking money away from people against their will, and there are bound to be many cases where citizens avoid, evade, or resist the tax authority. Traditionally, the governmental response to tax evasion was to apply brute force, to terrorize people into obedience. In Roman times, cities that reneged on their obligation to pay tribute were razed as an example to others. In18th-century France, those who attempted to evade the salt tax were subject to whipping and branding; more serious offenders were made galley slaves or were subjected to the torture-death of being broken on the wheel. In a more compassionate age, we limit tax officials in the steps they can take, and we give taxpayers the right to contest actions taken against them. But once again, this softening automatically brings with it increased complexity.

To take one specific example among the hundreds that might be cited, consider summons-enforcement practices. The IRS often wants to force third parties, such as accountants or bookkeepers, to testify against taxpayers by summoning them to give evidence or produce records. Before the mid-1970s, the IRS would have these summons issued without the taxpayer knowing about it, so that he could not make any move to block an unjustified gathering of evidence against him. The power to issue "secret" summons was taken away from the IRS in the tax reform act of 1976. After that time, the IRS was required to notify the taxpayer when it was summoning a third party to testify against him.

This curbing of IRS powers brought about a corresponding increase in paperwork. To begin with, the IRS now had to draft and mail notices to taxpayers in connection with the summons. And taxpayers, naturally, responded by more frequently contesting these summons in drawn-out legal proceedings. The number of summons enforcement legal actions went from 1,877 in 1975 to 3,698 in 1977—and on up to 8,254 in 1990. Thus, giving citizens more rights led to an increase in administrative and compliance burdens on all sides. This is the general pattern with efforts to make taxation rational and humane. Each taxpayer "right" means more work for those who have to spell it out on paper, more work for those who have to find out about the right, and more work for those who wish to challenge an IRS action on the basis of the right.

The Gentle, Legalistic Battle Against Cheating

What are tax managers to do about the growing problem of cheating? The old-fashion tactic of redoubling the level of violence is now out of reach. In this kinder and gentler era, the only tools left to enhance enforcement of the tax system are bureaucratic and legalistic weapons—weapons which complicate the tax system each time they are used.

For example, when it looked like too many taxpayers were declaring non-existent children as dependents, tax managers did not follow the practice of whipping and branding a few thousand of these cheaters as an example to the country. Instead, the response was to require that all children have a taxpayer identification number. See the tangled web this gentle, legalistic approach weaves. One has to add spaces on the tax return where the taxpayer has to fill in the taxpayer identification number of each dependent. If that number has been lost, the taxpayer has to write to the Social Security Administration. This may delay the filing of a tax return, and require filing for an extension, or incurring a late penalty, and a subsequent appeal of this penalty, and so on.

This same approach—demanding more information from the taxpayer—has been used by tax officials in an effort to curb cheating in many other areas including deducting home offices, moving expenses, and automobile costs, as well as establishing the amount of charitable deductions and establishing the value of donated art. The additional requirements may or may not reduce cheating, but they always increase the paperwork burden on the taxpayer.

Reporting requirements are another way that tax officials attempt to control cheating. Their theory is that if all economic transactions are reported to tax authorities, then taxpayers are less likely to cheat—and more likely to be caught if they do. Year by year the application of this theory has led to more reporting requirements. There are now over eighty of these requirements, covering a vast range of economic transactions, from wages, tips, and dividends to home sales, honoraria, and fish catches. In 1998, the IRS received 1.2 billion pieces of information, an average of over five for each taxpayer. Generating and transmitting all this data is only part of the workload that the information reporting system involves. A second burden is created when the IRS attempts to use this information to catch cheaters. In 1998, the

IRS sent out 4 million notices based on this information: 1.7 million "underreporter" notices that accused taxpayers of failing to report all their income, and 2.3 million "non-filer" notices that accused taxpayers of failing to file a tax return. Even if every one of these notices were valid and correct, they still involved additional tax compliance work for taxpayers. As it turns out, a majority of these notices are wrong—sometimes because the reported information was wrong, but more often because the IRS has gross and careless systems of interpreting the information given it (Payne 1993, 43-49). As a result, millions of taxpayers are falsely accused of making some kind of tax mistake—and the taxpayers, threatened by seizure of their property if they don't clear the error up, are forced to engage in many hours of frustrating labor to convince a slow-witted bureaucracy that it has made a mistake.

Another legalistic approach to discouraging cheating is to add new penalties: since 1954, the number of penalties has increased from 13 to over 150. This approach, too, adds to complexity. Each time a penalty is issued, it involves a further step for the taxpayer: he has to think about it, deciding whether to pay it or contest it. Since the IRS issues over 30 million penalties each year—34 million in 1998—this is no small workload. Since many of these penalties are erroneous, millions of taxpayers contest them. Each effort to contest a penalty involves considerable paperwork for taxpayers and their representatives. In 1998—the IRS abated 4.4 million penalties, agreeing that they were inappropriate or unjustified. Presumably additional millions of taxpayers went to the trouble of asking for abatement and were turned down.

Increasing the size of fines is another way tax officials have attempted to discourage cheating—but this also increases burdens. With more money at stake, it becomes more worthwhile for taxpayers to appeal a penalty—expending more energy and wasting more resources as they do so.

We can see, then, how the effort to control cheating with the mild, legalistic measures now in use today sets up a vicious cycle. The measures are too feeble to terrorize wayward taxpayers, but they always bring on a new round of complexity and frustration for everyone. The result is a growing climate of disrespect and hostility which breeds more cheating.

The Quest For Fair Taxation

A second source of complexity is the desire to make the tax system "fair." When the king's soldiers take two cows from Farmer Jones but only one cow from Farmer Smith, Farmer Jones is irate. It's an understandable reaction. Taxation involves a sacrifice. In order to defend it, and maintain it, both the public and the lawmakers need to feel that its burdens are spread across the society in an equal and appropriate fashion.

When most people refer to "fair" taxation, they speak as though there were a single, obvious principle for allocating tax burdens. Unfortunately, this is not so. "Fair" has a great variety of meanings when applied to taxes. Should the tax level be assessed on the basis of income, or on the basis of wealth, or on the basis of need (number of mouths to feed, etc.)? Should it take into account the sacrifices made to earn income or acquire wealth? For example, suppose a person has amassed savings as a result of virtually starving himself all his life. Should that savings be taxed at the same rate as money won in a lottery? The practice of taxation presents an almost infinite number of such moral conundrums.

A second source of confusion about "fair" taxation follows from the fact that people generally consider that a proper, rational tax should not harm any worthy social or economic effort. For example, if a poor widow is buying food to feed her children, a tax on her purchase of food would seem most unjust and socially counterproductive: in other words, unfair. So would a tax on medical services needed to sustain life, or a tax on shelter, or a tax on fuel needed to heat one's dwelling, and so on. The underlying assumption is that a "fair" tax system should not harm any worthy activity.

Unfortunately, this assumption is specious. Taxation inevitably harms virtually all human efforts, including moral and constructive activities. Politicians thus face a choice: either ignore all these injuries and turn a deaf ear to the pleas for relief, or embark on a never-ending effort to alter a tax system to exempt worthy causes from the burdens of taxation. Naturally, the politicians have opted to modify the tax code, and the result is a tax system riddled with exceptions and modifications.

Let us take a typical example. Suppose we agree on the principle that people with equal incomes should pay an equal amount of tax. At first glance, it seems that we have established a "fair" tax. But suppose one taxpayer has a child with a crippling disease that is very expensive to treat. So this taxpayer spends a large fraction of his income on medical bills for this child. In consequence, he has a much lower standard of living than another taxpayer with the same income who has no such burden. Is this "fair?" Most people—and all politicians—would say it is not, and that an exception ought to be created for medical expenses.

But look what the creation of this exception means for the complexity of the tax code. Regulations have to be written defining which medical expenses are included, and taxpayers have to master these regulations, collect records, add up expenses, make calculations, and fill in the extra lines on the tax form. More paperwork comes when IRS officials challenge a medical deduction, making more work for everyone involved in the appeals process. The pattern will generally be the same for any exception made to a simple tax principle: the modification leads to more complexity.

Ironically, the accretion of exceptions—each defended as an attempt to make the tax system fairer—has produced a tax system now widely considered to be. . . unfair! The exceptions—called loopholes—have resulted in a situation where a wealthy person might pay little or no tax at all. This person could direct his assets to the socially-constructive things Congress didn't want to punish with taxation—donating to symphony orchestras, turning land to conservation purposes, investing in local school bonds, and so forth. Yet most people find it outrageously "unfair" that a wealthy person might pay no tax. Political protest on this issue reached the boiling point in the 1970s.

The Congressional response—in the tax act of 1978—affords a chilling lesson for those who believe that Congress is capable of simplifying the tax system. If Legislators had proceeded logically, they would have seen that what made it possible for the wealthy to escape taxation was all the exemptions they had written into the tax code. They would therefore have eliminated some of these exemptions—starting, for example, with the exclusion of interest income from state and local bonds. This was not the avenue taken. Instead, lawmakers went in the opposite direction, *creating yet another layer of tax complexity in order to make the tax system "fairer."* This was the alternative-minimum-tax requirement. After they have filled out all relevant forms and tax returns, taxpayers are now obliged to make another set of burdensome calculations that may result in an additional tax liability beyond that calculated using the existing tax code.

The penchant for "fairness" explains why different tax systems—which might be much less complex—are consistently rejected in Washington. Some reformers argue, for example, that replacing the income tax with a uniform national sales tax would slay the dragon of complexity. In principle, it probably would. But in practice, it is most unlikely that such a tax would be adopted—because of its apparent unfairness. To begin with, it would be regressive, allowing the rich to earn and keep large untaxed incomes. Furthermore, when people saw that the burden of a high sales tax was penalizing socially desirable expenditures—food, medical prescriptions, college textbooks, pollution control devices—there would be great political pressure to exempt one field after another from taxation—bringing back the very complexity that reformers sought to avoid.

THE FUTURE OF THE MODERN TAX SYSTEM

This exploration of the causes of tax complexity suggests that the problem is deep-rooted indeed, one not amenable to simple reforms. At bottom, tax complexity arises from powerful imperatives, namely, the desire to humanize the tax system and to use humane methods to counter tax evasion, and the desire to make taxation "fair." It therefore follows that the tax system is on a fatal course, bound to see more of the complexity that is making it cumbersome and bringing it into disgrace. It is perhaps overdrawing the case to say that a collapse is imminent, but some erosion or deterioration seems almost certain to occur.

It does not appear that modern thinking about government and government spending programs has taken this possibility into account. From a distance, the welfare state seems well-established and secure. It has been around for many years and is now taken for granted by intellectuals, politicians, and the public. Government agencies like the Social Security Administration make calculations about tax revenues expected to be collected fifty or even 100 years hence. Such estimates reflect a strange confidence in continuity in a world where everything else, from religion and marriage to global climate, is undergoing major changes. This confidence in unchanging taxation is particularly naive for it overlooks the powerful trends working against the tax system.

After all, what is this system that provides the funds for government's programs of social improvement? It is not an arrangement recently devised by high-minded social reformers applying rational and ethical principles. It is an oppressive scheme handed down to us by history's tyrants. Taxation developed as a system of exploitation. Tribe conquered tribe, nation conquered nation, and to enjoy the fruits of their conquest the oppressors developed systems of taxation. Instead of making conquered peoples slaves and shipping them off at great expense and loss of life, they were allowed to continue to work in their own lands—where they would be more productive than slaves—and the conquerors extracted the wealth thus created using force and the threat of force. In effect, taxation is a system of slavery-in-place.

It is indeed paradoxical to find that a system with such a disreputable background should become the foundation of the modern welfare state. It is rather like finding a day care center set up in a medieval torture chamber. The arrangement may work for a time, but there is bound to be growing tension between sensitive modern values and the harsh violence of the ancient technology. So it is with taxation. The extraction of funds through force and the threat of force no longer fits in with modern values. Ethically, it clashes with our distaste for violence. Culturally, it contradicts the principle that people should be free to choose their own goals and aspirations. And politically, it transgresses the trend toward kinder, gentler government.

No one is willing to face this hard truth, of course, because taxation has become so central to modern social and economic arrangements. Society is not ready for an open debate on the moral and cultural liabilities of taxation. But our refusal to talk about these liabilities does not make them go away. The historical drift against taxation continues, taking a devious and unexpected route: tax complexity. Our modern values compel us to make taxation ever more burdensome and complicated, and this complexity makes taxation increasingly unworkable and increasingly disparaged.

In this analysis, the inability of the politicians to banish tax complexity should not be viewed with alarm or dismay. To the contrary, it is a hopeful sign, for tax complexity has a positive role to play in our national evolution. It is history's way of telling us we have the wrong system for raising funds for public purposes—and compelling us to find another.

REFERENCES

Doernberg, Richard L. (1988) The Market for Tax Reform: Public Pain for Private Gain. *Tax Notes*, November 28, 1988, pp. 965-969.

Lewis, Charles and Bill Allison. (2001) *The Cheating of America: How Tax Avoidance and Evasion by the Super Rich Are Costing the Country Billions—and What You Can Do About It.* New York, NY.: William Morrow imprint of HarperCollins.

Little, Arthur D. (1988) *Development of Methodology for Estimating the Taxpayer Paperwork Burden*, Washington, D. C.: Internal Revenue Service.

Payne, James L. (1993) *Costly Returns; The Burdens of the U. S. Tax System.* San Francisco: ICS Press.

Raby, William L. and Victor H. Tidwell. (1986) *Introduction to Federal Taxation*, 1987 edition. Englewood Cliffs, N. J.: Prentice-Hall.

Tax-Code Termination Act Debate. (1998) Congressional Record, June 17, 1988 (House), H4543-H4677.

10 SITE-VALUE TAXATION AND THE RULE OF LAW

Fred E. Foldvary

Site-value taxation (SVT) consists of basing public revenue on the value of real estate sites or the rental obtainable from such sites, excluding the value and rental of any improvements such as buildings. This chapter examines the economics of SVT and compares the economic effects of this method with that of other types of taxes. It then delves into the ethical and political nature of the rule of law and analyzes the comparative effects of site-value taxation versus other taxes on governance. Finally, the chapter examines how SVT facilitates a more decentralized governance and other constitutional provisions that could provide community services more congruent with the desires of the people affected.

THE ELEMENTS OF SITE-VALUE TAXATION

A "site" is a three-dimensional extent of space in a particular location. Its "site rental" is defined here as the periodic amount that would be paid by the highest-bidding tenant if the site were to be auctioned for tenancy. (Technically, in an efficient auction, the rental would be set by the second-highest bid, in order to avoid discouraging the highest bid. In practice, the rental is usually estimated from the market rentals in the neighborhood, when paid for the highest and best use of the sites.) Site-value taxation consists of a payment of a portion of the site rental to the governing agency. Mason Gaffney (1964, 18) calls it an "*ad valorem* tax on the base of site capacity."

The market value of a site is a return to all three factors of production: land, labor, and capital. Economic "land" includes all natural resources and natural opportunities. Capital goods are products which are used to produce more goods or which provide long-term services. Improvements to sites such as the leveling of the ground, the replacement of water with solid matter, and the buildings, swimming pools, and fences built on the site surface, are not really improvements to the *land*, since strictly speaking economic land excludes such alterations.

Mason Gaffney (1994) further points out several distinctions between spatial land and capital goods, spatial land being nonreproduceable, permanent and recyclable, fixed in supply, and immobile in space. Land sites do not turn over like capital goods do, i.e. space does not depreciate and thus does not need to be maintained.

The market rental generated by a site depends both on the value to users of the natural aspects (such as the climate, features such as bays and rivers, and minerals in the ground) and on value derived from the surrounding civic infrastructure such as streets and security services. The latter value is a return to capital goods and labor, including such elements as the alteration of the ground by clearing trees or replacing water with solid matter, and also including the value of having real-estate titles recognized and registered.

Nicolaus Tideman (1994) distinguishes three returns, 1) the value attributable to nature; 2) the value attributable to public services, and 3) the value attributable to private activities. James Buchanan (1989) calls the output value attributable to governmental services "social rent," some of which individuals may at the constitutional stage agree to use collectively.

The value of a small site, such as a typical city house or store, is not affected by the improvements on that site, i.e. the building, but is very much a result of the neighborhood and city civic goods and services. As Gaffney (1964, 18) puts it, "A site-capacity tax will move up or down as [the] environment improves or worsens, but remains frozen as individual landowners respond to the environmental challenge."

A site is fixed both in location and in extent. Each site has a unique location that cannot be moved, unlike labor and capital goods that are mobile, especially in the long run and ex-ante (i.e. one has a choice of where to construct a building). Unlike labor and capital, space cannot be imported to expand the supply. Unlike capital goods, the supply of ground space cannot be expanded within the boundary lines of some jurisdiction. The supply of raw land, apart from improvements, is therefore inelastic, meaning that the quantity of sites does not change when the prices rise or fall. One may of course increase the amount of land for any particular use, but not the totality of the space within some boundary. The supply of offers to sell land slopes up, with more owners willing to sell at higher prices, but they can only offer to sell plots of a totality of area whose supply is fixed. The fixed quantity of space needs to be distinguished from the variable quantities of offers to sell bits of space, just as the total shares of stock of a company is fixed while offers to sell shares increase with price.

As a general rule, the market price of an asset is based on its return relative to the prevailing rates of return to other assets and its risk relative to other returns. Abstracting away from risk, the real-interest rate (after subtracting the price-inflation rate) reflects the prevailing returns on assets. The general formula for the price of a perpetual asset is the expected returns divided by the interest rate, or 1) $p = r / i$, where **p** is the price, **r** is the annual return , and **i** is the real interest rate, since the return equals the interest rate times the principal or price of the asset, if **r** and **i** are expected to be constant. If **r** and **i** are expected to change, then one needs to discount each year separately and add up the terms, hence (1) is a simplification that abstracts away from expected changes, but the simplification does not change the essential relationships.

In the case of a site, the return is the rental net of expenses. If there is also a property tax or assessment on the site, it too is paid from the rental. In real-estate property taxes, there is some tax rate **t** applied to the price of the property, **p**. For example, if the tax rate **t** is 3 percent and the market price **p** of the property is $400,000, the tax paid would be $12,000 per year.

Since the rental both pays a normal return to asset value and pays the property tax, the market price of the site is capitalized down by both the interest rate and the tax rate. The interest and tax rates are therefore added together in the denominator: (2) p = r / (i+t), where **t** is the tax rate on **p**. Suppose, for example, that a plot of land has a market rental of $10,000 per year, and there is no tax. An interest rate of 5% will capitalize the rental to $10,000/.05 = $200,000. After a tax rate of 15% of the price is implemented, we add 15% to the 5% for a denominator value of 20% or .2, and the market price then falls to $10,000/.2 = $50,000. That is because 3/4 of the rental is paying the tax, and 1/4 is paying the normal return on assets, making the after-tax price 1/4 of the non-taxed price.

The relationships in (2) also enable us to determine what proportion or percentage of the rental is being taxed. Given the tax rate **t** based on **p**, the portion or percentage of the rental paid as the assessment or tax is (3) x = t / (i+t) where **x** equals the percentage of the rental that is paid. If the interest rate is 5% and the tax rate is 15%, then the percentage of the rental paid would be 15/20 or 75%.

Taxes on produced goods, such as general sales or value-added taxes, add to their market prices, because these goods have costs of production which are not reducible. Taxes on wages can add to the cost of hiring labor while reducing the net wage of the worker. In contrast, taxes on sources that are fixed and have no cost of production lower those prices. Since land has no cost of production, nor any opportunity cost (since sites do not have a leisure alternative), when taxed, the value of a site becomes capitalized down by the amount of rental taken. Income and sales taxes to some extent also reduce rent and become capitalized into lower site values.

In (2) above, as **t** rises, **p** falls. The formula providing the change in site value is (4) c = i / (i+t), where **c** is the proportional or percentage change in site value, i.e. the fraction of the pre-tax price that constitutes the after-tax price. For example, if a plot of ground has a market value of $100,000 with no tax, a rental of $5,000, and an interest rate of 5%, then a tax rate of 20% results in a price of 5000/.25 = $20,000, and the change in price is .05/(.05+.20) = .05/.25 = 20%, the after-tax price being one-fifth the pre-tax price.

We can see that the burden of SVT does not fall on the tenant, since the market rental does not change, but falls entirely on the owner as a reduction in the price of the site. This burden, however, falls only on the owner at the time of transition. A new buyer, once the tax change has taken effect, has no real tax burden, because the lower price of the land offsets having to pay a tax on the rental. What he pays in rental tax he saves in avoiding a mortgage payment (or opportunity cost of the funds if there is no debt) of a similar amount.

To implement SVT, the value of the site needs to be appraised or assessed separately from the value of the improvements. This distinction is also necessary for insurance purposes. To prevent insurance fraud, a company providing fire or earthquake insurance wants to avoid insuring the total property value, but only the value of that which can be destroyed, i.e. the improvements. Professional appraisers and assessors have several techniques for splitting the values. In some cases, there is data from the sale of nearby vacant lots, or leaseholds with separate titles for the land and the improvements. An assessor can also estimate the replacement value of the structures and subtract the depreciation of an older building. A tax assessor would also subtract the value of improvements that are permanent, such as the value added by leveling the ground or filling in water or clearing away trees and rocks. What remains is site value.

Assessors have maps, now often computerized, that show the site values in a neighborhood. They can extrapolate and smooth out variances in individual assessments and appraisals, so that similar sites in a locality have similar estimated values. The assessments should be a public record (and nowadays could be accessible on the Internet). The title holders can then appeal the assessments if they think they have been treated unfairly relative to their neighbors, or if they claim that the assessment as a whole overvalued the sites. A proper appeals process, ultimately to juries, is an important part of SVT. This process is quite different from the taxation of income, sales, or value added, which involve extensive record keeping and tax audits, and where the records are not public, making it difficult to avoid being discriminated against.

Would SVT be sufficient to finance all of government? It is quite possible for the total rental generated by a public good to be greater than its total cost at the optimal quantity. Studies of the impact of subways in New York City show that landowners could have paid for it and still made a profit. As another example, the George Washington Bridge across the Hudson River increased New Jersey site values by six times the cost of the bridge (Tucker, 1958, 11).

The totality of site rentals is much greater than generally recognized. Mason Gaffney (1970) has estimated that site values are more than half of all real-estate market value. The Bureau of Economic Analysis estimated the total value of real estate in 1986 to be $10.8 trillion (Miles, 1990). That would put the site value of the US at over $5 trillion in 1986, and that excludes the rent of material land (oil, coal, minerals, water), the electro-magnetic spectrum, airline routes and satellite orbits, and the fact that much of present-day site value has been negatively capitalized due to taxes, regulations, excessive litigation, and other imposed costs that reduce profits.

One could also argue that government should not be spending so much of public funds for services which either are not paid from genuine user fees (charges for beneficial services, rather than disguised excise taxes) or which do not generate more rental than the cost. Much of government spending is for transfer payments rather than providing public goods, and many of these transfers are the result of political pressure groups seeking subsidies that do not benefit the public. Still, if additional funds other than user fees and site rentals are desired, other sources of funding can include profits from government-operated enterprises as well as charges on negative externalities such as congestion and pollution (when such costs are not compensated for by negotiation or torts), and there is therefore no economic need to tax beneficial activities such as entrepreneurship, labor, investment, and the sale of goods.

COMPARATIVE ECONOMIC EFFECTS

The "excess burden" of a tax is the cost imposed on taxpayers and on society beyond the funds paid to government. For example, a sales tax is added to the price of a good, making the purchase more expensive. In a competitive market, the seller is typically making only a normal profit, and if the profit is reduced, firms leave the industry. So the tax cannot be absorbed in a lower profit. The producers and sellers also cannot lower their costs of production because of the tax, since they are already generally trying to minimize their costs.

Since general sales taxes are added to the prices of goods, this shifts up the supply curves by the amount of the tax. Since the demand curve typically slopes down, this shift of supply moves up along the demand curve to a higher price and lower quantity. An increase in the price results in a lower quantity demanded.

The excess burden extends beyond the taxpayer. Consider a shopkeeper who would have kept a store open on Sunday, but decides to keep it closed because the after-tax profit would be too low. Workers who would have been employed now do not have this opportunity, and customers who would have shopped there also lose that opportunity; their additional travel and loss of convenience is part of the social waste caused by the tax. This decrease in the quantity consumed is a social waste, because resources are not being allocated to where consumers most want them. As Wagner (1980) puts it, waste is "a lessened ability of an economy to satisfy people's wants." Buyers are willing to purchase more quantities at prices that cover the economic marginal costs, but the tax intervention prevents them from doing so. It is a loss of "consumer surplus," the gain to consumers of being able to get goods at prices lower than what they are willing to pay.

There is also a loss of producer surplus, the gain from selling above the marginal costs of production, since there is less production. Economists call this loss of consumer and producer surplus a "deadweight loss" because it is a pure loss with no corresponding gain. This waste is created by all taxes on productive activity, taxes that include sales taxes, income taxes, value-added taxes, and other taxes or so-called "fees" for engaging in business. The excess burden of the U.S. corporate income tax, for example, has been calculated as more than half the revenues collected (Congressional Budget Office, 1996). The total excess burden in the U.S. has been estimated at more than $1 trillion (Tideman and Plassmann, 1998).

The excess burden comes from the elasticity or responsiveness of quantity to changes in price, from the reduction in quantities produced and purchased. If this elasticity or responsiveness is low, the excess burden is likewise reduced. Since the supply of land is inelastic, the quantity of surface area not expanding or contracting with changes in the site rentals, the taxation of site rentals has little if any deadweight loss. Indeed, there can even be an excess benefit from tapping site rentals, since if some plots were not being used productively, the title holders would be induced to either increase the productivity, to pay the site charge, or else sell it to someone who would do so. Vacant lots and surface-parking lots in the center of a city would soon be converted to office buildings, hotels, and apartments, increasing the supply of improvements. Such infilling would reduce the demand to build on the fringes of a city.

The elimination of income, value-added, sales and other excise taxes by SVT would eliminate the disincentives and burdens that stifle production and growth. The on-going study *Economic Freedom of the World 2000* (Gwartney et al, 2000) provides empirical evidence that countries with greater economic freedom have higher per-capita incomes and faster growth than those with less. Taxation is a key element of the degree of economic freedom, especially, as emphasized by that study, marginal tax rates, or the added tax for additional income. SVT reduces marginal tax rates to zero, thus being the ultimate in production-enhancing supply-side policy.

Site-value taxation also eliminates the implicit subsidy of landowners by government when it finances public works from taxes on labor. As noted above, civic works become capitalized in higher rentals and site values. When the site owners do not finance these works, in effect the government imposes a transfer of income from wages, profits, and other non-rental income to site-rentals. Consumers and workers pay twice for the public works, first with higher rentals and then again with taxes. SVT is also therefore neutral with regard to socially optimal speculation, i.e. in decisions as to the timing of construction, (Feder, 1996, 44), whereas taxes on labor and capital that capitalize up site values are distortive.

Site-value taxation helps inhibit the expansion of unproductive government debt. As Richard Wagner (1986, 209) notes, "When property comprises the tax base, liability for debt amortization rests on property owners in proportion to their ownership shares.... Hence, debt choices are capitalized into property values." Wagner adds that this is not equivalent to a personal debt choice. Nevertheless, when government debt is not related to productive investments which add to site rentals, landowners have an incentive to oppose the budget deficit, since it will come out of the rentals in the future if not now, and future payments will include interest not offset by future benefits.

The result of these effects is that the taxation of income, sales, and produced property creates a moral and economic imposition. There is not just a waste of resources but a redistribution of resources, the taxes being an instrument of domination hitting workers and enterprises with two burdens, the excess burden and the redistributive burden. In contrast, the use of site rentals for public revenue has little excess burden and avoids the subsidy to landowners. Site owners pay back to the government that value added by the civic works. SVT is a means of communal provision consistent with maximal prosperity and justice.

Urban sprawl can be defined as a greater amount of land use than would be the case in a pure free market. Current urban policy subsidizes sprawl first with zoning and other restrictions that reduce the intensity of urban land use, and second with taxes that subsidize the urban fringes at the expense of the center. New developments require more civic infrastructure, schools, and other services, mostly paid for from taxes other than the site rentals.

The sprawl induced by such interventions increase the cost of urban living and enterprise, reducing the effective standard of living and the profitability of investments. Pushing the urban margin outwards also increases the rentals of the city center, since the relative cost of transportation is lower there. An artificial lower density also inhibits the use of public transit, including privately provided transit such as jitneys, which are often also restricted by law. The effect is an increase in congestion. Even when suburb-to-suburb commuting mitigates the congestion and commute times, cities worldwide still face congested streets and highways that reduce the mobility essential to urban life.

Site-value taxation not only induces a more market-based compactedness of cities, but also facilitates urban mass transit. While jitneys and taxicabs offering flexible and personalized service at higher prices can be valuable elements in urban transit, large rail and bus systems typically have high fixed costs and low marginal costs. Their efficient funding (leaving aside the question of whether alternative transit would be more efficient) would charge the user only the marginal cost, or even provide gratis service, much like hotel elevators and department-store escalators do. The fixed cost of the capital goods and overhead would be paid for from the site rentals that have been increased by these transit services. SVT thus induces the natural density that makes public transit feasible and provides the means to finance the costs (Vickrey, 1977).

THE RULE OF LAW

The relationship between site-value taxation and the rule of law requires not just an analysis of this type of public finance, but also an inquiry as to the nature of the rule of law itself. The "rule of law" implies not merely that there are governmental laws enforced on a population, but the stronger principle that policy adhere to law rather than the caprice of officials. The rule of law also connotes the yet stricter principle that the laws themselves are stable and do not change with the whims of the governing officials.

The supreme law of an organized society makes up its constitution, such that all other laws must adhere to that highest-level framework. In any society, there is always a constitution, whether explicit in writing or implicit in custom and authority. The stability and constraints implied by the rule of law imply a constitution that is itself more stable than operating laws, and thus that the requirements for changing constitutional law are broader, such as requiring supermajorities and wider ratification requirements such as consent also by the voters or by other levels of government.

The rule of law is not an end in itself, but a means to something greater. There could be a rule of law under a regime in which slavery is legal or private enterprise is prohibited or free expression is suppressed. Most people presumably hold as a normative ideal not just a stability of law, but also that the content of the law provide for justice, liberty, and a basis for prosperity. Indeed, the purpose of the rule of law is to help preserve the provisions of a constitution that prescribe for liberty and justice, so that in practice the implementation is not eroded and evaded by power-seeking officials.

The question then is whether such principles of liberty and justice are themselves arbitrary, or whether they are grounded in stable, indeed eternal, foundations. If liberty is purely "socially constructed" so that it is a function only of the preferences of a particular society, then the law can change with the ebb and flow of political fads and erroneous economic doctrines. Tax rates can then rise or fall in response to changing economic conditions, the victory of a political party, or the influence of a demagogue. In the U.S. there is a continuous pattern of tax cuts followed by tax-rate increases as well as an ad-hoc hodge-podge complex of federal, state, and local taxation. There seems to be no consistent rule in the practice of taxation other than to extract revenue from the explicit flows with the least political resistance.

In its deepest sense, the rule of law implies that the desire of most folks for a legal infrastructure providing for genuine justice requires a constitution itself grounded in moral principles beyond the whims and caprice of the people themselves. The long-run and more important desire of people for justice must prevail over their short-run temptations to gain favors from government or attempt remedies for urgent problems such as poverty or crime which in the long run endanger their liberty and property.

If the foundation for the rule of law does not merely come from the arbitrary predilections of the public, from what could it derive? The natural-law philosopher John Locke (1690 [1947], 123) proposed that "The state of nature has a law of nature to govern it which obliges every one; and reason, which is that law, teaches all mankind who will but consult it that, being all equal and independent, no one ought to harm another in his life, health, liberty, or possessions..."

If there is a natural law in the "state of nature" apart from governmental law, then it must be inherent in human nature rather than coming from culture or personal views. Locke above states as premises of human nature the equality and independence of human beings. Independence, in the biological sense that each person has his own mind and body, implies that values are subjective to each individual rather than being inherent in things or even in society as a whole. Moral equality gives these values an equal standing, and also implies that there is in nature no inherent basis for master-slave relationships. This concept of moral equality, that human beings are "created equal," together with the independent determination of each individual as to his own good, provides the fundamental moral basis for constitutional constraints that limit governmental power.

A universal ethic that formulates the natural law derived from these Lockean premises provides for three basic moral rules (Foldvary, 1980):

1. Acts that are welcomed benefits to others are morally good.
2. Acts that coercively and invasively harm others are morally evil.
3. All other acts are morally neutral.

This natural law or universal ethic implies the existence of natural rights, which are merely another way of expressing the ethic. A right is a correlative of a wrong, such that the right to do or have X means that the negation of X by theft is wrong. Thus, having the right to own property means that it is morally wrong for others to steal it.

A constitution of liberty, with justice as a universal principle rather than based on arbitrary cultural norms, prohibits and penalizes only acts prescribed as evil by the universal ethic, leaving acts prescribed as neutral or good to the voluntary choices of the people. Moreover, the prohibition of coercive harm to others implies the principle of self-ownership, that a person may not be legally restricted in the exercise of peaceful and honest activity, and that arbitrary costs may not be imposed on peaceful and honest human action. If a person rightfully owns his body, time, and life, the logical implication is that a person fully owns his labor and his wages and products of labor.

By this analysis, natural law proscribes the arbitrarily taxation of wages, goods, and exchanges, i.e. taxing stocks of wealth or flows of income simply because they exist or because government "needs" the funds. Therefore, if the rule of law is to be based on natural and eternal moral principles, public finance must find other sources. These sources exist, since it is ethical to provide collective goods voluntarily by contract. Beyond voluntary exchange, it is not arbitrary to obtain restitution from human action that imposes significant costs upon others. Finally, since self-ownership does not extend to the benefits of natural resources, apart from the value due to human action, it does not violate the right to one's wages to tap rents due to natural opportunities and resources.

The 19th-century economist and social philosopher Henry George (1879 [1975], 561) proposed that economic and moral principles are in harmony: "the social law runs into and conforms with the moral law." In the most fundamental sense, site-value taxation implements the rule of law by providing justified rules grounded in individual sovereignty, yet also providing independence from social and political whims.

COMPARATIVE EFFECTS ON LAW AND GOVERNMENT

The effects of site-value taxation are not merely theoretical, since there have been numerous implementations. While almost all of these have been partial, used in combination with other taxes, nevertheless the empirical cases provide data for comparative analysis.

Many countries and localities have taxed site values aside from improvements, including cities in Australia, New Zealand, South Africa, and Pennsylvania (Cord, 1979; Chandler, 1982; Andelson, 2000). In Pennsylvania, cities may split their property tax into separate rates for land and improvements, and where they have done so, those cities having lower rates on buildings have had greater growth compared to nearby cities of similar size (Saunders, 1999). In Japan during the latter 1800s and Taiwan after 1950, the national taxation of land rent was a significant element of their rapid economic development (Chandler, 1982; Harrison, 1983). Some places, such as Hong Kong, have obtained substantial revenue from site leaseholds. (For a survey on the implementation of land-value taxation world-wide, see Andelson (2000)).

The most complete implementation of site-value taxation occurred in Kiaochow (now Jiaoxian), the German colony in China from 1898-1914, whose main city was Tsingtao, now Qingdao. The imperial commissioner, Ludwig Wilhelm Schrameier, a member of the German Land Reformers, established a land-value tax of six percent (Silagi, 1984; Peterson and Hsiao, 2000). Sun Yat-sen, China's revolutionary leader, was impressed with this example, and proposed land reforms and land-value taxation, which would later be put into the Chinese constitution in 1930, but only implemented in some cities until the Nationalists came to Taiwan and implemented it nation-wide in 1950 (Chandler, 1982).

Since the empirical examples are in accord with theoretical expectations, it should be possible to project a theory of the effects of a complete implementation of site-value public finance. A constitution that fully implements site-value taxation would consist of the following elements:

1. There shall be no taxation of labor, produced goods, exchanges, profits, value added, or persons, as such, other than on negative external effects as in (4) below.

2. Title holders of all land, including governmental, religious, and non-profit owners, pay an assessment based to the relevant communities based on the market value of the sites when put to their highest and best current use. The assessments for all sites shall be a public record, and site owners shall have the opportunity to appeal the assessments to impartial boards and ultimately to juries, paying the legal expense only if their assessments are found to be proper.

3. The improvements of and to a site, including buildings and the preparation of the ground, are exempt from any taxation. The value added by privately provided civic works and services by developers, civic associations, and enterprises shall not be taxed or assessed by government.

4. Significant negative pollution and congestion externalities imposed on others, when not compensated for by negotiation, arbitration, or civil law suits, shall be subject to payments to the relevant communities based on the imposed cost.

5. The title holders of sites in communities may form voluntary associations that provide for public goods and services, and deduct such payments from site-revenue charges for services that would otherwise be provided by government. Such consensual communities may have whatever internal payment methods they choose.

The effects of this Constitution on politics and the rule of law can now be compared with the alternative Constitution, that of taxing productive activity aside from any negative externalities. In practice, both income and sales taxes are applied selectively, with some income and goods exempt and with widely differing tax rates. We get the well-known effect of government using taxation to influence behavior as well as for revenue, and also perhaps unintended consequences such as the marriage-penalty of taxing a married couple at a higher rate than two single persons having the same total income.

The taxation of all explicit flows also has a high variance, with tax rates continuously changing, making it difficult for an enterprise to plan long-term projects, since future tax rates are uncertain. So far, there has been no futures market for tax liabilities that would enable firms to hedge against future tax risks the way they can hedge against changes in currency and commodity values.

Variance in time and among sites would also make SVT more uncertain and costly to enterprise, but this problem would be less severe than with other taxes. The site-revenue assessments would be based on market prices. A tax on site rental cannot be greater than the rental, providing a market-based upper limit to that revenue source. Ideally, the percentage of the site rentals assessed would be stable; the rate could even be a constitutional rule.

No human institution is perfect, but we can design institutions to minimize the opportunity for corruption and privileges. These institutions are more feasible for SVT because land has inherent public and immobile characteristics. Land cannot be hidden or moved out of the jurisdiction. The assessment records would be public, as they generally are today. It would therefore be easy to compare one's assessment with that of one's neighbors for discrepancies. As noted above, an appeal process would enable landowners to challenge assessments they deem to be greater than that of similar neighboring sites, or for a group of owners to challenge too-high assessments. A high rate of appeals could be a public signal that the assessments were being set too high.

However much SVT facilitates a more thorough rule of tax law, it is not sufficient for truly consensual governance and communal provisions that avoids domination. The residents and land-title holders should also be able to choose alternatives to the prevailing governmental services when feasible, in accord with the fifth constitutional principle set forth above. People could form lower-level governments or contractual associations that provide services such as street and lighting maintenance, garbage collection, schooling, and parks. Such private places already exist for the streets in St. Louis, as well as in residential associations (Foldvary, 1994). A constitutional provision for service and tax substitution, being able to withdraw some services from a jurisdiction and substitute private or local provision and funding, would reduce the scope of inefficient, corrupt, or biased governance.

Spencer MacCallum (1965, 58) has noted that in our relationship with government, contemporary society "suffers a schizophrenia," whereby "the same agency that provides wanted public services also performs such public disservices" in "cannibalizing the society" by taxation. Government becomes ambiguous, both benign in its services and yet also a threat to society. "The modern dilemma is that we have a continually growing need for community service that we know no way of getting except through the technique of sovereignty, which in turn exists by ... the abrogation of ownership." This is similar to the statement by Vincent Ostrom (1984) that public finance involves a "Faustian bargain" whereby government must use force, an evil, in order to obtain tax revenues needed to provide a good, the services wanted by the public.

MacCallum (1970) offers a way out of this dilemma, proprietary community as a vehicle that resolves the twin public-goods dilemma, free riding and transfer seeking, by combining governance with market. While MacCallum focuses on single-owner proprietorship, civic associations, such as condominiums and residential associations also provide a contractual medium that overcomes this schizophrenia, since these too are in effect if not explicitly financed from the rental value generated by the association's civic goods (Foldvary, 1994).

The contractual financing of public goods amounts to a unanimous consent of the members of the community. Knut Wicksell (1896 [1958]) sought to implement unanimity in requiring that each item of government expenditure be linked to its financing. Though for large groups unanimity may be impractical for operating decisions, unanimity can be implemented at the constitutional level, that of the initial agreement on and subsequent changes to the basic rules of a community and the choice of joining or leaving a community. Consensual provision works best, however, when governance is decentralized.

Gordon Tullock's (1994) analysis of decentralization concludes that the two major benefits of decentralized governance are the flexibility of local governance in adapting to local conditions, and the greater control of governance by residents.

Site- value taxes are amenable to local public finance, since sites can't run away when taxed and does not impose a marginal cost on the activity of the title holder. In contrast, enterprises and investment flee when their profits, sales, investments, and labor are taxed. Rent-based public finance is ideal for the bottom-up governance which I have elsewhere labeled "cellular" (Foldvary, 1999).

In cellular democracy, the foundational unit of governance is a small neighborhood district (cell) of several hundred persons. The residents elect a council, whose members may be recalled by petition and a special election at any time. In such small-scale voting, there is no need for mass media campaigns, and therefore little demand for campaign funds, relative to mass democracy where candidates much reach thousands or millions of voters. In a small neighborhood, it is easy to contact and meet the voters personally. Political parties may still operate and attempt to influence the voting, and special interests may attempt to bribe or sway the candidates and council members, but with a small population and limited local power, and with only the local council to monitor, council members who abuse their position will be watched and recalled much more easily than with mass democracy and multiple representatives.

A score of neighborhood councils form a higher-level association and elect representatives chosen from the first-level councils to the second-level council, also recallable at any time. The second-level council provides coordination among the first-level cells and provides public goods more efficiently provided at the second level, reducing spillover effects. The second-level council taxes the first-level councils for revenues rather than taxing the people directly. Individual households and firms are only taxed by their first-level council, although the site-value assessments are determined by boards of assessors selected by the councils of several levels to avoid fiscal bias.

A score or so of second-level councils then elect the next higher, third-level council from its second-level council members. Note that a third-level council member has been elected thrice, as he represents a first, second, and third level electorate. If he is removed at the first level, he is automatically removed from all higher-level seats.

Power as well as public revenues thus flow from the bottom to the top. Moreover, the associations are voluntary, a lower-level council being able to withdraw from the next-higher level council and join some other one. Combining small-group voting, bottom-up elections and funding, secession from higher levels, and representatives removable at will, the opportunity for "rent seeking" or privilege and transfer seeking by special interests, and the ability of officials to exploit their positions, becomes quite limited.

The diseases of mass democracy become cured much more readily with small-group voting than with mass-democratic constitutional structures such as separate branches of government and federal structures, because the root cause of transfer seeking is voting in large masses.

The scope of government has grown to leviathan size as an ever larger population creates an ever larger mass of voters whose incentives are to be ever more rationally ignorant because each vote becomes an ever smaller portion of the total. An ever larger mass of wealth provides an ever greater incentive to be taken by concentrated interests, the cost of each program spread so thinly among the voters and consumers that the cost of individual resistance is greater than the cost of the transfer.

This dysfunction is like a large river that overwhelms attempts to dam it with restrictions such as campaign-finance limitations that only treat its effects. If the basic cause is the incentives inherent in mass democracy, the remedy must remove the cause, which implies the opposite political structure, small-group voting where an individual voter votes for just one representative body. The public finance complementary to such a constitutional structure is SVT, since very local income and sales taxes drive out residents and enterprises unless the rates are uniform, and their collection is more efficient if centralized, given that people live and work in different areas, and that enterprises have presences in multiple jurisdictions.

A shift in taxation away from sales and income and towards a site-value base would create incentives to decentralize rather than move towards greater centricity. With centralized taxation, local government must seek transfers and "revenue sharing" or "matching grants" from higher-level governments, which typically come with "strings" that control the expenditure. With SVT, the revenue is efficiently collected locally, and the local demand would be to retain the funds rather than seek restricted grants from the top. Moreover, with bottom-up voting, officialdom would be more responsive to that demand.

Decentralized governance, even if not as complete as cellular democracy, would also provide for both more efficiency and choice because it would be more feasible for residents to choose the particular mix of public goods they desire. The seminal model of competition among communities in the provision of collective goods is that of Tiebout (1956), in which consumer-voters, voting with their feet, select the communities which best satisfy their preferences regarding local collective goods. This competition among communities provides a second source of efficiency, besides site-value public revenue.

Relevant to the concept of competition among communities is Friedrich Hayek's (1985 [1978]) treatment of competition as a discovery procedure. How can we determine the scarcity of goods, and the social value of the goods? As Hayek states, these are discovered by competition, by the bids and offers of goods in a rivalrous market. Two types of efficiency emerge for decentralized communities that finance their collective goods via rentals: the most efficient provision of goods within the community where marginal costs equal the marginal rents induced, and the marginal choice of a bundle of goods among various competing clubs. One community may be providing goods in a technically efficient way, given the choice of good, but then a second community may come up with superior goods, revealed by the fact that members of the first community migrate to the second, thereby inducing the first community to improve its provision of goods.

External effects are often pointed to as a problem for markets, distorting the prices by imposing costs and receiving uncompensated benefits from others. Buchanan and Goetz (1972) find that the internalization of the externalities could occur if the communities are proprietary and competition equalizes the value of the externality. "Tax shares would have to be related to the size of the *locational rent* component in individual income receipts" (35). "If all valued 'space' should be privately owned and if competition among proprietary ownership units were effective in all respects, allocational efficiency might emerge" (40). Many territorial externalities become capitalized into land rent, and when that rent is tapped for public finance, this eliminates the external effect, since compensation removes the externality.

Competition among communities is necessary, but not sufficient, to prevent site exploitation, i.e. the shifting of public revenue to spending that benefits the governing officials rather than the public, as well as wasteful spending. The corrupt and inefficient spending would become capitalized into lower site values, as the paid assessments would not be offset by corresponding benefits. Democracy may help in providing a "voice option" to the residents in addition to their exit option, but politics by itself does not eliminate site exploitation, since in a democracy, a faction may induce the government to grant it benefits at the expense of the others. Besides the exit and voice options, efficiency and equity require the contract option.

Constitutional provisions to protect the public from opportunistic exploitation include provisions for liberty, such that government may not restrict or impose costs on peaceful and honest human action, including speech, assembly, and enterprise. The constitution may also split government into branches and levels, and provide for elections. For nondemocratic governance by proprietary communities such as hotels or the corporate ownership of real-estate complexes and towns, contracts can and do specify in detail the terms of tenancy and the fees and assessments. This is even more critical when the proprietor owns title to the land and the site tenant owns the improvements.

Brennan and Buchanan (1977) note that the political-bureaucratic process maximizes revenues within the constitutional constraints. One could add that when the constitution prescribes site-value taxation as the major tax base, such maximization can be beneficial. The maximization of government revenues then implies the maximization of the site rentals. Since productive public works raise rentals and wasteful spending reduces rentals, such capitalization induces efficient governance when maximization is sought.

Brennan and Buchanan (1977) also note that maximum revenue is inversely related to the elasticity of the tax base. An inelastic base such as land can therefore yield a larger amount of revenue relative to the size tax base. There is no "Laffer curve" with site-rental taxation. The limitation of the tax base to site rentals and significant negative externalities provides an upper limit to a power-seeking Leviathan government. With site-rental taxation, the seeking of government transfers becomes rent seeking in two senses, the economic rent sense of returns not based on productive contributions, and in the sense of the return on site value. As a wasteful endeavor, rent seeking reduces the benefit stream that is the counterpart of the tax stream. Site owners therefore have an incentive to organize to limit such rent seeking. Unlike today, site owners themselves would not be able to rent seek on taxes imposed on returns to labor and capital.

While site owners would seek to minimize tax rates on site values, the reduction of government revenues also reduces the source of productive rental-generating public works. The political equilibrium would therefore likely be tax rates that are not so low that valued public works are starved of financing. Site owners would be residual claimants on generated site values. Site-value taxation has an inherent Wicksellian link between spending and revenue.

The provision of communal services without domination by government thus includes several interrelated strands. Site-value taxation provides public goods with economic efficiency and with a suitability to local governance.

Decentralized voting and governance would provide the political structure that keeps governance responsive to public desires while minimizing the influence of transfer-seeking special interests. Contractual communities provide for even greater consent and efficiency by their voluntary provision and competition. Rental-based public finance complements the rule of law in the most fundamental sense of basing its constitutional rules on principles of justice while also providing the means for society to enjoy as much growth and prosperity as people desire.

REFERENCES

Anderson, Robert V., ed. (2000) "Land-Value Taxation Around the World," 3rd ed. Annual supplement of Volume 59, *American Journal of Economics and Sociology*. Malden, MA.: Blackwell Publishers.

Brennan, Geoffrey and Buchanan, James. (1997) "Towards a Tax Constitution for Leviathan." *Journal of Public Economics* 8: pp. 255-273. Rpt. *The Theory of Public Choice II* (Buchanan and Tollison 1984, pp. 71-89).

Buchanan, James M. (1984) "Constitutional Restrictions on the Power of Government." In Buchanan, James and Tollison, Robert (eds.) *The Theory of Public Choice II*, pp. 439-452. Ann Arbor, MI.: University of Michigan Press.

Buchanan, James M. (1989) "Coercive Taxation in Constitutional Contract." In Tollison, Robert and Vanberg, Viktor (eds.) *Explorations into Constitutional Economics*. College Station, TX.: Texas A&M University Press: pp. 309-328.

Buchanan, James M. and Goetz, Charles J. (1972). "Efficiency Limits of Fiscal Mobility." Journal of Public Economics 1: 25-43. Rpt. *Explorations into Constitutional Economics* (Tollison and Vanberg 1989, pp. 246-263).

Chandler, Tertius (1982). *The Tax We Need.* Berkeley CA.: The Gutenberg Press.

Congressional Budget Office (1996). "The Incidence of the Corporate Income Tax." CBO Paper (March).

Cord, Steven (1979). "Catalyst! How a Reform of the Property Tax Can Revitalize Our Cities and Counter Inflation and Recession." Indiana, PA.: Henry George Foundation of America.

Feder, Kris (1996). "Geo-economics." In Foldvary, Fred (ed.) *Beyond Neoclassical Economics: Heterdox Approaches to Economic Theory*, pp. 41-60. Aldershot, UK: Edward Elgar Publishing.

Foldvary, Fred E. (1980). *The Soul of Liberty*. San Francisco, CA.: The Gutenberg Press.

Foldvary, Fred E. (1994). *Public Goods and Private Communities*. Aldershot, UK: Edward Elgar Publishing

Foldvary, Fred E.(1999),"Recalculating Consent." Buchanan Festschrist http://www.gmu.edu/jbc/fest/files/foldvary.htm.

Gaffney, Mason (1964). *Containment Policies for Urban Sprawl.* Lawrence, KS.: University of Kansas Publications, Governmental Research Series No. 27.

Gaffney, Mason (1970). "Adequacy of Land as a Tax Base." In *The Assessment of Land Value.* Daniel Holland (ed.) Madison, WI: University of Wisconsin Press.

Gaffney, Mason (1994). "Land as a Distinctive Factor of Production." In *Land and Taxation*, pp. 39-102. N. Tideman (ed.) London, UK.: Shepeard-Walwyn.

George, Henry (1879 [1975]). *Progress and Poverty.* New York, NY.: Robert Schalkenbach.

Gwartney, James, Lawson, Robert, and Dexter, Samida (eds.). (2000) *Economic Freedom of the World 2000.* Vancouver, B.C., Canada: The Fraser Institute.

Harrison, Fred (1983). *The Power in the Land.* New York, NY.: Universe Books.

Hayek, Friedrich A. (1978[1985]). "Competition as a Discovery Procedure." In *Studies in Philosophy, Politics, Economics, and the History of Ideas.* Chicago, IL.: University of Chicago Press, pp. 179-90.

Locke, John (1690[1947]). *Two Treatises of Government.* New York, NY.: Hafner Press.

MacCallum, Spencer (1965). "The Social Nature of Ownership." *Modern Age* 9, No. 1 (Winter 1964-65), pp. 49-61.

MacCallum, Spencer (1970). *The Art of Community.* Menlo Park, NJ.: Institute for Humane Studies.

Miles, Mike (1990). "What is the Value of All U. S. Real Estate?" *Real Estate Review 20*, No. 2 (Summer), pp. 69-75.

Ostrum, Vincent (1984). "Why Governments Fail: An Inquiry into the Use of Instruments of Evil to do Good." In Buchanan, James M. and Tollison, Robert D. (eds.). *The Theory of Public Choice II.* Ann Arbor, MI.: University of Michigan Press, pp. 422-435.

Peterson, V.G. and Tseng Hsiao (2000). "Kiao-chau." In *Land-Value Taxation Around the World,*

Robert Andelson (ed.). Balden, MA.: Blackwell Publishers.

Saunders, Vernon I. (1999). " In Defense of the Two-Rate Property Tax."In *Land-Value Taxation: The Equitable and Efficient Source of Public Finance*. New York, NY.: M. E. Sharpe. pp. 269-276.

Silagi, Michael (1984). "Land Reform in Kiaochow, China: From 1898 To 1914 the Menace of Disastrous Land Speculation was Averted by Taxation." *American Journal of Economics and Sociology* 43, No. 2 (April), pp. 167-177.

Tideman, T. Nicolaus (1994). "The Economics of Efficient Taxes on Land." In *Land and Taxation*. Tideman, T. Nicolaus (ed.). London, UK.: Shepheard-Walwyn, pp. 103-140.

Tideman, T. Nicolaus and Plassmann, Florenz (1998). "Taxed Out of Work and Wealth: The Costs of Taxing Labor and Capital." In *The Losses of Nations*. Fred Harrison (ed.). London, UK.: Othila Press, pp. 126-174.

Tiebout, Charles M. (1956). "A Pure Theory of Local Expenditures." *Journal of Political Economy 64*, pp. 416-424.

Tucker, Gilbert M. (1958). *The Self-Supporting City*. New York, NY.: Schalkenbach Foundation.

Tullock, Gordon (1994). *The New Federalist*. Vancouver, B.C., Canada: Fraser Institute.

Vickrey, William (1977). "The City as a Firm." *Economics of Public Services*. Fedstein, extra Martin and Inman, Robert (eds.). pp. 334-343. Rpt. William Vickrey (1994). *Public Economics*, pp. 339-349. Cambridge, UK.: Cambridge University Press.

Wagner, Richard E. (1980). "Boom and Bust: The Political Economy Of Economic Disorder." *Journal of Libertarian Studies* 4, No. (Winter) pp. 1-37. Rpt. *The Theory of Public Choice II*. (Buchanan and Tollison 1984) pp. 238-272.

Wagner, Richard E. (1986). "Liability Rules, Fiscal Institutions, and the Debt." In *Deficits*. Buchanan, James M., Rowley, Charles K., Tollison, Robert D. (eds.). New York, NY.: Basil Blackwell.

Wicksell, Knut (1958). " A New Principle of Just Taxation." In *Classics in the Theory of Public Finance*. Musgrave, R. A. and Peacock, Alan T. (eds.). London, UK.: Macmillan & Co.

11 ZONING, SMART GROWTH, AND REGULATORY TAXATION

Samuel R. Staley

INTRODUCTION

The debate over urban sprawl and Smart-Growth has thrust land-use planning to the forefront of public debate in the United States. State Legislatures throughout the nation are considering sweeping new laws that could radically change the nature and character of land development in urban as well as rural areas. In some cases, such as Florida and Oregon, these laws are explicitly top-down—the state sets goals and objectives and local governments are expected to tow the line. Indeed, Florida's law (enacted in 1985) is quite clear that growth-management should actively shape the urban form of the state by encouraging higher density, mixed uses, and mass transit (Audirac, Shermyen, and Smith 1990; Holcombe 1994). More recently, Wisconsin enacted Smart-Growth legislation that included the design of a model zoning ordinance that all large cities would be required to adopt as a way to combat urban sprawl.

While the nation periodically moves through waves of new planning theories and experimentation, few trends seem to have the staying power or visibility embodied in the contemporary Smart-Growth movement. In fact, the very character of the current wave of zoning reforms is fundamentally different from previous eras of planning reform and has been shaped by past economic and political successes. At no other time in U.S. history has planning, particularly zoning, had such widespread acceptance, nor citizens been willing to use the levers of local government to pursue planning goals.

This chapter examines Smart-Growth planning reforms at the state and local level through the lens of public finance and economics. More specifically, it uses an economic perspective of taxation to understand both the political motivations behind support for Smart-Growth initiatives and the potential impacts of imposing some of the new wave of growth controls. Zoning and Smart-Growth, it turns out, are simply alternative ways local governments can redistribute wealth from one (usually politically powerful) group to another (less politically powerful) group although they often using quite different rationales in the public debate. Rather than using the 20th century method of using taxes to directly generate revenues for social programs to benefit certain groups (e.g., the poor, senior citizens, etc.), Smart-Growth has emerged as a regulatory mechanism local and regional governments use to redistribute wealth within cities and regions. Indeed, the growth-management movement is, in many respects, distinctly 21st century in its character and impacts, a product of an affluent society well versed in the use of government to accomplish objectives and maximize personal gain.

Government action can, in principle, enhance community welfare by encouraging the efficient and productive use of resources and securing private property rights. Unfortunately, many of the tools and recommendations of the Smart-Growth movement may likely have the opposite effect—creating uncertainty and destabilizing private property rights. The consequences, however, of adopting many of these growth controls are not fully vetted in the public debate. In part, this is because the rhetoric of planning reform focuses on potentially legitimate functions of government—the protection of property rights, reducing spillover impacts, and protecting public goods—even though the tools are fundamentally redistributive in their effects and, in many cases, intentions.

ZONING AND SMART GROWTH

In the case of Smart-Growth, citizens and public officials use the tools of the urban planner to avoid conventional forms of taxation to provide public goods and services. Rather than purchase land for parks, open-space preservation, or recreation, growth-management advocates use land-use regulation to prevent the development of open space for urban uses. In other words, they use the regulatory process to provide a good or service the private market is unwilling to provide through normal, consumer-driven market transactions. In other cases, interest groups may use land-use regulation as a way to protect themselves from changes in their industry that potentially threaten their profitability. Farmers, for example, facing a globally competitive market, use development controls to protect a key asset—land—from competition from nonagricultural uses such as housing or commercial development. In each of these cases, the regulatory framework of growth control is used to transfer wealth from one group to another, behavior which is sometimes called "rent seeking." (Tullock 1967; see also Mueller 1989)

Zoning, not surprisingly, has become the tool of choice for executing this redistribution of wealth through growth management. As the most pervasive planning tool in the United States, zoning has the benefit of widespread acceptance and familiarity in state and local politics. In fact, despite its inherently centralized approach to land use and regulating markets, zoning receives bipartisan support. Conservatives and liberals use it when they believe it serves their interests, whether preventing development of a neighbor's property or attempting to script a centrally planned vision of their community. Ironically, zoning and planning have received some of their strongest support on the national level during Republican Presidencies:

- The Standard City Planning Enabling Act was published in 1928 under the auspices of U.S. Department of Commerce Secretary and future President Herbert Hoover;
- During the Eisenhower Administration, the Housing Act of 1954 created the basic features of the urban-renewal program and required these projects to be part of a comprehensive city plan. Title 1, Section 701 provided federal funding for planning, creating "vast employment opportunities for planners" as well as seeding "a major private urban development consulting industry in America." (Gerckens 1979, p. 47);
- Significant expansions of programs in the U.S. Department of Housing and Urban Development, including the full implementation of the Model Cities program and large-scale public-housing subsidies, occurred during the Nixon Administration. In fact, more public housing units were funded or subsidized between 1968 and 1973 than in the previous two decades (Feldman and Florida 1990, p. 41).

On the local level, zoning has emerged as the planning tool of choice for property owners hoping to protect themselves from nuisances or changing market conditions in their communities. Zoning has also evolved into a cumbersome and unwieldy mechanism for regulating the spillover impacts of land development and has codified centralized land-use control as the cornerstone of development regulation in the United States.

The modern wave of Smart Growth, however, superimposes a new function on zoning and land-use regulation—centralized land-use planning to implement a utopian vision of the future. This may be best illustrated by the Coordinated Planning Act (CPA), a planning-reform proposal introduced in the Michigan Legislature in 2001. The Act, using public concern about urban sprawl as its lightening rod, would require cities and towns to adopt comprehensive plans that conform to a 20-year vision of what the community should look like, how it should function, and what kinds of housing and businesses would locate there. In this respect, the CPA follows the model pioneered by states such as California, Hawaii, Oregon, Florida, and Washington.

Advocates, however, have completely ignored the redistributional consequences of further politicizing the land-development process by broadening the scope of development regulation. In Michigan, as well as other states, additional political controls over land development are likely to create new incentives to use regulation as a mechanism for redistributing wealth from less-favored to more-favored groups through the legislative policymaking process. As a consequence, its role as a way to protect property rights and create certainty in development erodes. In addition, most often the redistribution is away from future and low-income residents and toward existing homeowners and wealthy interest groups. Understanding how this process works is not obvious, but a better grounding in the economics of taxation, regulation, and wealth distribution helps illuminate the issues and improves our understanding of growth management's impacts on the policy process.

REGULATION, TAXATION, AND RENT SEEKING

From an economist's perspective, regulation serves several purposes. In the classic textbook case, regulation tries to correct for real or perceived failures in the private market to produce necessary goods and services in a way that maximizes society's welfare (Holcombe 1996, 117-118). In some cases, private parties might not have an incentive to incorporate the full social costs of their behavior into their actions. Many in the Smart-Growth movement, for example, would argue that property owners—mainly farmers—need to be regulated more stringently because they would sell their land for housing when the "socially optimal" use would be to leave it as open space. This has emerged as a primary justification for urban-growth boundaries, agricultural zoning, and large minimum lot sizes to prevent development (Staley, Edgens, and Mildner 1999). A second reason government might regulate behavior is because private parties might not have sufficient information to make the "right" choice—if one is not fully informed about costs and benefits of a transaction, the outcome might not be efficient or socially optimal.

The quality and completeness of information is particularly relevant in discussions of public subsidies to new development. If local governments extend water, sewer, and other infrastructure to residential developments, for example, the full costs of providing those services will not be incorporated into the market price of the house. Thus, the homebuyer will not be fully aware of the costs of supporting the new housing with infrastructure paid for by existing residents. Thus, the market price of the house will be lower than if the full costs of infrastructure were included. As a result, homebuyers might buy a larger home or a larger lot than they would have when faced with the full costs of the purchase. These issues, however, have been addressed elsewhere and are beyond the scope of this chapter, which focuses on the redistributive qualities of regulation and taxation. For a more complete discussion of infrastructure pricing and costs, see Staley, Edgens, and Mildner (1999).

Beyond these "instrumental" functions, a more fundamental role of regulation may be to protect property rights. Laws regulate human behavior by creating boundaries and accountability for individual human action in a broader social context. Laws codify rules of civil society, providing a foundation for social and economic order. They become a critical element of market economies because they provide an institutional framework for voluntary transactions—they provide a foundation for contracts and contract enforcement. In land development, laws establish the legal rules of the game that make markets effective and efficient. Regulation, like law, puts binding constraints on private actions to prevent people from doing certain things—like selling farmland for housing, or putting too many houses on a specific plot of land. Whether a local government has "taken" private property is determined by whether the property was seized for a legally valid public purpose. Zoning, in principle, is a legally defensible restriction on property owners because it prevents them from using private property in a way that diminishes the public good. In general, the courts have defined public purpose very broadly, but the principle remains intact: private action can be regulated if it serves the general welfare.

If planning and zoning reduce the transaction costs associated with land development and create certainty in the development approval process, community welfare can be enhanced through the more efficient and productive development of land (Staley 2001c; Lai 1997). In fact, the creation of area-wide zoning often serves this function by subjecting similar parcels of land (if not use) to the same development rules and constraints (Lai 1996). But, regulation's purpose in general, and land-use regulation in particular, is not limited to these functions. It has another, redistributive quality that makes it both politically popular and sustainable. In fact, this redistributional quality may be the most salient factor explaining the popularity of current Smart-Growth initiatives since the protection of open space on the urban fringe is often the principle justification for more extensive land-use regulation to curb urban sprawl (Staley 2001d).

Taxation vs. Regulation

The purpose of taxation is both functional and political. Functionally, taxation raises revenue to finance government services and programs. The purpose of these programs, of course, is to provide goods and services that individuals can not consume individually through the private market. The classic case is national defense, but an entire range of services potentially fits this bill—subsidized housing for low-income families, retirement income for the poor, health care for senior citizens, etc. Decisions about who receives the benefits of government action, and who pays, are fundamentally political, not economic. In short, politically, taxation is used to extract wealth from one group to redistribute it to another group and represents a wealth transfer. Regulation can and does serve the same purpose (Peltzman 1976; Stigler 1971).

Conceptually, the redistributional elements of taxation are noncontroversial, at least in academic circles. Taxation, the dominant form of raising revenues to pay for public services, usually implies an explicit transfer of wealth from one group to another. In fact, the definition of taxation requires that the revenue is separated legally and functionally from expenses for specific goods and services. Indeed, this makes sense for a host of public services. User fees, for example, would defeat the purpose of providing a housing subsidy to poor families.[1] The purpose of any social-welfare program is to use the compulsive powers of taxation to transfer wealth from higher-income families to poorer families in an effort to enhance the quality of life for those less well off (e.g., provide a house or apartment they could not afford to buy on their own in the private market).

Taxes and user fees, however, are often unpopular, and, in many cases, would be too onerous to achieve some policy goals. This is particularly true in the area of land use (as the next section points out), but it highlights regulation as an alternative way to transfer wealth using public policy. Unfortunately, the redistributional quality of regulation is not as intuitive or obvious as direct taxation. Some regulation is protective in nature, and its purpose (if not effect) is to protect property rights, civil liberties, and public welfare. For example, criminal law is used to ensure the personal safety of citizens from acts of aggression and fraud from others (e.g., assault, robbery, murder, etc.). Civil law is used to resolve disputes among people (or businesses) when a crime has not been committed but someone's action negatively impacts someone else. If a tangible harm can be shown, often the party inflicting the damage compensates the victim, and the issue is resolved through civil court proceedings. These protective qualities can enhance community welfare, particularly in land use, if they create certainty and consistency during the land development process or protect property rights by ensuring the mitigation of, or compensation for, spillover impacts from development. If a property owner agrees to sell his land and signs a contract promising to sell the property for a specific amount, the buyer can sue the property owner if he reneges and the prospective buyer can show significant, tangible harm. Breaking a contract is not necessarily against the law, but it can inflict damages that can be recovered through the tort system (civil courts). This, in effect, is a protective function that provides the foundation for exchange and contract.

One of the purposes of the legal system is to provide certainty and specificity and create an environment in which decisions can be made now based on reasonable expectations about the future. If someone breaks the law, and they are likely to be caught and held accountable through punishment or restitution, security is increased for citizens through both the deterrent effect of law enforcement as well as the knowledge the perpetrator(s) will be unable to commit the same crime again. Similarly, the protective quality of land-use regulation can enhance community welfare by ensuring some groups do not unfairly burden others in the community by their actions. Land-use regulation, for example, can help mitigate the spillover effects of stormwater runoff by requiring detention and retention basins that more adequately regulate the flow of water off some properties and onto others (or in streams, lakes, or tributaries).

The protection of property rights and providing accountability in contract are fundamentally different from using regulation to redistribute wealth. Protecting property rights and ensuring the integrity of contracts is a positive-sum game: both parties benefit from the contract or exchange because they promote investments in the future based on expectations about responsibilities and commitments made now. Conventional planning, in fact, attempts to achieve this in principle by creating certainty about future land uses and development patterns (Staley 2001c; Lai 1997). In practice, however, planning is a political exercise (see the discussion in Staley 2001b). Planning decisions are approved through the legislative process and professional planners can influence but not dictate land-use policy. The open-ended nature of the legislative process creates uncertainty for land developers which is unavoidable as long as these decisions are made (directly or indirectly) via the electoral process. Politics, then, can transform the planning process into a zero-sum game (where winning depends on someone else's loss) as interest groups compete for a share of the existing pie. To the extent the political system is used to transfer wealth from one less-favored group to another more politically powerful group without a consensus on objectives or social benefits, social welfare will be reduced. Thus, the institutional setting of land-use decision making provides an incentive to focus on short-term political gain. Often, elected and appointed officials, even professional planners, can take advantage of the relatively arcane and technical nature of development control to extract "rents" from landowners and property developers. A developer may be unwilling to legally challenge a city council for fear of future reprisals, and thus succumb to current restrictions on the project or privately finance products and services (e.g., bikeways or road widenings) that are in reality public goods.

In fact, the regulatory process can create a system where this kind of political activity is common. Since regulation can be used to prevent entry into markets, firms can lobby elected and appointed public officials to create a noncompetitive market by limiting entry, pushing prices higher than would exist under competitive, open-entry conditions. These potential rents from a regulation-protected monopoly (or oligopoly), create strong incentives for special-interest groups and firms to lobby governments to limit competition (Mueller 1989, pp. 235-244). Economists have found evidence of rent-seeking behavior in lobbying efforts of various businesses and special-interest groups to regulate utilities and international trade. Consumers and citizens may also use the political process to increase regulation and secure benefits unavailable through a competitive market (e.g., subsidized electricity). In fact, a savvy politician may well recognize the political benefits of restricting private markets if they believe it will benefit the majority of his constituents (Peltzman 1976).

SMART GROWTH, REGULATION, AND WEALTH REDISTRIBUTION

Zoning and other forms of land-use controls are increasingly used to promote public-policy goals beyond protecting property rights, mitigating harm, and recovering losses (financial or otherwise). Indeed, most growth-management strategies may be fundamentally redistributive in nature, not protective, even though they are justified under the "police powers"—the authority of national, state, and local governments to regulate private activity—granted by the federal and most state constitutions. Judicial deference to local governments on land-use matters created opportunities for rent seeking. Thus, the infusion of politics into the land development process, a trend likely to be encouraged under Smart Growth (Staley 2001b), has the potential of shifting the focus of regulation from protecting property rights and providing legitimate public goods to rent-seeking behavior.

Legally, planning and zoning are legitimate exercises of police powers if they link regulation specifically to the policy goals of zoning codes and master plans. As long as property has some economic value (literally, a value greater than zero), and planning is tied explicitly to the purpose of promoting the general welfare and community interest, local governments are effectively given free reign over development regulation. Thus, local growth controls can impose moratoria on new developments as long as they are not permanent, or do not have the effect of permanently preventing development at some future date. This judicial support for local planning allows many communities to create and implement detailed land-use plans that (in principle) can plot out the future development of a community.

In reality, these plans are rarely successful. Many Smart-Growth advocates assume the political process will work effectively and efficiently and unrealistically presume an ability to predict future population and economic trends that effectively makes the plans obsolete as soon as they are approved (see the discussion in Staley and Scarlett 1998). Yet, comprehensive plans are rarely updated in a systematic or methodical way, trends and forecasts are riddled with uncertainty, and zoning maps are routinely amended ad hoc as local planning boards and city councils adapt to the realities of the market place. Even when changes are not made ad hoc, the planning process and zoning maps have often inefficiently locked land into proscribed uses irrespective of actual market trends, demand, or evolving needs within the community. While paying lip service to how communities evolve, comprehensive planning is not an organic process; it operates largely within a static, "closed-system" framework, where land uses are established in an existing map geared toward an abstract, long-term "vision" of what a community will look like. Most of the realities of urban development—new residents, changing community values, elected-official turnover, changing market conditions—are ignored, compromising the integrity of the planning process.

The inconsistency between the planning ideals and the realities of plan implementation provide unique opportunities for rent seeking. If zoning maps and comprehensive plans need to be amended to accommodate changing market conditions or a community's evolution, special-interest groups can use the development-control process as a way to extract rents from less politically powerful groups (e.g., future residents, low-income residents, niche-housing markets). In fact, several of the more popular Smart-Growth recommendations lend themselves to this kind of rent-seeking activity through the land-use regulation process.

Urban-Growth Boundaries

Urban-growth boundaries are politically established lines around urban areas that place some land off limits to development (Staley, Edgens, and Mildner 1999). The effect is to increase the value of land inside the boundary as land outside the boundary becomes difficult to develop. Within the first year of establishing Portland, Oregon's regional-growth boundary, for example, land values inside the boundary were four times the value of land outside the boundary (Knaap 1985). Thus, wealth is transferred from rural land owners outside the boundary to urban land owners inside the boundary.

Attempts to promote infill housing over large-scale development on vacant land also has a redistributive effect. Infill housing is typically more expensive to build because land prices are higher in urban areas, demolition and renovation costs are typically greater than building from scratch, and builders have difficulty achieving economies of scale for their projects (Staley, Edgens, and Mildner 1999). In addition, building at higher densities is more expensive because high-rise buildings require different designs and engineering standards. Florida State University Economist Randall G. Holcombe estimates that a mid-rise apartment building of four to seven floors would cost 26 percent more to build per square foot than a low-rise apartment buildings of one to four floors (Holcombe 2000, pp. 34-35). Not surprisingly, housing production is lower in neighborhoods that depend on infill and higher density housing to meet housing needs. An analysis of housing development in Portland, Oregon found that neighborhoods depending on infill or redevelopment of existing properties had lower overall rates of housing production than neighborhoods depending on new housing (Conder 1999). Public policy that explicitly relies on infill to increase housing supply is likely to encourage housing price appreciation, in effect transferring wealth from first-time homebuyers and renters to existing residents and property owners.

Minimum Lot-Size Requirements

Many communities are attempting to manage growth or slow development by adopting minimum lot sizes of 10 or 20 acres per housing unit in rural areas. This has the effect of slowing overall housing production and protecting open space, but also reflects a wealth transfer through regulation from existing land owners (often farmers) interested in selling their land for development to other property owners who want to protect the aesthetic qualities of their current lifestyle.

Minimum lot-size regulations may be the most widely used zoning technique to protect farmland (Daniels and Bowers 1997, pp. 117-118). In fact, consultants have been asked explicitly by members of planning boards how large the minimum lot size should be to discourage development. In these cases, the intent is obvious if not openly stated: The regulatory process can be used effectively to discourage development with minimal financial impact on the local government because it will not legally be considered a Fifth Amendment "taking" and require compensation to the landowners. In short, they can be financially cheap ways to keep large parcels of land as open space.

The political benefits are fairly easy to see. In November 2000, Ohio voters approved a $200 million bond initiative to finance the purchase of development rights and conservation easements for farmland and open space. The initiative was promoted as a way to curb urban sprawl and mitigate farmland loss due to urbanization. The initiative, however, even if fully financed, would only protect about 15,000 acres per year (The Buckeye Institute 2001). Over a ten-year period, the initiative might protect 2 percent of the state's farmland, clearly an insufficient amount to curb urban sprawl. If the state wanted to replicate New Jersey's initiative, fully funding a program to protect half of the existing farmland, the Ohio legislature would have to approve funding equivalent to more than $15 billion dollars (excluding interest on bonds). This level of funding is clearly beyond the willingness of most politicians to bare, particularly one that obviously and openly benefits an already well-off population (most suburbanites).

Ballot-Box Zoning

Another increasingly popular feature of Smart-Growth policies is expanding public participation in land-use regulation. In California, a series of growth-management initiatives dubbed "SOAR" (Save Open-Space and Agricultural

Resources) has led to the adoption of restrictive growth controls in dozens of cities and counties. Most SOAR initiatives include broad-based citizen participation through referenda and initiatives, and most of these efforts have been promoted as a form of rational planning. In the San Francisco Bay Area, for example, Citizen Activists for Public Planning (CAPP) supported initiatives that would subject housing developments of 10 units or more to public vote, arguing the proposals were not intended to discourage growth but improve its quality (Staley 2001c). One of the more heralded cases is Ventura County, California where growth boundaries were established around each of the county's ten cities and any expansion of the growth boundary, or rezoning of the property from agricultural to urban uses must be approved by popular ballot. Similarly, the Sierra Club has supported grass roots civic activism at the ballot box as a way of mobilizing "voter concern" about sprawl (*The Dark Side of the American Dream*, n.d.). Ballot-box zoning, in essence, gives citizens more "voice" in land-use decisions, implying that greater public participation in the land-development process would, in fact, improve the efficiency of land development and maximize social welfare.

Unfortunately, the reality of ballot-box planning is inconsistent with the hope. An analysis of ballot-box zoning in 63 Ohio cities found citizen-initiated referenda on site-specific rezoning requests had a consistent, negative impact on housing-unit growth, regardless of whether the community voted in favor of the request or against it (Staley 2001c). Communities that subjected rezoning issues to a public vote experienced an annual "growth penalty" of between 19.4 to 28.7 housing permits for every 1,000 population. For a city of 50,000 people, this translates into a penalty of almost 1,000 building permits, suggesting that the uncertainties introduced into the planning process by broad public participation in the details of plan implementation may have significant impacts on building activity and growth.[2] The mere fact that citizens place land-use decisions on the ballot appears to be a signal to developers that their projects will be subject to higher levels of uncertainty and delay compared to cities that resolve land-use decisions through more conventional legislative or administrative process.

Another study of comprehensive plans and amendments (rezonings) in Ventura County, California and its 10 cities found that the development projects were approved at densities 45 percent lower than the planned capacities (Fulton, Williams, Jones, 2001). Similarly, in Oregon, actual densities inside the growth boundaries ranged from 33 percent to 75 percent lower than the levels permitted by local comprehensive plans (Howe 1993, p. 70). In Portland, densities were one-third lower than those permitted by local land-use plans (Howe 1993). Combined, this evidence suggests that planning goals are often inconsistent with development realities, increasing the scope for rent seeking to use the development-approval process to meet narrow private goals. In fact, the evidence in Ventura County suggests that one reason actual development densities are lower than planned densities is a "knock down" that occurs in the pre-application process (Fulton, Williamson, and Jones 2001).

Staff planners realize that planning commissioners will not approve high-density projects, so they recommend reducing overall densities to ensure their acceptance by the board and city council (see also Seigan 1990).

Implications for Planning

The implications are important for understanding the dynamics of planning reforms, their impacts on housing markets, and their distributional effects. Even as proponents of more restrictive growth-management policies and development controls argue their intent is to manage growth more effectively, the effects can be to slow (or even stop) growth. Historically, citywide zoning was adopted more quickly in cities with ward systems of voting, suggesting that protecting existing land uses from market pressure had politically important, geographically targeted benefits independent of nuisance mitigation (Clingermayer 1993). In fact, high homeownership rates were important factors in whether a city adopted a comprehensive zoning ordinance, indicating many politicians could use zoning to protect existing land uses from a competitive land market by limiting competition from other uses and bolster their popularity at the ballot box (Clingermayer 1993). Thus, using the political system, anti-growth special interests can use the regulatory process as a mechanism for taxing the wealth of future residents and existing property owners via the land development process. Regulation thus becomes a form of redistributional taxation.

In short, so-called Smart Growth, the emerging conventional wisdom over how growth should be managed on the local level, represents a series of growth-control policies that focus largely on redistributing wealth from one group to another. The current environment for planning reform is different from previous ones primarily because:

(1) The pervasiveness and acceptance of modern planning in communities;
(2) The willingness of local residents to use the political process to achieve narrow political goals;
(3) The judicially unrestrained and legally undisciplined environment in which growth controls are created, promulgated, and implemented at the state and local levels.

The analysis so far, however, has been relatively abstract. But, redistribution of wealth from one group to another in the development-control process can have significant, concrete impacts. The next section illustrates how these impacts manifest themselves in the real-estate market using an example from a historic preservation effort in a Midwestern city.

THE CASE OF HISTORIC PRESERVATION

Cities and towns are increasingly using historic-preservation ordinances and districts to preserve cultural amenities and landmarks. Indeed, this is encouraged in the current Smart-Growth environment because older buildings and landmarks are used to create a distinct sense of place. Historic preservation has also become popular because of its emphasis on maintaining and redeveloping the urban core as a way to lower demand for housing on the urban fringe. In practice, historic preservationists have focused primarily on downtown areas, promoting preservation as a tool for protecting the residential and commercial character of specific neighborhoods. To the extent these ordinances protect or produce a public good, or create certainty about development regulation, they can enhance community welfare.

But, as the previous sections suggest, historic preservation ordinances can be viewed as part of a broader movement to use the regulatory process to extract concessions from private developers. The concessions could include parks, recreation areas, schools and public facilities, and other amenities (see Ross and Thorpe 1992). The use of exactions to obtain public amenities, also called "linkages," are often viewed positively in the economic-development planning literature (Nelson, Frank and Nichols 1992) because they represent mechanisms for mitigating market failures and preserving the aesthetic qualities of neighborhoods and cities.

In the case of historic preservation, local ordinances allow a city council, planning board, or council-appointed review board to subject private property to strict development controls. These designations can be applied broadly to entire neighborhoods through district-wide regulation or to individual buildings. Buildings subject to historic-preservation ordinances are required to go through more rigorous review processes over improvements, renovations, or demolition. More importantly for this discussion, historic-district ordinances allow a public body to mandate changes to private property without bearing the financial burden of compliance. For example, historic preservation ordinances often regulate colors, facades, architectural detail, as well as the structural characteristics of new and renovated buildings.

Historic-preservation ordinances, however, are implemented in an open-ended political environment, where policy goals and standards can shift with the membership of the review boards and city councils. Since historic-preservation ordinances allow government agencies to impose strict controls on development and building renovation at little direct cost to the local government, the potential exists for political and economic inequities to emerge in their implementation. Thus, they also provide important insight into the dynamics of regulatory taxation. In the case of new development, these costs can be passed on to future residents through legally enforceable mandates. The analysis below is based on a case from a wealthy suburban city in Ohio that designated a nineteenth century farmhouse on a 30-acre undeveloped tract as an historic landmark.

Background and Context

The City of Centerville, Ohio rests in the center of a growth corridor directly south of Dayton, a metropolitan area consisting of four counties and a population of a little under one million residents. Centerville benefited from central-city out-migration during the 1960s and 1970s and the decentralization of manufacturing in the 1970s and 1980s. Rapid growth pushed the city's population from fewer than five thousand in 1960 to more than twenty thousand in 1990. Not surprisingly, more than half of its land, 51.3 percent, is developed residentially.

Centerville's commercial base is growing at a higher rate than the average for other cities in urban counties in Ohio, but less than 15 percent of the land in the city is used for industrial or commercial property. The city has expanded through annexation, and 36 percent of the land inside its borders is either vacant or agricultural. The zoning code and development-approval process is explicitly designed to protect the residential character of the community. Centerville is also relatively wealthy with a median household income significantly higher than the state average and a poverty rate that is one of the lowest in the state.

The city has also adopted numerous vehicles for expediting planning and zoning applications. Staff are assigned as case managers to applications as they are submitted, and voluntary preapplication meetings with the staff and planing board are encouraged. These features of the planning process help ensure the application is consistent with the general tenor of development as embodied in the comprehensive plan, community concerns, attitudes of staff, planning-board members, and city council. As a result, only applications with a high likelihood of success actually make it to public hearings before the planning board.

Estimated Fiscal Impact of Historic Preservation

In 1998, the Centerville, Ohio city council voted 5-2 to designate the Opdyke farmhouse, sitting on 30.6 acres of developmentally prime vacant land inside its boundaries, as a historic landmark.[3] The farmhouse dated to 1814 and was remodeled in 1827, 1851, 1863 and had a series of owners. K&S Enterprises purchased the property in 1983 before the creation of the Centerville-Washington Township Landmarks Foundation. In fact, the historic significance of the building did not become a factor until K&S Enterprises applied for a demolition permit for the house, barns, and other outbuildings, all of which were in severely deteriorated condition. The Foundation argued for the preservation of the farmhouse, barns, and other outbuildings along with Joseph C. Williamson, the great-great grandson of Eleazer Williamson (who purchased the property in 1851). At the April meeting, the council designated the farmhouse an historic landmark and cleared the other buildings for demolition. The burden of maintaining and renovating the farmhouse lay with the property owner, not the Foundation, city, or the Williamson Family.

Land and Renovation Costs

Meijer, Inc., a national "big box" retailer, submitted an offer to purchase the property from K&S Enterprises for $100,000 per acre, or $3 million, contingent on the demolition of the house and buildings. (The application for demolition triggered an inquiry by local citizens into the historical significance of the farmhouse.) Given the property's proximity to a major transportation artery and accessibility to residential and commercial uses, $3 million is likely a lower-bound estimate of the parcel's market value. Discussions with local land developers suggest the property may be worth closer to about $130,000 per acre, or $4 million, for more intense commercial development. Thus, the market value of the property, fully developed, ranges from a lower bound of $12 million ($392,000 per acre) to $20 million ($654,000 per acre) given that property values are consistently 25 percent of the cost of development in this region.

The property owners estimate that a renovated and restored house with a paved driveway would require at least one acre. The farmhouse is located near the center of the property, interrupting standard traffic flow patterns for this kind of development. Any further development would require "creative" design to reconfigure land uses and businesses optimally. The farmhouse land is also not a commercially viable use at current market prices, so the property owners would likely subsidize tenants in the house or leave it vacant once restored. Since the property is zoned for Business Planned Unit, which allows for retail shopping uses, the market potential for the portion of the property occupied by the house is further diminished.

Consultants retained by the property owner estimated that bringing the farmhouse up to code and renovating the barns for commercial purposes would cost about $600,000. Bringing the farmhouse up to code would cost between $85,000 and $100,000. The property owner (who is also a developer), however, estimates that adding the amenities to the building to make it "livable"—indoor plumbing, extra bathrooms, extending water and sewer, and paving the driveway—would bring the total costs to over $200,000.

Commercial Development Impacts

The total impact of local planning regulations consists of combining the revenue impacts of taking land off the market and dedicating it through government fiat to historic preservation and the renovation costs imposed on the property owner to bring the farmhouse up to a livable condition. The total regulatory impact would be $592,000 at the lower estimate and $694,000 at the higher estimate. The lower bound estimate is based on a market price of $100,000 per acre and the higher bound estimate is based on a market price of $130,000 per acre.

Historic designation lowers expected revenues from the project since the land cannot be developed for marketable commercial purposes. The estimated fiscal impact on the project is equivalent to between 4.4 percent and 5.1 percent of the market price per acre at build out (Table 1). The average dollar impact is $20,000 per acre at the lower price and $30,202 at the higher estimated market price.[4]

Table 11.1. **Commercial Development Impact on Planning Regulation For Opdyke Farmhouse Property**

	Low Estimate	High Estimate
Development potential	$12,0000	$20,000,000
Revenue impact (excluding farmhouse)	$392,000	$694,000
Revised revenue estimate	$11,608,000	$19,306,000
Total regulatory impact	$592,000	$894,000
Average per developable acre	$20,000	$30,202
% of market value (per acre)	5.1%	4.4%

Source: Estimates by author based on information provided by the City of Centerville and interviews with developers.

Residential Development Impacts

The property could be developed for residential rather than commercial purposes although this would require rezoning the parcel to residential planned unit development (PUD). In fact, this use would be more compatible with adjacent land uses since the property is bordered by single-family residential uses on three sides (although less efficient given the property location along major roads). An analysis of the impact on residential development also provides an alternative lens through which the impacts of planning decisions and historic preservation can be viewed.

Based on Centerville's zoning code, a single-family residential development would require a maximum of two housing units per acre. This could be achieved by developing the property under standard zoning on half-acre lots, or using the cluster development option that allows developers to dedicate open space in exchange for higher densities. Irrespective of the developer's choice, the property could not average more than two units per acre for the entire project.

Given the city's zoning requirements, sixty houses could be built on the property. The market for new housing in the immediate area suggests new home prices ranging from $200,000 to $250,000 for new three and four bedroom homes with about 2,000 to 2,500 square feet of living area. If these homes were sold for $250,000 each, the anticipated revenue from the development would be $15.0 million (Table 2).

Table 11.2. **Residential Development Potential for Opdyke Farmhouse Property**

Developable acreage	30.6 acres
Number of houses (1/2 acre min.)	60
Average home value	$250,000
Total anticipated revenue	$15.0 million
Average lot cost	$50,000

Source: Estimates by author based on interviews with Centerville Planning Department and local land developers.

Total anticipated revenues from the housing project would also fall by $500,000 (a reduction of two houses) to $14.5 million (Table 3). Since the property owner is still required to restore the house and dedicate land to the farmhouse, the net fiscal impact for this regulatory decision is $900,000 using the lower-bound estimate of $100,000 per acre. The impact on housing in this area would be $15,517 per unit, or 6.2 percent of the price of the house.

Table 11.3. **Development Impact of Planning Regulation for Opdyke Farmhouse Property**

Farmhouse	
Farmhouse renovation	$100,000
Farmhouse improvements	$100,000
Land dedication (1 acre)	$200,000
Development Impact	
Housing unit reduction	2
Revenue reduction	$500,000
Net Revenue Impact	
Revised revenue estimate	$14,500,000
Total regulatory impact	$900,000
Average cost per housing unit	$15,517

Source: Estimates by author based on information provided by the City of Centerville and interviews with developers.

Historic Preservation as Regulatory Taxation

By using its regulatory discretion to designate buildings as historic landmarks, the City of Centerville has legislated additional costs of between $600,000 and $900,000 on the private-property developer. These costs range from $15,517 per acre for residential development to as high as $30,000 for commercial development. Whether these costs will be born by the developer or future property owners is an empirical question and depends on the strength of the housing market (Dresch and Sheffrin 1997).

Since the private property owners are responsible for the renovation and restoration of the building and property and the cost will be born by the developer (in a slumping market) or future residents (in a strong housing market), the city and existing residents do not bare the burden of the regulation. Using the residential case, a small neighborhood of 58 *future* households will pay for a $900,000 amenity for the entire city. If the cost of preserving the historic farmhouse were spread over the entire city, the cost would have been equivalent to a $97.5 assessment on each housing unit. Since future residents do not vote today, and the courts do not require compensation for partial takings, these inequities are implicit in current planning policy.[5] In short, rent-seeking behavior used the regulatory process to transfer wealth from the current and future property owners to the special interests in the community at large, a wealth transfer worth almost $1 million.

SMART GROWTH, ZONING, AND REGULATORY TAXATION

This chapter has argued that zoning and development control can be viewed as regulatory taxation. From an economic perspective, taxation is a mechanism used by government to raise revenues to produce goods and services that would not normally be traded in an open market. Taxation, as an instrument of government, compels one group of citizens to finance the production of a good or service that will be consumed more broadly.

Regulation can be used the same way: by restricting the land development process for some members of society, wealth can be redistributed to other members or groups. Regulation can be used to protect community interests, but many conventional Smart-Growth techniques lend themselves to rent-seeking behavior. Many of the contemporary proposals bundled as part of the Smart-Growth movement—urban-growth boundaries, large-lot zoning, ballot-box zoning—can be characterized this way. Citizens are reluctant to buy specific goods (e.g., open space) on the open market and resort to land-use regulation to compel property owners to provide a public service to the broader society without compensation. In short, by preventing someone from subdividing and developing their property, planning boards and city councils allow politically influential groups to benefit from open-space preservation while the burden is born by property owners subjected to regulation. This is most clearly evident in the case of urban-growth boundaries, but the process can also be seen through the indirect effects of agricultural zoning, ballot-box zoning, and other land-use controls.

The fiscal impacts of this wealth transfer was illustrated using a case of historic preservation in a fast-growing suburban community in Ohio. The regulatory burden of historic preservation ranged from $15,000 to $30,000 per acre in the case study. Almost all the costs would be born by future residents or commercial tenants even though the primary beneficiaries were the historic preservation community.

The redistributive qualities of zoning and development regulations are not in and of themselves a justification for their elimination. Local communities may well decide that the collective benefits of regulation are warranted and, in some cases necessary. Elected officials, citizens, and planners, however, should still recognize the political ramifications of the redistributional character of regulation.

ENDNOTES

1. Governments have other forms of raising revenue. The most direct way to finance government services, for example, is a **user fee**. User fees are direct payments by the users of services (e.g., water, sewer) to cover the costs of providing them. User fees also imply a transfer of wealth, but, unlike taxation, the transfer is voluntary in the same way buying food at the grocery store is voluntary. Restrictions may exist on the number of providers (utilities are often protected monopolies), but the amount of a product or service used is determined by the consumer. Thus, by choosing how much of the product they will use, consumers determine how much of their wealth will be paid to the service provider in a way similar to buying goods and services in private markets for cars, groceries, or clothing. Moreover, user fees are directly related to costs, and, ideally, they should perfectly offset each other.

2. Importantly, this would be the gross impact. Other facts, including income and population growth, contribute to higher levels of building permit growth that would offset these impacts. Thus, the *net* growth in building permits could still be positive.

3. The property is in a prime development location at the intersection of two major transportation arteries, Wilmington Pike and State Route 725. The East Side is bordered by a two lane road that separates the vacant property from an older single family residential subdivision built in the 1960s in an adjacent city. Directly to the parcel's north is a gasoline station. Further north, beyond the intersection, is a 2-mile commercial strip consisting of an automobile dealership, "big box" grocery stores and retail outlets, more than a dozen restaurants, and specialty retail shops. To the West and South are single family residential housing subdivisions developed on half-acre lots. The property is zoned for business planned-unit development which requires comprehensive site-plan approval. The parcel is also the last large, undeveloped plot of land in the city.

4. Importantly, these calculations may under-estimate the true cost to the developer. Legal and consultant fees are not included, nor are the costs of delaying the project until historic designation issues were resolved. The controversy surrounding the historic designation added at least six months to the project and could delay it for another year if the property owner appeals the city's decision or attempts to secure another demolition permit from Centerville's Architectural Review Board.

5. A more equitable approach would be to either: 1) have the city buy the property and house and restore it using general-revenue funds, or 2) have a private foundation such as the Centerville-Washington Township Landmarks Foundation raise private money to buy and restore the farmhouse. If neither of these groups are willing to use or raise resources to buy and preserve the farmhouse, it's public purpose is suspect to begin with.

REFERENCES

Audirac, Ivonne, Shermyen, Anne H., and Smith, Marc T.. (1990) "Ideal Urban Form and Visions of the Good Life: Florida's Growth Management Dilemma." *Journal of the American Planning Association* 54: pp. 470-82.

Clingermayer, James. (1993) "Distributive Politics, Ward Representation, and the Spread of Zoning." *Public Choice* 77: pp. 725-738.

Conder, Sonny. (1990) *Residential Refill Study*. Growth Management Services Department Technical Report, Portland Metro, February 10.

The Dark Side of the American Dream. College Park, Maryland: Sierra Club, n.d.

Daniels, Tom and Bowers, Deborah. (1997) *Holding Our Ground*. Washington, D.C.: Island Press.

Dresch, Marla and Sheffrin, Steven. (1997) *Who Pays for Development Fees and Exactions?* San Francisco: Public Policy Institute of California.

Feldman, Marshall M.A. and Florida, Richard A.. (1990) "Economic Restructuring and The Changing Role of the State in U.S. Housing." In Vliet, Willem and Weesep, Jan van, (eds.), *Government and Housing: Developments in Seven Counties*, pp. XXX. Newbury Park, California: Sage Publications.

Fulton, William, Williamson, Chris, and Jones, Jeff. (2001) *Smart Growth and the Ballot Box: The Impact of SOAR on Plan Implementation in Ventura County, California*. Los Angeles: Reason Public Policy Institute, November.

Gerckens, Laurence Conway. (1979) "Historical Development of American City Planning." In So, Frank S., Stollman, Israel, Beal, Frank, and Arnold, David S. (eds), *The Practice of Local Government Planning*,. Washington, D.C.: International City Management Association, pp. 21-57

Gyourko, Joseph. (1991) "Impact Fees, Exclusionary Zoning, and the Density of New Development." *Journal of Urban Economics* 30: pp. 242-56.

Holcombe, Randall G. (1994) *Florida's Growth Management Experiment*. Tallahassee, FL: James Madison Institute, December.

Holcombe, Randall G. (1996) *Public Finance: Government Revenues and Expenditures in the United States Economy*. New York: West Publishing Company.

Holcombe, Randall G., (2000) *Land Use Planning for the 21st Century*. Washington, D.C.: Joint Economic Committee.

Howe, Deborah A. (1993) "Growth Management in Oregon." In Stein, Jay M. (ed.), *Growth Management: The Planning Challenge of the 1990's*, Newbury Park, California: Sage Publications, pp. 61-75.

Lai, Lawrence W.C. (1996) *Zoning and Property Rights: A Hong Kong Case Study*. Hong Kong: Hong Kong University Press.

Lai, Lawrence W.C. (1997) "Property Rights Justifications for Planning and a Theory of Zoning." In Diaman, D. and Massam, B.H. (eds.), *Progress in Planning: Recent Research on Urban and Regional Planning*,. Oxford, England: Pergamon Press. pp. 161-246.

Mueller, Dennis C. (1989) *Public Choice II*. New York, NY.: Cambridge University Press.

Nelson, Arthur C., Frank, James E., and Nicholas, James C. (1992), "Positive Influence of Impact-Fee in Urban Planning and Development." *Journal of Urban Planning and Development* 18: pp. 59-64.

Peltzman, Sam. (1976) "Toward a More General Theory of Regulation." *Journal of Law and Economics* 19: pp. 211-40.

Ross, Dennis H. and Thorpe, Scott Ian. (1992) "Impact Fees: Practical Guide for Calculation and Implementation." *Journal of Urban Planning and Development* 18: pp. 106-118.

Seigan, Bernard (1990), "Land-Use Regulation Should Preserve Only Vital and Pressing Government Interests." In Cooper, John W. (ed.) *Private Property Rights, Land-Use Policy and Growth Management*, Tallahassee, FL.: Montpelier Books, pp. 17-37.

Staley, Sam. (1992) *Drug Policy and the Decline of American Cities.* New Brunswick, NJ: Transaction Publishers.

Staley, Samuel R. (2001a) "The Political Economy of Land Conversion on the Urban Fringe," In Anderson, Terry L. and Yandle, Bruce (eds.) *Agriculture and the Environment:Searching for Greener Pastures*, pp. 65-80. Palo Alto, California: Hoover Institution Press.

Staley, Samuel R. (2001b) Markets, Smart Growth, and the Limits of Policy. In Holcombe, Randall G., and Staley, Samuel R. (eds.) *Smarter Growth: Market-Based Strategies for Land-Use Planning in the 21st Century City*,. Westport, CT: Greenwood Press, 2001. pp. 203-219

Staley, Samuel R. (2001c) "Ballot-Box Zoning, Transactions Costs and Urban Growth." *Journal of the American Planning Association* 67: pp. 25-37.

Staley, Samuel R., Edgens, Jefferson G., and Mildner, Gerard C.S.. (1999) *A Line in the Land: Urban Growth Boundaries and the Future of Growth Management*, Policy Study No. 263. Los Angeles, California: Reason Public Policy Institute.

Staley, Samuel R. and Scarlett, Lynn. (1998) "Market-Oriented Planning: Principles and Tools for the 21st Century." *Planning and Markets* 1: electronic journal http://www-pam. usc.edu.

Stigler, George J. (1971) "The Theory of Economic Regulation," *Bell Journal of Economics and Management Science* 2: 1-21.

Tullock, Gordon. (1967) "The Welfare Costs of Tariffs, Monopolies, and Theft." *Western Economic Journal* 5: pp. 224-232.

Wagner, Richard E. (1988) "Morals, Interest, and Constitutional Order: A Public Choice Perspective." *Oregon Law Review* 67: pp. 73-92.

Weitz, Jerry and Moore, Terry. (1998) "Development Inside Urban-Growth Boundaries: Oregon's Empirical Evidence of Continuous Urban Form." *Journal of the American Planning Association 64.*

12 EMERGING PROPERTY RIGHTS, COMMAND-AND-CONTROL REGULATION, AND THE DISINTEREST IN ENVIRONMENTAL TAXATION

Bruce Yandle

INTRODUCTION

This chapter addresses a puzzle that has to do with the economic instruments chosen by U.S. and other regulators for managing environmental quality. The political-economy puzzle is about the prevalence of apparently more costly and less effective command-and-control regulation over efficiency-enhancing emission taxes, effluent fees, and property rights operating under a rule of law. Buchanan and Tullock (1975) have explained why polluters prefer cartel-enhancing, command-and-control regulation enforced at the national level to taxes and emission fees, but their story only partially addresses the apparent disinterest in property rights protected by common law. In any case, polluter preferences alone cannot likely explain national political action. There is more to the politics of environmentalism than what industry alone might want.

In 1990 Greve (1990) explained why national environmental organizations prefer the citizen suit enforcement features of command-and-control regulation that can only be provided by the central government.[1] When Greve is combined with Buchanan and Tullock, we get a double cartel story that finds polluters and purity lovers seeking similar political action, yet another Bootlegger and Baptist story (Yandle 1983, 1999a). When rational ignorance is added to the political recipe, the combination seems to provide a robust theory of command-and-control dominance.

While the theory just sketched explains the dominance of command and control for pollution control purposes, we are still left searching for an explanation as to why environmental taxes are imposed on certain products and activities, and why broadly-based environmental taxes that never get adopted are nonetheless a perennial favorite item of political debate. To complete the discussion of environmental control, we must also deal with the fact that the oldest form of environmental protection, property rights operating under a rule of law, seems to be completely lost in the political shuffle that responds to the demand for environmental protection.

In truth, any form of environmental regulation, whether it be taxes, command-and-control, or private property rights, embodies some form of property rights. A discussion of instrument choice is therefore a discussion of property-rights evolution. The chapter is accordingly organized first to present a discussion of the evolution of environmental property rights that becomes focused on the political choice between private property rights (common law) and regulatory property rights (command and control). The chapter then gives an expanded treatment of Greve's theory of regulation by litigation, which of course fits and is accommodated by the Buchanan-Tullock theory that explains polluter preference for command-and-control regulation. The last major part of the chapter then turns to a discussion of the renewed interest in environmental taxation and the potential for taxation to replace command-and-control regulation. Brief final thoughts conclude the chapter.

THE TRANSFORMATION OF ENVIRONMENTAL PROPERTY RIGHTS

The evolutionary process that builds bundles of environmental property rights begins with a commons where rights are unspecified and ends with a bundle of specified rights that may be traded in political or private markets (Yandle and Morriss 2001). Along the way, benefits and costs drive the process by which rights to a resource emerge. As Demsetz (1964, 1967) explained, steps are taken through the property-rights stations when the relative benefits of defining, defending, and devising property rights make it worthwhile for entrepreneurs in a human community to enclose the commons or establish rules for rationing and allocating valuable environmental resources. Each of the property-rights stations—common, public, private—provides an interesting setting for economic analysis, but it is fully transferable private property rights that give rise to markets and the creation of wealth through specialization and gains from trade.

The schematic in Figure One provides a highly stylized view of the property rights evolution process. As indicated by the arrows, a particular resource may at times be treated as a commons, then as common property, and later as public property, with transaction costs, custom and tradition affecting the property-rights outcome. Then, when relative scarcity dictates change, a resource that may have been treated as private property can cease to be protected as such and may once again become a commons where the law of capture determines ownership. Government and politics obviously play an important part in property rights decision-making (Libecap 1989). After all, property-rights define wealth and who controls it. With wealth hanging in the balance, it is understandable that politicians would be interested in assisting the birthing process that favors particular interest groups with politically determined rights to what was formerly a commons. But more often than not, politicians are altering existing property rights arrangements instead of providing first-time rights to a previously unrationed and unowned resource. Still, there are political profits to be made when rents are reassigned.

Figure 12.1: **Property Rights Evolution**

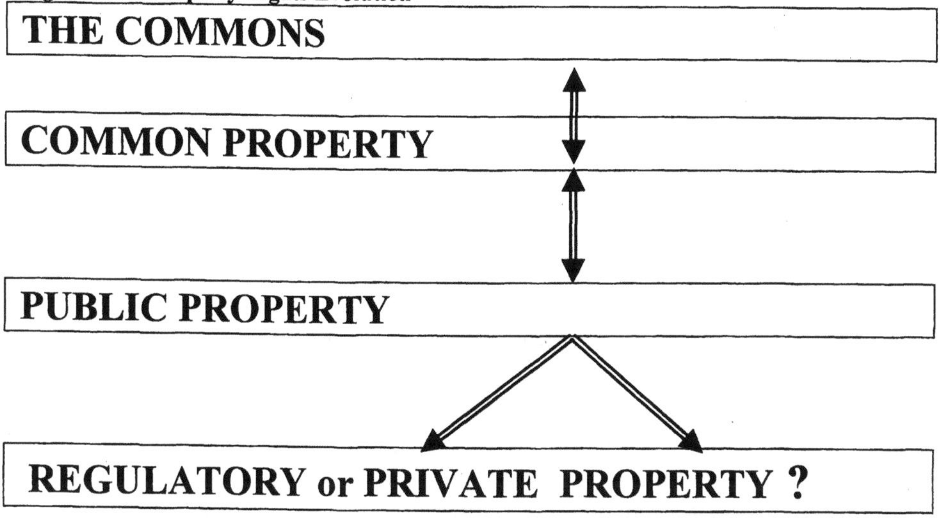

Most environmental resources have been around long enough to have traveled through the property-rights stations. For well over a century, the common law of nuisance defined rights to air and water quality, avoidance of harm from hazardous waste, noise, and even sunlight. In terms of Figure One, certain features of environmental resources in the United States had traveled from commons to private property long before the federal government became involved in environmental regulation. Put in the simplest of terms, common law theory said that ordinary owners and occupiers of property had the right not to be harmed by the actions taken by others that might alter the rightholders' beneficial use of such things as air, water, and light. At common law, environmental rights were transferable; a rightholder could contract with another party to accept specified levels of pollution, noise, heat, or shade (Brubaker, 1998, Meiners and Yandle, 1999, Yandle 1999b). When an individual rightholder was harmed by the actions of another party, the rightholder could bring a private nuisance suit against the harming party. The common-law remedy was payment of damages and injunction. When multiple parties were harmed, common law provided for a public nuisance remedy, where an attorney general or public defender would bring suit on behalf of the harmed parties. Common law provided defenses for private and public goods.

Prior to the federal government's takeover of the management of environmental resources, common law was seldom the only or even the principal property rights-based defense for protecting environmental assets. In the vast pre-1970 U.S. federalist system, one searching for environmental property rights protection would have found a rich array of common law, city ordinances, state laws, regional compacts, private trusts, associations, and other forms of action. In some cases, the underlying property rights were public; which is to say, a city council managed and allocated the rights. In other cases, the rights were common to particular Indian tribes and community members. In still other cases, the rights were private and common law controlled their protection.

When a combination of social and political forces moved environmental decision making to the federal government level, the institutional structures that had evolved for well over a century were suddenly placed on hold and then reshaped. With environmentalism in full sway, federal politicians took action to redefine rights. The major environmental statutes nationalized each element of the natural environment. While many of the pre-existing institutions might continue to have some bearing on outcomes, federal law and regulation were to be constitutionally dominant. The politicians had the power to convert private property rights to regulatory property rights and to change state public property to federal public property. In terms of Figure One, the political focus was on the fork in the property rights process where either private or regulatory rights might be defined and defended. As seen through the eyes of a rent-seeking politician, consider now the relative merits of the instruments that might be chosen for managing environmental assets.

The common-law process had nothing to offer the rent-seeking politician. Based on protection of private property rights, common law was a decentralized, judge-managed process. Actions taken at common law applied only to the parties in court and could not be extended beyond the plaintiff showing harm and the defendant causing the harm. While lacking political appeal, common law was also unattractive to industrial firms that wanted uniform and predictable rules that they could expect to find anywhere in the nation. Industrialists had little interest in maintaining the common law status quo. Environmentalists seeking tough federal controls were also looking for change. They too wanted strict and uniform standards imposed from the top down. Politicians were not alone in seeking to move from private property to regulatory rights based on command-and-control regulation. Of course, these considerations were based on a rent-brokering politician's motivation.

THE DOUBLE ENVIRONMENTAL CARTEL

Even those who claim efficiency for the command-and-control regulation that dominates much of U.S. environmental policy grant that government-enforced output restrictions can result in a regulatory cartel. The basic cartel story, told many times, hinges on the fact that federal regulation is technology based and is based on inputs, not environmental outcomes. The regulation applies across the board to every firm in an industry, no matter where the firm is located, and generally requires more costly controls for new than for old plants (Buchanan and Tullock 1967). In short, once a set of EPA effluent guidelines is made final, all existing firms face the same environmental constraint, and new firms systematically face a stricter constraint. Any growth in demand for an affected industry's product offers the prospect of "polluters' profits." Clearly, the same result cannot obtain where pollution is limited by taxation, fees based on environmental use, and cap-and-trade discharge permits. And of course, it is inconceivable that an entire industry could cartelize itself by being sued in state common-law courts nationwide and thereby obtaining uniform verdicts to be applied to the industry. When it comes to rents induced by regulation, command-and-control takes the day.

No cartel is better than its enforcement mechanism, and this is where the second cartel story enters. As outlined here, the polluter cartel story relies on federal regulator gatekeepers who restrict the entry of new polluters and keep existing polluters in line. In addition, the gatekeeper (cartel manager) must find a way to monitor polluters by the tens of thousands and make certain they are abiding by their restrictive permits. With the output restriction yielding higher prices, there is a natural tendency for cartel members to cheat. The regulator must find low cost ways to maintain the cartel. In actual fact, the federal government delegates to the states the enforcement of most major environmental statutes. To make matters more difficult for cartel managers, there is compelling empirical evidence of considerable variation in the stringency of enforcement across the states (Helland 1998). With limited resources and variation in enforcement across the states, it is reasonable to see provisions for private enforcement of environmental law in the major federal statutes. And of course, there is an enforcement problem faced by members of the Buchanan-Tullock cartel.

But while the industry cartel story is now a standard part of regulatory lore, the story of cartelization induced for environmental organizations remains largely uncelebrated. First developed by Michael Greve (1990) and then expanded upon by Barnett and Terrell (2001), the prospect for this cartel story relies on command-and-control regulation with a special enforcement feature of U.S. environmental regulation. Private individuals and organizations are made enforcement deputies by statute through the provisions for citizen suits. Precluded from making a profit in their enforcement endeavors, private citizens join public agents to enforce the law. Given technology-based command-and-control regulation that focuses on inputs, permits, and reporting, environmental organizations, and any others concerned about compliance, can readily examine the individual plant reports filed regularly with state and federal regulators. Private parties can read the required reports and identify firms that have failed to report properly or that have reported pollution excedances and other permit violations.

With evidence in hand, private parties can sue the polluter and, if successful, recover the cost of their legal action. Just cost recovery is not all that attractive, of course. In addition, the resulting fines levied against the convicted polluter must be paid to the U.S. Treasury. The statutes make it clear that private parties cannot earn a "profit" from their enforcement litigation activities. However, there is another payoff for environmental organizations, and herewith are some of the seeds of the environmental cartel. Environmental organizations bringing suit can fully recover litigation costs and obtain for environmental purposes court-ordered grants above and beyond the penalties and fines paid by a convicted polluter. The court-ordered credits cannot redound to the direct benefit of the environmental organizations bringing suit, but can be designed by the plaintiffs so that organizations they favor will obtain the grants.

The prospects for profitable regulation by litigation is made even more attractive by virtue of the fact that most permit violation suits brought by private parties are won by the plaintiffs. When informed that a suit is pending, the affected polluter has a powerful incentive to settle out of court. A well-crafted settlement accomplishes several important cartel-enforcing functions. The polluter's opportunity cost of settling is represented by the expected value of fines, legal costs for both parties, and environmental credits that may be demanded by the judge in the case. Given the fact that most polluters lose, the polluter is likely to settle for some amount close to this full opportunity cost. The settlement payments discipline firms that may have broken the cartel's output constraint, and the environmental organization bringing suit helps to enforce the regulatory cartel. Then, the design of the credit program to be undertaken by the polluter provides a way to reward good environmental organizations and punish bad ones. Organizations that have cooperated in going after violators can obtain court-administered revenues. Those organizations that favored economic incentives, property rights, or some decentralized alternative to federal command-and-control regulation can be omitted from sharing in the litigation largess.[2]

Bootleggers and Baptists to the Rescue

The operational success of the double-cartel is reinforced by the fact that seemingly disparate interest groups are working diligently toward the same end. Of course, this is where the Bootlegger/Baptist (B&B) element of the story becomes compelling. The B&B theory draws its name from the fact that illicit sellers of booze and members of some religious organizations both favor the imposition of limits if not selective prohibition on the consumption of alcoholic beverages. Obviously, Sunday closing laws that shut down the corner liquor store expand the market for the bootlegger's sales. As an aside, one hardly ever finds state or local ordinances or laws that prohibit the

Sunday consumption of alcoholic beverages by adults. Restrictions on consumption would destroy the B&B alliance.

The B&B story forms a small footnote to the rich special-interest theory of regulation most notably associated with Stigler (1971) and Peltzman (1976).[3] B&B explains how it is possible for public-interest arguments to serve special-interest demand for regulation. The footnote says that rhetoric matters a lot in the world of politics but that neither well-varnished moral prompting nor unvarnished campaign contributions can do the job alone. It takes both.

The technology-based scrubber regulations required by the 1977 Clean Air Act offers a prime example of Baptist-delivered regulatory benefits (Ackerman and Hassler, 1981). The statute required costly scrubbers to be installed on all newly constructed coal-fired electric utilities whether they burned dirty coal or not. Special-interest groups tied to high sulfur coal production in the Eastern United States celebrated the statute, as did most environmental groups. The unorganized miners of Western low-sulfur coal and highly dispersed and rationally ignorant consumers of electricity had no cause for celebration.

The much-celebrated efforts to protect the Northern Spotted Owl that began in the early 1990s provides an example of "bootlegger" benefits delivered by environmental "Baptists" by way of the courts. Following a series of court decisions and regulatory actions, millions of acres of federal forest land and owl habitat in the Pacific Northwest were placed off limits to the woodsman's axe.

The Wall Street Journal (1992) explained how Weyerhaeuser Corporation employed wildlife biologists to search for owl habitat, but not on Weyerhaeuser's timberland.

> Weyerhaeuser says it has restricted logging on 320,000 acres to comply with federal and state rules protecting the birds. On the other hand, logging restrictions to protect the owl have put more than five million acres of federal timberland in the Pacific Northwest out of loggers' reach—and driven lumber prices through the roof.

The story noted that Weyerhaeuser's "[o]wl-driven profits enabled the company to earn $86.6 million in the first quarter, up 81% from a year earlier." Environmentalists celebrated the expanded protection of owl habitat while the owners of Weyerhaeuser and other timber products companies celebrated abnormal positive returns.

A more recent B&B example is found in the "struggle" that has occurred between environmentalists and North Carolina hog farmers. North Carolina, the nation's number two hog producer, has imposed a moratorium on new large-scale hog farms; other leading hog producing states have imposed similar strict entry restrictions. Indicating that he welcomed the restrictions, Joseph W. Luter III, CEO of Smithfield Foods, Inc., North Carolina's and the nation's largest hog producer/processor said: "Nobody can duplicate what we've done" (Kilman 2001). As it turns out, the North Carolina regulation paralleled proposals from the U.S. Environmental Protection Agency (EPA) for stricter standards on confined animal feeding operations. The EPA's proposal came as result of a citizen suit brought against the agency by Natural Resources Defense Council in 1999.[4]

Putting Enforcement to Political Advantage

The combination of private and public enforcement enables command-and-control regulation to become a vehicle for forming and maintaining industry and environmental cartels. The resulting barriers to entry generate rents for the cartelized industry, and the payments extracted through settlements and litigation reward environmental organizations that rally to help maintain the industry cartel. While the resulting rents may be dissipated through the process of getting them, the regulation that yielded the rents in the first place become capitalized in the resulting social structure. The resulting symbiotic relationship leads to high-cost environmental protection, and thus less of it, and reduced production of goods and services. Like most biological symbiotic relationship, there is little direct control that either party can exert over the other. Both parties are rent seekers. Industrial polluters hope to avoid common law suits and environmental taxes while using pollution control to wall out competitive entry. The environmental organizations play an important role in policing members of the cartel that break the output constraint. However, the environmental litigators cannot perfectly identify the polluter that deliberately breaks the cartel from the firm that experiences an accidental discharge or simply fails to maintain required records. In other words, regulation by litigation is no more precise than any other regulation. All forms of regulation are crude.

Unfortunately, the litigation process is more than just unguided. It is misguided. The citizen-suit litigation introduces a distinct bias to the enforcement process. Environmental organizations seeking litigation-generated revenues will not likely target farmers and municipalities, which are the leading sources of water pollution, but will go for deep pocket, high profile, industrial firms run by executives who have a high incentive to settle out of court. Along with this unfortunate bias, as noted by Ashford and Caldart (2001, 113), the crude private litigation process chills the prospects for any experimentation that EPA and other agency might wish to undertake.

Regulation by Litigation

There are no good data on out-of-court settlements and private litigation. However, the pace of these activities under the various statutes enforced by the EPA can be inferred from the pace of actions taken by EPA and federal prosecutors. Mark A. Cohen (1992) notes that only 25 criminal environmental cases were prosecuted in the entire decade of the 1970s. Then "from 1982 through April 1995, the agency brought charges against roughly 443 corporations and 1068 individuals and obtained convictions against roughly 334 organizations and 740 individuals."[5] As shown in Table One, the pace of federal action can also be observed in the number of criminal cases referred to the U.S. Department of Justice by the EPA. It should be noted that infractions of EPA regulations can result in civil penalties as well as criminal action and jail sentences. The data here reflect the more serious charges.

Table 12.1: **Criminal Referrals to the Department of Justice**

Fiscal Year-	Criminal Referrals-	Months Sentenced	-Defendants
1987	41	456	66
1988	59	278	97
1989	60	325	95
1990	65	745	100
1991	81	963	104
1992	107	1,135	150
1993	140	892	161
1994	220	1,188	250
1995	256	888	245
1996	262	1,116	221
1997	278	2,351	322
1998	266	2,076	350

Source: Nicholas C. Yost, The State of Environmental Law Enforcement: A Speech Presented at the American Bar Association's 1998 Annual Meeting, ELR News & Analysis, 28(December 1998)12: 10711-10720, at 10717.

As might be expected, the data in Table One are affected by changes in federal environmental statutes. For example, there is a sustained increase in the pace of activity and total length of sentences after the Environmental Crimes and Enforcement Act of 1996 was passed. The 1996 law strengthened existing laws and provided additional resources for the Department of Justice to investigate and prosecute environmental crimes.[6] It should also be noted that even before the 1996 law, EPA had made agreements with the FBI, IRS, SEC, and OSHA to share investigation data.[7] Industrial firms and industrialists notified that they were being sued by environmental organizations had even more reason to settle quietly.

Another indirect glimpse of regulation by litigation is seen in data on state and federal court environmental nuisance actions reported by Frank Cross (1999). Cross gathered data on the number of reported cases where the plaintiff included a common-law nuisance pleading. Going far beyond what might be termed traditional common-law actions, these cases included citizen suits as well as actions by regulatory agencies; both would have been filed in federal court. The data in Table Two show how federal court action experienced explosive growth after 1970 and the passage of major environmental statutes.

Table 12.2: **Reported Environmental Nuisance Actions**

Year	State	Federal
1945-50	145	18
1955-60	207	31
1965-70	228	31
1975-80	378	149
1985-90	447	324
1990-95	610	504

Source: Cross (1999, 970).

To give perspective to the data, consider that real GDP grew almost 4.5-fold from 1945 to 1995, which is more than the growth of state court nuisance cases. Also, notice that federal court cases grew by 28-fold during the same period. Again, these data may indirectly reflect the pace of out-of-court settlements entered into by environmental litigation organizations.

THE RENEWED INTEREST IN ENVIRONMENTAL TAXATION

Since the 1960s, when the environmental saga began in the United States and other developed countries, economists pursuing a normative treatment of pollution have relentlessly, but unsuccessfully, argued for regulation by taxation. Harking back to A.C. Pigou's (1920, 1932) treatise on the matter, modern economists urged implementation of pollution taxes and effluent charges as a way to convert marginal social cost to marginal private cost and thereby induce socially efficient behavior. The deceptively simple notion requires a public authority to identify the cost being imposed by a polluter on others against their will and to place a tax on marginal units of pollution equal to the cost imposed by the polluter. Upon feeling the pain of his pollution activities, according to the theory, the formerly unrepentant polluter will cut back on pollution to avoid the tax. Ergo, the world is made cleaner, and those who buy the polluter's product no longer escape paying the opportunity cost of their consumption.

Captured by the power of the taxation idea, few modern advocates seem to recognize that Mr. Pigou recanted and argued against the use of Pigouvian taxes (Pigou 1932, 332). He recognized that calculating efficient environmental taxes would be practically impossible and that if calculated, no legislative body worth its political salt would ever adopt taxes just for the sake of efficiency, which is to say income redistribution drives the political process, not efficiency. In other words, Mr. Pigou said that Pigouvian taxes were nice in theory but not in practice. Modern economists who advocate regulation by taxation still believe that what is good in theory must be good in practice. In spite of this, and the fact that the European Community officially embraced the "polluter pay" policy, pollution taxation has not been used generally or systematically to achieve some optimal levels of air and water quality. Even so, a call for pollution taxation has been a regular part of the environmental policy chorus.

The Search for a Double Dividend

Starting around 10 years ago, a new variation on the Pigouvian theme began to be heard in European countries that have historically imposed burdensome taxes on labor (Bosquet, 2000, Patterson, 2000). Faced with high structural levels of unemployment that seemed resistant to even the most salutary levels of economic activity, policy analysts became enamored with the idea of substituting environmental taxes for taxes on labor. Doing so perfectly would produce a double dividend, it was argued. The tendency to pollute would be chastened and workers facing lower taxes would be eager to expand their hours of labor. Water would be cleaner and unemployment rates would fall. Indeed, a tax substitution package could be designed that would leave total revenues at the same level, while national output expanded. The idea seemed as good as perpetual motion and the ever-evasive free lunch. With talk of double dividends in the air, proposals for environmental taxes became more frequent and fervent.[8]

As good as it may sound in theory, the prospects for gaining a double dividend from environmental taxation are dim indeed. This is so for three fundamental reasons. First, in the very context of environmental taxation, Pigou (1932, 332) noted:

> [W]e cannot expect that any public authority will attain or will even wholeheartedly seek, that ideal. Such authorities are liable alike to ignorance, to sectional pressure, and to personal corruption by private corruption by private interest. A loud-voice part of their constituents, if organized for votes, may easily outweigh the whole.

In other words, efficiency-seeking politicians will be diverted by their rent-seeking brethren. Environmental tax reform is not a politically viable alternative. Second, even if the politics did not matter, it is not clear that even the brightest politicians aided by a host of bright economists would be able to make the socialist calculations necessary to design an appropriate set of environmental taxes with offsetting taxes on wages and capital. A review of environmental tax studies that encompassed 139 simulations from 56 studies by Bosqet (2000) concluded that it was indeed theoretically possible to induce employment increases by offsetting employment taxes with taxes on CO2.[9] The first theoretical dividend (environmental) effect is fairly certain. However, the findings for the second dividend were more tentative and in application required a sophisticated understanding of the effects an environmental tax will have on prices and then on demand for affected products and consequently, the demand for labor.

Finally, to embrace fully environmental taxes as the principal instrument for environmental control means that command-on-control regulation will be dismissed. In terms of property rights evolution, taxation implies public ownership of the environment; command-and-control gives regulatory property rights to polluters that will be difficult to take away. Industry long accustomed to the use of the environment at zero marginal cost will fight long and hard before paying environmental taxes on an activity that is now seen as a property right. In other words, the search for the double dividend may be as treacherous and disappointing as the search for the Holy Grail.

In early 2000, eight countries were reported to be involved explicitly in the search. These included the Nordic countries, Denmark, Finland, Norway, and Sweden, and Germany, Italy, the Netherlands and the United Kingdom.[10] Denmark expected to obtain six percent of total tax revenues from taxes imposed on carbon, sulfur dioxide, automobiles, and gasoline. Taxes had been cut for personal income tax and social security. At the other end of the spectrum, the United Kingdom had imposed a landfill tax that accounted for 0.1% of total tax revenues; the country had reduced social security taxes in tandem with the landfill tax increase.[11] It is impossible to determine if a double dividend has been generated in any of the eight cases or if taxes that would have been imposed in any case are now being celebrated as part of a double-dividend strategy.

The Apparent Case for Environmental Taxation

Environmental taxation is yet another case that reveals the Nordic countries' affection for top-down control of the economy. And while those countries may be making extensive use of taxation as opposed to command-and-control regulation, it must be remembered that the countries are small and rely heavily on export markets for their income. The possibilities of cartelization around environmental regulation are decidedly slim, and there is no litigation tradition that might support industry cartelization. We should not expect to see cartelization efforts where cartelization is not possible. Perhaps this is the reason that we find far more talk about double dividends and environmental taxation than we find action. Command-and-control regulation must be dislodged if extensive use of environmental taxation is to take hold. Along these lines, Patterson (2000) indicates that the U.S. federal government has imposed taxes that might be labeled environmental on ozone depleting chemicals, gasoline, gasoline-guzzling vehicles, heavy equipment tires, chemical and petroleum feedstocks, and coal. None of these replace EPA regulation on the same industries. It is also true that environmental taxes are imposed extensively across the 50 U.S. states. These include taxes on fuels, tires, batteries, as well as environmental fees for landfill use and waste discharge. Again, none of these replace cartel-forming command-and-control regulation.

CONCLUSION

The political economy of regulatory instruments for managing environmental quality is a study in property rights, how they are formed, and who obtains wealth in the process. For many years, economists engaged in the normative analysis of environmental control have been puzzled by the demise of common-law protection of environmental rights and the rising dominance of higher-cost technology-based command-and-control regulation that imposes uniform standards across vast industries and locations. The same efficiency theorists were equally puzzled by the apparent lack of interest in the use of environmental taxes and fees for rationing environmental use. This apparent puzzle was partly solved when Buchanan and Tullock described the rent-generating aspects of the regulation and showed how federal regulators can generate polluter profits. Greve showed how the same command-and-control regulation could become a rent generator and cartelizing force for environmental organizations. When combined, the two theories described a double cartel that can apparently withstand political competition from efficiency seekers.

In spite of the durable dominance of command-and-control regulation, a drive for environmental taxation continues to surface in the industrialized world. Partly driven by the old and discredited Pigouvian logic, some advocates still believe that politicians can design taxes for an entire economy that will internalized the externalities perceived by the same advocates. Other advocates are simply searching for new sources of revenue that might fund their favored government projects. Recently, however, these two groups have been joined by a third that hopes to generate a double dividend by shifting welfare-reducing taxes on labor and capital to efficiency-enhancing taxes on pollution. Of course, the social engineering required to accomplish this feat is daunting. Still, hope springs eternal in the hearts of those who seek a larger central government.

The theory that supports command-and-control regulation also predicts that environmental taxation will be limited to consumer goods and products where it is impossible for producer cartels to form. This means that we should find a vast set of environmental taxes in municipalities, states, and in countries with small, open, economies.

In the United States, it seems logically impossible to dislodge command-and-control regulation as the principal form of environmental control so long as citizen suits fund national environmental organizations and regulation-induced output restrictions generate polluter profits. For private property rights and common-law protection of environmental assets to rise from near death, either the environmentalists or major industries must turn away from the common source of wealth. This, of course, can happen, but only when command-and-control becomes more burdensome than profitable to industry and environmental outcomes generated by command-and-control cease to satisfy the environmental community.

ENDNOTES

1. For an elaboration on Greve's insight, see Barnett and Terrell (2001).
2. Greve (1990) reports that a 1983 review of consent orders indicated an amount equal to about 400 percent of the penalties paid to the U. S. Treasury was paid to environmental groups for attorney fees. In addition, the value of the credit projects required of the convicted pollutes amounted to millions of dollars and far exceeded the value of fines. His report of an analysis of thirty enforcement actions brought in Connecticut between 1983 and 1986 shows the cases were settled for payments in excess of $1.5 million. See Greve (1990, 259).
3. For a survey of this literature as it relates to environmental regulations, see Yandle (2001).
4. See *Natural Resources Defense Council, Inc., et al. v. Reilly* Civ. No. 89-2980 (RCL)(D.D.C.).
5. Susan F. Mandiberg and Susan L. Smith, *Crimes Against the Environment.* Charlottesville, VA: Michie, 1997:3.
6. The Pollution Prosecution Act of 1990 authorized the dramatic expansion of the force of EPA agents from 50 in 1990 to 200 in 1996. The EPA collected approximately $200 million in fines and penalties from 1989 to 1991. In 1992, the EPA passed a milestone in collecting over $135 million in civil and criminal penalties. The significance of these figures is best illustrated by contrasting them to the total of $166 million in fines and penalties that were collected in the entire 15 years prior to 1989. Court decisions since 1988 indicate it is no longer necessary to prove knowledge of illegal action to convict. (See Edward Stead, Michael M. McKinney, and Jean Garner Stead Institutionalizing Environmental Performance in U. S. Industry: Is it happening and what if it does not? Business Strategy and the Environment, 7 (1998): 261-270 at 263.
7. Sandee Blabolil, Ines Cho, and Scott Haenni, et al. "Environmental Crimes" (Twelfth Survey of White Collar Crime), *American Criminal Law Review* 34 (Winter 1997) 2: 491-554, at 510.
8. For example, Susan Lee (2001) gives a popular discussion of the double-dividend possibility that was discussed in a Congressional Budget Office study. Also, see Rojas (2002) for more U. S. relevant discussion of the double-dividend argument. For an example of political discussion of the topic in 1990, see Patterson (2000, 139). At that time, Congressman Stark read into the record a double-dividend presentation made by economists at a Ways and Means Committee hearing. Later, in 1996, Congressman Stark stated: "I am preparing legislation to move to the next step and gradually increase taxes on pollutants that contribute to global warming and the degradation of the environment. The money raised from these taxes can be used to fund lower taxes on wages and incomes." (Patterson, 2000, 140).
9. For another survey and comments on the complexities involved in designing taxes that might offer the double-dividend prospect, see Metcalf (2001).
10. See Bosqet (2000, 21) for data and discussion of environmental taxes in the eight countries discussed here. Also, see European Environment Agency (2001).
11. Patterson (2000, 127) indicates that the United Kingdom had no environmental taxes through the 1980s. By 1995, the U. K. had imposed taxes in the name of the environment on gasoline, water, sewage, solid waste, and "employer paid commuting expenses." Justification for the shift was based on a need for more tax revenues, preparing to meet the requirements of the Kyoto Agreement, and a desire to deal with the inefficiencies of direct regulation. None of the taxes replaced command-and-control regulation.

REFERENCES

Ackerman. Bruce A. and Hassler, William T. (1981), *Clean Coal/Dirty Air*, New Haven, CT: Yale University Press.

Adler, Jonathan. (1996), " Green Politics and Dirty Profits," *Regulation* (1996): pp. 26-34.

Ashford, Nicholas A. and Caldart, Charles C. (2001), "Negotiated Environmental and Occupational Health and Safety Agreements in the United States: Lessons for Policy," *Journal of Cleaner Production* 9 (April): pp. 99-120.

Barnett, Andy H. and Terrell, Timothy D. (2001), "Economic Observations on Citizen-Suit Provisions of Environmental Legislation," *Duke Environmental Law & Policy Forum* (12): pp. 1-30.

Blaboli, Sandee, Cho, Ines, and Haenni, Scott, et al. (1997), "Environmental Crimes: Twelfth Survey of White Collar Crime," *American Criminal Law Review* 34, (Winter) 2: pp. 491-554.

Bosquet, Benoit. (2000), "Environmental Tax Reform: Does it Work? A Survey of the Empirical Evidence," *Ecological Economics* 34: pp. 19-32.

Brubaker, Elizabeth. (1998), "The Common Law and the Environment: The Canadian Experience," Peter J. Hill and Roger E. Meiners (eds.) *Who Owns the Environment?* Lanham, MD: Rowman & Littlefield Publishers, pp. 87-152.

Buchanan, James M. and Tullock, Gordon (1967), "Polluters' 'Profit' and Political Response," *American Economic Review* (65): pp. 139-147.

Cohen, Mark A. (1992). "Criminal Law: Environmental Crime and Punishment: Legal/Economic Theory and Empirical Evidence on Enforcement of Federal Environmental Statutes," *Journal of Criminal Law & Criminology* 82 (Winter): pp. 1054-1098.

Cross, Frank B. (1999), "Common Law and the Conceit of Modern Environmental Policy," *George Mason Law Review* 7(Summer): pp. 965-982.

Demsetz, Harold. (1964), "The Exchange and Enforcement of Property Rights," *Journal of Law & Economics* 7(October): pp. 7-26.

Demsetz, Harold. (1967), "Toward a Theory of Property Rights," *American Economic Review* 57(2): pp. 347-359.

European Environment Agency. (2001), Environmental Taxes: Implementation and Effectiveness. http://org.eea.eu.int:80/documents/issuerep/EnvTaxes/default.htm.

Greve, Michael S. (1990), "The Private Enforcement of Environmental Law," *Tulane Law Review* (65): pp. 339-382.

Helland, Eric. (1998), "The Revealed Preference of State EPAs: Stringency, Enforcement, and Substitution," *Journal of Environmental Economics and Management* 35: pp. 242-261.

Kilman, Scott (2001) "Smithfield Foods CEO Welcomes Backlash Over Its Hog Farms," *The Wall Street Journal* (August 31): p. B4.

Lee, Susan (2000) "How Much is the Right to Pollute Worth?", *The Wall Street Journal* (August 1): p. A15.

Libecap, Gary (1989), *Contracting for Property Rights*. Cambridge,MA.: Cambridge University Press.

Mandiberg, Susan F. and Smith, Susan L. (1997), *Crimes Against the Environment*. Charlottesville, VA: Michie.

Meiners, Roger E. and Yandle, Bruce (1999), "Common Law and the Conceit of Modern Environmental Policy," *George Mason Law Review* 7 (Summer) pp. 923-963.

Metcalf, Gilbert E. (2001), "Market-Based Environmental-Policy Instruments," *NBER Reporter* (Summer): pp. 12-15.

"Owls, of all things, Help Weyerhaeuser Cash in on Timber," (1992), *The Wall Street Journal*, (June 14): p. A1.

Patterson, Charles D. (2000), "Environmental Taxes and Subsidies: What is the Appropriate Fiscal Policy for Dealing with Modern Environmental Problems?" *William and Mary Environmental Law and Policy Review* 24(Winter): pp. 121-159.

Peltzman, Sam. (1976), "Toward a More General Theory of Regulation," *Journal of Law & Economics* (August): pp. 211-240.

Pigou, A.C. (1920), *Economics of Welfare*. London: Macmillan.

Pigou, A.C. (1932), *Economics of Welfare*. 4th ed. London: Macmillan.

Rojas, Warren. (2000) "Clean Air vs. Clean Wallets: The Emissions Tax Debate Continues," *Tax Notes* (December 4): pp. 1206-1207.

Stead, Edward, McKinney, Michael M., and Stead, Jean Garner (1998), "Institutionalizing Environmental Performance in U.S. Industry: Is it happening and what if it does not?" *Business Strategy and the Environment* 7: pp. 261-270.

Stigler, George J. (1971), "The Economic Theory of Regulation," *Bell Journal* (Spring): pp. 3-21.

Yandle, Bruce. (1983), "Bootleggers and Baptists: The Education of a Regulatory Economist," *Regulation*. (May/June): pp. 12-16.

Yandle, Bruce. (1999a), "Bootleggers and Baptists in Retrospect," *Regulation*, 22(1999): pp. 5-7.

Yandle, Bruce. (1999b), "Grasping for the Heavens: 3-D Property Rights and the Global Commons," *Duke Environmental Law Forum*, 10(Fall): pp. 13-44.

Yandle, Bruce. (2001), "Public Choice and the Environment," William F. Shughart II and Laura Razzolini, (eds.) *The Elgar Companion to Public Choice*. London: Edward Elgar Publishing, Inc.: pp. 590-610.

Yandle, Bruce and. Morriss, Andy P. (2001), "The Technologies of Property Rights: Choice among Alternative Solutions to the Tragedy of the Commons," *Ecology Law Quarterly* (28): pp. 123-168.

Yost, Nicholas C. (1998), "The State of Environmental Law Enforcement," A Speech Presented at the American Bar Association's 1998 Annual Meeting, *ELR News & Analysis*, 28(December)12: pp. 10711-10720.

INDEX

MIX
Papier aus verantwortungsvollen Quellen
Paper from responsible sources
FSC® C105338

If you have any concerns about our products,
you can contact us on
ProductSafety@springernature.com

In case Publisher is established outside the EU,
the EU authorized representative is:
Springer Nature Customer Service Center GmbH
Europaplatz 3, 69115 Heidelberg, Germany

Printed by Libri Plureos GmbH
in Hamburg, Germany